About

Introduced early to 'God' as the eldest child or parents who helped establish a new Baptist church in post-war Birmingham, Ann eventually trained to become a Church of England Reader during the early years of raising a family of five, before also studying for an MA in Contextual Theology.

Her talented seamstress-mother perhaps sowed a seed of intuitive interest in the way clothes reflect personality throughout life's stages and contexts. Hospital Chaplain, county-wide preacher, mother of Oxford choristers, founder of a retreat centre in Bedfordshire – such further experiences coalesced into a mould-breaking appointment as a lay minister to three rural Anglican parishes in North Yorkshire for seven years.

Retirement saw a return to her non-conformist roots, playing a varied role in the outreach of an enterprising United Reformed Church in the nearby market county town.

From all this fertile soil grew the autobiographical book, Naked and You Clothed Me, and now the present anthology, showcasing stories from a wide range of her enthusiastic and empathetic readers.

Threads

or

Thresholds

Naked and You Clothed Me

A Spiritual Retrospective
From the Yellow Satchel!

Ann Bowes

We choose them; they shape us; they define us in intimate relationship with our flesh. We grow in them, work in them, play in them, sleep in them. We make mistakes in them... and out of them! We die and are buried in them.

Clothes weave a unique message into the fabric of our lives.

The clothes-line of my own life has numerous distinctive garments pegged along it – starting in the Midlands and moving, via Northamptonshire, Buckinghamshire and Bedfordshire, on to North Yorkshire.

From quality little outfits handmade by a dressmaking Mum; to the stylish purchases of my heady teenage years; to an unorthodox era as a mother of five in my thirties; to a mid-life phase as clothing embraced my blossoming spirituality and ministry; to later life in creative ensembles...avoiding beige!

Glimpse the seven decades of my busy and varied life in a series of revealing vignettes – trimmed with a rich seam of Bible-based clothing reflections.

A selection of responses to the editor's autobiographical
'Naked and You Clothed Me'

The following reactions emanate from a wide audience, including a museum curator, a grammar-school Head of English, a medieval historian, a poet, a therapist, a Christian minister, a counsellor, and several teachers, amongst many others.

"I thought I would dip into it before 'lights out'. Two and a half hours later I finally did turn out the light, with more to read tonight. It is a page-turner ... a very happy book as well, looking for the good in everything."
- E.C.

"A treasured gift ... a store house of so many delights ... the variety hinted at in the headings and sketches. Your inspiring spiritual reflections provided me with much food for thought, several times sending me back to the Bible to re-read in a different light. Above all, your quirky sense of humour brings the whole account sparkling with life ... A wonderful miscellany ... a heart-warming read!"
- M.H.

"Congratulations on your first-class wonderful book. I couldn't put it down. It made me laugh, cry, and moved me and has really helped and encouraged me so much."
- E.W.

"I enjoyed your book very much, for the exploration of colour, and the discernment of joy, even in the middle of pain."
- A.L.

"Wonderfully uplifting! I loved every bit of this enthralling book ... written with humour, pathos and energy ... poignant ... fabulous!"
- C.C.

"What a wonderful book. Fascinating reflections ... the illustrations are superb."
- M.G.

"How special – I read it too greedily and now I want to read it again and taste every morsel ... I love the honesty, warmth, humour, humanity and spirituality of your writing."
- G.C.

"It felt as if we were having a talk together. It felt as if God was with us. I think it has changed my life. I laughed and I cried."
- P.W.

"I read it with great pleasure, as a lovely holiday read. I didn't want it to finish, but I can see that there is another layer on which to read it, and I am going back to do just that!"
- H.W.

"It made me laugh. It made me cry and it made me think."
- M.E.

"A beautiful read. It flowed seamlessly between spirituality and re-membering. It was so evocative of the heady giddiness of trying on an ensemble. Thank you for the sharing of your highs and horrendous lows and most importantly the love and pathway to strength."
- J.G.

"This is a book of joy, life-affirming. I had no grandparents, nor any siblings, so it has been fascinating for me to read of these dynamics of family life and just begin to sense what it must have been like."
- C.B

"Wow and wonderful! A liminal threshold for our 70th year and how we are experiencing the past."
- S.H.

"I love it because it chimes so very much with my own childhood. The illustrations and photos are such a pleasure to look at. I look forward to reading a little each day before I go to sleep."
- A.O.

"I have really enjoyed it. The detail that has been included in each section has been fascinating to read. Learning about how different aspects of life, such as clothing, can impact on parts of society has been very compelling."
- J.B.

"This book has become a catalyst in my life. So much that you write about the church, I absolutely feel and share. Person-focused ministry is so much my calling and passion too. I am hugely grateful for what you have written."
- C.H.

"I couldn't stop reading it. You are here with me and speaking about God to me. You are the only person who has ever done that and now you still are."
- W.A.

"My Auntie B. gave me your book and I have chuckled. Knicker elastic on hats and dungarees for your son with no flies! I am nearing the end, so don't tell me anything else about it!"
- G.D.

"Absolutely wonderful. I can't put it down. I'm loving it. Thank you. It's been an amazing gift and will continue to be so. I'm honoured to have read it ... it has touched my soul."
- H.V.

"Your writing is wise, enlightened. The book has been a blessing to me."
- A.B.

"A varied and stimulating read. Your sermons/pieces on the Remnant, Transfiguration, Babette's Feast and the final one on clothing were very thoughtful and thought provoking."
- A.S.

In Threads or Thresholds, the contributors expand on similar issues...and many more

Threads or Thresholds

A Transformational Anthology

From the Yellow Satchel!

Compiled and edited by Ann Bowes

'God made man and woman because he loves stories.' Elie Wiesel

Anthology - mid 17th Century, via French or Medieval Latin from Greek, anthologia, denoting a collection of the 'flowers' of various authors.

By the same author:

Naked and You Clothed Me, ISBN: 978 1 906632 15 1

#

Threads or Thresholds published by Book Castle Publishing, November 2021

ISBN: 978 1 906632 16 8

Printed in Great Britain by TJ Books Ltd

Editorial material and arrangement © Ann Bowes 2021

Other text © as named 2021

Line drawing vignettes throughout © Gillian Causley 2021

Additional artwork as credited © RMc Becky McMurray, EB-R Emma Bowes-Romanelli, HB Harry Buckledee, LB Lottie Bowes, ISR Irene Robinson, MK Michael Kilpatrick, CS Cherry Shore, PB Paul Bowes, CW Cameron Whapples, GW Georgia Wilkinson, JK Judy Kennedy, GT Gillian Tucker, GH-D Gillian Harris-Douglas, HL Harry Lobley 2021

Cover paintings © Becky McMurray 2021

Back cover photograph © Harry Lobley 2021

The moral right of the editor and contributors has been asserted.

Special thanks to Joshua Buckledee for his practical expertise in preparing this book for publication; to my husband Paul for editorial oversight; to Tracey and Steve Moren at Moren Associates Limited for the cover design and layout; and to the talented illustrators who have so enlivened the text, especially Becky McMurray and Gillian Causley.

Dedicated to:

Maureen, who picked up all the threads, as well as the loose ends, and wove them into the colourful fabric of church life in Brafferton, the Parish on the Boundary.

Heather, my feisty, forthright friend from Thormanby, who would have been astonished that the beautiful, cream silk and cashmere pashmina, which she bequeathed to me as she lay dying, is now my prayer shawl. It enfolds me like a tent, a shelter for my journey.

Ruth, at the Coach House in Kilmuir – that resting place, my causeway when the high tide came in.

Sue, who held me up until I could swim again.

Bible quotations are taken from the New International Version.

Contents

Preface	ix
Introduction	xi
In a Jar by the Door...	1
IDENTITY	
Through the Wardrobe Door (contributors)	3
Sue Thorne, Sally Wise, Maureen East, Bren Sainsbury, Nicky Coope, Sue Kennedy, Pippa and Lottie Brown, Lesley Bustard, Gill Causley, Ian Stewart, Helen Radcliffe, 'Sally', Rachel Faulks, Sandra Purrett, Liz Styan	
Through the Vestry Door (editor)	19
Reflection, Homilies, Musing	
'ee, That's Champion...	27
VILLAGE	
Through the Wardrobe Door (contributors)	29
Liz Oldfield-Beechey, Pete Nelson, Maureen East, Jess Hayne, Irene Robinson, Hilary Porter, Gareth Dadd, Anon	
Through the Vestry Door (editor)	43
Reflection, Homilies, Musing	
To Be Busy or Not to Be Busy...	49
WORK	
Through the Wardrobe Door (contributors)	51
Nick Ramsden, John Reveley, Iris Wilkinson, Barbara Taylor, Christine Roddam, a Funeral Director, Anne Miller, Hilary Vinall, Alistair Calman, Sister Catherine Wybourne, Chrissy Fincham, Jane Oglesby, John Lansley	
Through the Vestry Door (editor)	67
Reflection, Homilies, Musing	

Can I Help You? **COMMUNITY**		73
Through the Wardrobe Door (contributors) Chris Kilpatrick, Mo Penson, Micky Wood, Olive Davey, Anon, Eileen Bennet, Rachel Faulks, Julia Barker, Louise Denison, Liz Styan, Roger Tucker, Audrey Wilson		75
Through the Vestry Door (editor) *Reflection, Homilies, Musing*		90

Stop, Look, Listen... 99
DRAMA

Through the Wardrobe Door (contributors) 101
Sue Thorne, Pam Jackson-Vickers, Heather Shone, John Henderson, Sue Thorn, Gillian Tucker, Geoff Oxley, Alexa Barber, Hazel Sumsion, Kerry Bass, Jan Portlock-Barker

Through the Vestry Door (editor) 114
Reflection, Homilies, Musing

Hither and Thither... 121
TRAVEL

Through the Wardrobe Door (contributors) 123
Nicky Coope, Liz Styan, Janet Stow, Jane Price, Sue Gibson, Chris Kilpatrick, Sue Bush, Paul Bowes, Sheana Barby, John Lansley

Through the Vestry Door (editor) 141
Reflection, Homilies, Musing

Time for Change... 149
LETTING GO

Through the Wardrobe Door (contributors) 151
Sue Woolmore, Gill Montia, Sue Graham, Alexa Barber, Cris Reay Connor, Jackie Marsden, Hilary Clark, 'Threshold Singers', Sue Thorn

Through the Vestry Door (editor) 161
Reflection, Homilies, Musing

The Maypole Dance... 169
POSTSCRIPT

Through the Vestry Door (editor) 171
Re-Configuring

Preface

'You cannot discover new horizons until you consent to lose sight of the shore.' Andre Gide

Someone once said to me that one of the things they like about immersing themselves in a book like this one – with so many different contributors – is all the varied voices, helping them to feel like part of another community of hope and inspiration.

So, Threads or Thresholds then. Maybe we will together discover here threads which link us; thresholds which we recognize, or which maybe we are relieved that we do not! Some will challenge us hopefully towards a new understanding of how, when and where we choose, and sometimes where we do not choose, to cross them.

I distinctly remember first hearing the word 'threshold' as a little girl of about seven years of age. I was on the top deck of a '55 buzz' in Birmingham one afternoon, going to town with my Grandma. Upstairs on the 55 was a decidedly smoky, smelly area, but with the compensatory advantage of a bird's eye view over the tattered remnants of a bombed city. A city certainly on the threshold between war and peace. Rows of houses with no fronts, exposed inner staircases, and shredded, peeling wallpaper. Behind lay other very humble dwellings, still miraculously whole. I would imagine with horror the stories of these people of the bombed houses. Then a never-to-be-forgotten moment. 'Grandma, Grandma, there is a sailor in his bell-bottom trousers and a hat like daddy wore in the war on his ship, carrying a bride into a house.' She replied, 'Well, he is carrying her over the threshold of their new home, because they have just been married.'

As on that occasion, clothes are often a significant feature at many times of transition. In an airport recently, surrounded by thousands of travellers in transit from threshold to threshold, one woman stood out like a beacon amongst all those tightly packed streams of baggy, tired and dishevelled looking hordes, dressed mostly in denim blue, black, grey, brown, beige, with holes and rips even. She walked proudly, upright and dignified. Very black and shiny skin, wearing a full-length garment which sculpted her body shape as it moved languorously amongst the crowds and queues. A turban crowned her head in the same brilliantly coloured fabric as the garment...bright blue, red, yellow, orange, white. Picasso-style shapes and designs rioted across the fabric. Oh, my goodness, could she be a queen?

How we cross the threshold matters. In Judaism you have a minimum of three names: one that your parents gave you, one that others call you, and one that you make for yourself, because Judaism understands that every time you cross a threshold you will be intrinsically changed. Anthropologists have brought many insights into why we respond to thresholds when they are woven into the fabric of our lives...and that metaphor brings us to our clothes. I was reminded again of the truth of this recently, one day in the middle of the recent pandemic and isolation, when a virus had brought the world to its knees. A lady in her 70s wrote to me, 'I am fed up with wearing my pyjamas all day or my gardening clothes just because no one will see me, so today I have worn my wedding dress and strappy stiletto sandals!'

So, is what we wear and how we wear it in that liminal experience significant, in the spirit of who we are?

Of course it is...

Taste and see...

Church of St. Peter, Brafferton © HL

Church of St. Mary, Myton-on-Swale

Church of St. Mary Magdalene, Thormanby

Zion United Reformed Church, Northallerton

Introduction

'How to thrive through life's transitions, to live fearlessly and regret free.' Sherre Hirsch

I am inviting you to move from the hallway, through the door and into my study. There to meet over fifty inspiring 'others' in my life – many encountered during my experiences in churches in North Yorkshire. Partly in an unorthodox role as a fully licensed but un-ordained minister to three rural Anglican parishes. Partly whilst contributing from the congregation to the spiritual life and outreach of a market-town church in the Reformed tradition.

On my desk are their responses to my autobiographical 'Naked and You Clothed Me'. Sometimes their reminiscences involve me, sometimes not. Sometimes their threshold memories involve transformational garments, sometimes not. Sometimes their experiences will evoke familiar images in your own life's kaleidoscope, sometimes their circumstances will be unique to them.

Under the broad umbrella of 'Threads or Thresholds', their highly individual reflections range widely across seven thematic sections. Enjoy them just as they are, without any additional direct commentary of mine. However, instead I have supplemented each topic with revealing accounts of my own 'ministerial' challenges and perceptions, along with brief homilies and a 'musing'. And in a closing postscript I highlight an underlying fundamental conundrum that still raises more questions than answers for the future of the Church.

So, in this anthology you may not only relive the excitement at a success, a new job, a passionate hobby, the joy of a child…but also echo the pain of illness, divorce, death, uncertainty. Either way, such moments bring definition, meaning, purpose, empathy, revelation.

In their rich variety, in their distinctive voices, these contributors offer a celebration of many lives and lifestyles.

Meet them all now…

Interwoven

We are part of the fabric of each other's lives.

I am not I, alone,

apart from you, and you, and you.

I am I in and through you

as you in me.

And when my 'I' responds to your felt need,

And yours responds to mine,

we grow and all our lives

become more than the sum of separate identities.

We are held by gossamer threads

interwoven, into an absolute pattern.

*With thanks to Rosemary May Wells for permission
to include this poem from her 'God is an Onion'*

In a Jar by the Door...

IDENTITY

What we know matters, but who we are matters more. – *Brené Brown*

It doesn't matter how great your shoes are if you don't accomplish anything in them. – *Marine Boone*

Don't be into trends. Don't make fashion own you, but you decide who you are, what you want to express by the way you dress and the way you live. – *Gianni Versace*

There is a shade of red for every woman. – *Audrey Hepburn*

Mrs Panabaker is ten years older than God and probably smarter. She stops…to tell my dad what she didn't like about his sermon the previous Sunday… She always wears a matching hat. Last week it was draped in fake fruit. I wanted to try to eat one of the grapes just to see what she'd do, but I value my life. – *A.C. Williams*

Beauty comes from the spirit. It is the spirit that 'dresses' the body, not the clothes that are added to it. – *Margo Anand*

The smell of naphthalene pervaded the air as we checked through a cluster of Medieval caps. Lots of these had been found in London, as ever-taller buildings required ever-deeper excavations. The felted wool was designed to be warm and waterproof and, although the caps were hundreds of years old, looked as if it still might be. In the next drawer along there was a group of top hats dating from 1820 – 1930. Each was sealed in a clear plastic bag marked with a skull and crossbones because mercury was used during their making and they were *still* toxic – caused madness. We detected the museum numbers through the safety of the hats' protective membrane. – *Claire Wilcox*

Through the Wardrobe Door
(Contributors)

Experimental Sixties, an embarrassing 'milk-maid' outfit and a ghastly first kiss...
Windscreen Wiper Eyelashes!

Clothes make a statement. From an early age, I have felt mine express my identity. Their design, colour, fabric and style. I think this came from my mother who, although only a paintress at Wedgwood earning a small wage, used to buy the best fabric she could afford and have her clothes made by an excellent seamstress. She had style and so did my father, a handsome man a few years older than her. One such tailored jacket from her twenties I still wear, as does my daughter, sixty five years later.

Mum spent much of her hard-earned cash on buying or making clothes for me, her only child. When I was four, she knitted a one-piece blue swimming costume for our happy annual trip to Blackpool. It's strange, isn't it, how in our memories the sun always shines on our childhood holidays. However, one difficult incident was never forgotten. My costume was made of beautifully soft wool – I can still feel it under my fingers – and I strode proudly into the waves till disaster struck. I was waterlogged. My mother was horrified as I struggled to return to her, bowed down by the weight of it full of sea water. The horror was soon forgotten, because I was taken to the expensive dress shop in Fleetwood and returned as the proud owner of a pink bubble costume which I adored for years.

However, one maxi milkmaid dress, worn to my first teenage party, still haunts my dreams, as I spent most of that evening hiding in the toilet! And a peasant dress was a real favourite at the time – light, floaty, with a see-through lace band at the waist. It took me on my first date and my first proper kiss... ghastly, but a rite of passage. The dress was flimsy, paisley patterned in beautiful pale peacock colours. I realized with this dress that certain colours and shapes enhanced my colouring and body and gave me confidence. The relationship with the boy was short lived but the love affair with the dress lasted years.

Along with clothes I must add makeup to my dressing up. My teenage years saw great experiments with Biba, Mary Quant and Vidal Sassoon, Carnaby Street and magazines showing me how to look and be. False eyelashes worn under glasses like windscreen wipers. Freckles painted on my face and stars stuck to my eyelids. Mini dresses, hot pants, pvc boots and snakeskin chokers – all aided by my Mum who now worked at C & A, giving me access to their trendy Clock House range. I was beginning to

In a Jar by the Door…

develop a style and loved putting together a look.

I have so many memories of my clothes for good or ill; sometimes items were relegated to the back of the wardrobe never to be worn again if I'd had a bad experience wearing them. Clothes are so important, reflecting what we want the world to think of us, making us feel good and allowing us to slip into a role. We are all doing it, presenting various faces to people and to ourselves. Put on a dress, a coat, high heels and immediately feel different. You grow a few inches, strike a pose and off you go. Somehow we learn this and work our way through childhood, teenage traumas, womanhood, motherhood and eventually into our mature years where hopefully we are comfy in our own skin and relish the clothes we wear, avoiding mutton dressed as lamb, of course, because there are always pitfalls!

Sue Thorne

**

Meet a shepherd who partied in her youth in her grandmother's 'flapper' dress…
For Everything there is a Season

Attending boarding school from the age of five, my sartorial life was dominated by school uniform until I reached 17. My mother was an excellent seamstress, so most of my holiday clothes were home made. I began to hate being dressed identically to my older sister in styles that *she* had chosen – and which certainly didn't suit me…full skirts on a rather

plump body followed the smocking of the early years. Just imagine my delight at that first visit to a 'posh' dress shop in Harrogate at the age of 16 to choose a close-fitting, royal blue jersey dress; and I felt a million dollars! The next purchase was a smart grey two-piece suit for a wedding complete with winkle-picking, white high heels – I had never felt so stunning!

I had not been to many dances – I remember one at the village hall when I had plaits down to the waist – I must have been about 10 as my plaits were simply cut off at secondary school age. (I still have them, complete with blue ribbons.)

For a 21st party, I made myself a tight, emerald green, satin dress and wore it with a matching diamante necklace. It encouraged me and I made a very bold play for the elder brother of our escorts. (Reader, I married him about three years later!) I still have both dress and husband 50 years later!

My own 21st birthday dress was a striking 'shift' of navy, green and white. I wish I had kept it but I'd left a brooch on the white stripe and it had deposited a rusty mark. My other favourite was a black and white evening dress which I lent many years later to the daughter of a very close friend and she cut it 3 or 4 inches shorter and ruined the whole look and shape of it. If you have read 'Flowers for Mrs. Harris', you will know the feeling, but it still holds the memories.

My maternal grandmother once made herself a flapper dress from a metallic Indian shawl – one never knew which way round to wear it, but it has since done the rounds of fancy dress parties and some day my own granddaughter might wear it…

Identity

I enjoy wearing second hand clothes, often wondering who has worn them before. I refer particularly to a 1950s style dress and jacket which I wore during the first summer when I had got my figure back after three children in quick succession. My maternity clothes had been wonderful voluminous 'shrouds', but this very different dress had a WAIST – it's still in the wardrobe for my granddaughter. (Nowadays, of course, with maternity wear the growing embryo is celebrated by outlining the bulging belly, or sometimes even showing naked!) There is a saying that 'children should be seen and not heard', well, I think babies should be kept under wraps until in the pram.

As for my clothes nowadays, I really couldn't care less – comfort before beauty is the order of the day, especially shoes. My daughter is horrified that I go 'out' in my scruffy gardening clothes, but thankfully my legs are still good enough to wear shorts. Sleeveless is 'no go', definitely. My 'potato picking' coat has done 30 years service since I found it in a charity shop. Perfect for ripping off as you work, and throwing into the dust. Will it eventually become a scarecrow? Oh dear. Probably!

I hope I shall never become 'mutton dressed as lamb', (I am a real shepherd after all!) and my mother-of-the-bride outfits have been worn many times since. In the end the most important thing to wear is your smile - on a face enhanced by a trip to the hairdresser!

Sally Wise

**

A cornucopia of garments for life from scratchy grey wool to yellow taffeta...
Enter, the Sartorially Diverse Verger

As a child I took it for granted that clothes would always be there for me. I didn't take much notice of what I wore until my mother made me a school skirt in a wool material, grey with white stripes, very heavy and scratchy to wear. I was pleased when it was too short for me and I no longer had to wear it. The only memorable 'bought' outfit was a royal blue skirt with nylon bodice, a white blouse and blue and white checked waistcoat, only worn on Sundays when we went for long walks or visited relatives. The outfit was passed down to my two younger sisters and somehow never looked worn. My favourite dress was in yellow taffeta, worn as a bridesmaid at my auntie's wedding. Very light and floaty, with a wire cage underneath which made it look like a crinoline dress. I later wore it to a school Christmas party minus the wire cage, and I felt like a princess.

At secondary school all girls had sewing and cooking lessons (housecraft as it was called then). My first achievement was a white cotton apron for cookery lessons, followed by a blouse with a low neckline which I proudly wore as often as I could. My mother also taught me to knit jumpers and cardigans for my sisters, my young cousins and myself. We would sit like two old maids whilst chatting about everything and nothing. I even made myself a knitted dress, using red sparkly wool in 4 ply no less, on very thin needles.

By now I had started work as a stenographer in a building firm where one of the

In a Jar by the Door...

secretaries and I joined a pen pal club called 'Internationally Yours'. We once attended a conference at a hotel in Scarborough and wore our knitted dresses, mine red and hers dark blue, which drew many appreciative stares and comments from other delegates. Eventually I bought myself an electric sewing machine and, as I worked in the middle of York, I could pop into Renders fabric shop in High Ousegate, spending many hours browsing and choosing fabrics and dress patterns. Whilst making my own clothes, some very practical for work and some fancy, frilly dresses, I would still ask my mother for advice on how to do the 'tricky' bits such as zips, button holes or fancy pleating.

My wedding dress was the most important challenge so far, as I couldn't afford the shop version. However, not only was my sewing machine still in York and too heavy to carry back to my temporary work-base in Bridlington, but I also wondered how I was going to have time to make both my own and the three bridesmaids' dresses. A borrowed, old hand sewing machine came to the rescue. The left-over pieces of turquoise and white satin even made a shirt and trousers for my eighteen-month-old brother.

When a mother eventually, I still knitted cardigans, jumpers and even blankets for cot and pram, then for toddlers I made dresses, skirts, trousers and shirts, sometimes from scraps left over from my own dresses, such that mother and daughter often went out in matching outfits. One outfit was a pink and white gingham dress with daisy trimming. I even made a knitted poncho for each of us. Child minding other parents' offspring and keeping my own entertained on a wet day is very exhausting. One cold January my eldest daughter asked me to make her a new dress for her doll. I took out my bag of scraps of material, lace, tape, buttons etc. and, with a book to guide me, taught the children too. Great fun was had, amidst all the mess. My son was not to be left out and he knitted a pair of yellow dungarees for his teddy. Teaching a left-handed child to knit when you are right-handed is quite tricky but we managed. Even a new Christmas Action Man was dressed in knitted army outfit. The girls' Cindy dolls had makeovers with knitted outfits too. Whole dolls were created from fabric, stuffed with kapok and wool hair, plus button eyes and stitched mouth (health and safety laws were not as strict as today). One Christmas my nine in-laws received a pair of knitted gloves or mitts, even scarves. I think I started making them in January. A great money saver!

The Church Nativity required many special outfits for the characters. So, with pieces of cotton either bought or given, even old counterpanes and curtains, we created a huge range, including some angel dresses made of taffeta, most of which are still going strong nearly fifty years later. More have been added over the years. None have been shop bought, which makes them look authentic. Branching out, the outfits have also come in useful for school plays or to retell the Easter story to a full Church. Then, in a team of adults dressing up to present stories from the bible (Open the Book) to the children at school in a most unique way, brilliant skills in dressmaking and carpentry were displayed, including the creation of some awesome props. I was volunteered to take on the role of 'Jesus' many times and have been 'crucified' with my arms stretched out on a wooden cross on more than one occasion! The children and staff at the school were mesmerized

and silence fell when I bowed my head at the end of the story, and cried out...
   'It is done.'

Maureen East

**

A political mole works for change. Dig deeper...
Underground Political Mole...in Brown Velvet

My open wardrobes, and a rail of what I'm wearing this week, are an autumn landscape. These are the earthy colours that suit me. It is fortunate that orange is an autumn colour, as it is a truth universally acknowledged (well, among those who know me) that orange is my favourite colour. The contrast of orange montbretia (crocosmia) flowers with bright green leaves in the late summer Irish hedgerows fills me with joy, and wearing these colours brings images of those beautiful places to mind.

Brown velvet or velour – reminiscent of the mole working out of sight until suddenly appearing and disrupting the apparently smooth surface – is another favourite colour and fabric. In some of the work I have done in the past I have described my role as that of a mole, busy working underground to change things.

These clothes also conform to the criteria of being as stylish as possible within the parameters of comfortable. They form collections or groups of clothing for different activities - so that, to some extent, they provide uniforms, protective coverings or disguises. Momentarily, I wonder 'if I need disguises, who am I really?'

In the spring and early summer of 2020 there was no need for disguises or clothes for events or activities as I hid, at home, from the novel coronavirus pandemic. The early weeks of 'lockdown' were spent wearing a dark brown velour maxi skirt and hoodie. In the hot summer days that followed, brown linen shifts and a jacket became the favourites.

Now, as I attempt to navigate returning to some kind of 'normality' whilst also worrying about the risks of contagion, I notice what I am choosing to wear every time I leave the safety of my own home:
- Item: a homemade, washable, 3-layer face mask (in brown, green or orange);
- Item: (or 2 items if you are the Secretary of State for Health) nitrile gloves

In a Jar by the Door...

(which I decontaminate and re-use, as I don't want to be a plastic polluter). Sadly, these only come in blue;
- Item: sensible shoes – for moving quickly to safe distances (brown);
- Item: slim trousers – as above (also brown);
- Item: T-shirt (brown, green or orange);
- Item: high tech walking jacket – with everything I need zipped into the pockets (bright scarlet).
- Missing: accessories – the orange satchel awaits the vaccine or cure; jewellery does not fit well into nitrile gloves, so that stays at home too.

Every outing is an expedition – but I realise this hyper-vigilance has its roots in my uniforms, disguises and protective coverings.

So, who am I really? Which uniform is the real me? As I reflect, I recognise that they all are – each and every outfit or collection is an aspect of who I am now, the many and different activities that I enjoy, the life I have experienced and the person I am still (in my 70s) growing into and becoming. I realise that I am happy to be a chameleon, changing to match my surroundings, adapting to the circumstances – as long as I can still wear orange.

Bren Sainsbury

**

Mundanely, it's the way you wear your jeans and T-Shirts that matters...
Spray-on Jeans

I am definitely not an avid follower of fashion, ever anxious to be seen in the latest, skinny, leopard-skin jeans or similarly trendy garment. I have always been, according to my stepfather, 'a jeans and T-shirt kind of girl'. That 'look' is always in, isn't it, and really it is how you wear your jeans and T-shirt that matters.

Nevertheless, at school, I remember coveting the clothes that my friends wore, but had to settle for a tank top that my grandma converted from an old school jumper. The sleeves, which had developed holes in the elbows, were unceremoniously cut off and the shoulder part of the garment finished off with crocheted caps. This was very innovative of my dear grandma and could perhaps have been the birth of a new trend; but no, not really what a teenager trying to 'fit in' needed at that time.

I also recall wanting Dunlop Green Flash trainers when I began playing tennis but instead getting white, lace-up plimsolls from the market. Actually, I remember using my new-found Home Economics skills, 'thank you Mrs Greenwood', by employing the sewing machine at home, the old Singer belonging to my grandma, to sew a line along the length of my unfashionably too baggy jeans legs. Single handed, I thereby transformed them from ordinary jeans from the market into the type of skinny jeans which all my cool friends wore, presumably purchased from the top high street shops. My only mistake was in sewing the legs a little too tight for my already well developed, strong 'hockey girl thighs'. I had to adopt the skills of a contortionist, acquiring a deep purple face, with sweat

threatening to ruin my eighties, bouffant hair creation, in order to ease them on further than my knees. The resulting 'look', which I had been tempted to so crave, attracted comments alluding to 'spray-on jeans' from the mature and sensible grown-ups in my life – who clearly had no idea whatsoever about the latest in fashions!

So, because I was not a follower of fashion, I needed to avoid the pressure of making stressful conscious choices after I left school. I began to become more comfortable with who I was, preferring to spend my money on a new hockey stick or a swanky tennis top. I can still be heard saying, at around fifty years old, that 'I can't go to that posh 'doo', as I've got nothing to wear and I look too frumpy' – the same excuses I used long ago to avoid the school disco. Hello! Would anyone go proudly to a school disco in an old, cut down jumper with crocheted, capped sleeves and a green corduroy, home-made, flared skirt with the letter 'N' elaborately embroidered on to it? The trauma has left its mark!

Nicky Coope

**

That christening outfit; less the smart centre of the party than the symbol of a new identity...
Hatch, Match and Despatch

I'm not really into clothes. Don't get me wrong, I obviously don't run around naked, but I can't really remember any clothes that have a special significance in my life. That is apart from two – my wedding dress and the christening robe that has been handed down through my husband's family. Now, that is special, for it was handmade, naturally, probably sometime in the early 1900s. And having had to repair it after my grandson's christening, I know that it must have taken a lot of time and effort to create. We probably wouldn't bother now but in those days being welcomed into the Church was a huge threshold and the occasion deserved a special robe. It was the beginning of a child's life of faith, even if any lasting effect on the child was not guaranteed!

I can also bring to mind several other personal threshold moments in a church setting. I have almost always been involved in Sunday School /Junior Church. Firstly, I attended and then graduated to teaching there and I've done that pretty well continuously ever since. I have taken many children over various thresholds in their Church life – the youngest with their need for help in creating things, rising up to the faith challenges provided by teenagers. Demanding certainly, but I think in many ways that is what has kept my faith going when it has wavered a little along the way.

Then, of course there are the thresholds that don't require 'threads' at all – firstly, a new birth. While the primary responsibility for caring may belong to the parents and immediate family, a new life lays on all of us a collective responsibility for the world in which they will have to survive and, we hope, prosper. It would be good to say that we all work together and do this without any problems, but of course we don't.

Secondly, the inevitable end of life as we each try to understand it. A very frightening threshold for some and yet for others a step into a new everlasting life with their Lord. How do you help someone over that threshold? How do you help yourself, for that

In a Jar by the Door...

matter? In the end, while you can say that what you believe is to come makes death non-threatening because it is a new beginning, no-one actually knows any detail of that future. In the final words of one of the booklets published by Christians on Ageing, *Death and Dying* by Gerry Burke, when we die we may well get the greeting, *'You weren't expecting this, were you!'* Oh well, one thing is for certain – we will all get to find out one day.

Sue Kennedy

**

Speaking of T-Shirts, we meet two 'allegedly' identical ones...
Sandpit Encounter

One gloriously sunny midsummer afternoon, I perched on the edge of a sandpit and chatted to the two beautiful little girls who are our landlord's twin daughters. They were together busy constructing and moulding impressive sandy sculptures. As they are normally quite shy little people, I was thrilled that they had agreed to be interviewed about being identical twins...so I went to where they were and that was in the sand pit!

I am not sure who is Lottie and who is Pippa, which is not surprising as they really do look identical, but the first thing they told me was, 'We are not genetically identical at all. It is a coincidence that we look just the same!' Well there's a conundrum for a start!

'People get very confused. We like the same sort of clothes. We like to shop and buy new clothes and Mum knows what we like. We might choose the same style but in different colours. To help people at school, we have different colour shoes with the same uniforms that everyone else has, but we have different button badges to help tell us apart. There are lots of mix-ups!

'It is annoying when people try to set us up. They even sometimes call to us as if we were one person, Plottie! Or try to point out not very nice differences between our looks. It can be hard if we get wildly different marks in school or are not doing as well as each other in sports. Subs time-out from the game is especially hard if it's just one of us. We understand, but it can feel upsetting. 'But there are lots of advantages. We always are each other's best friend. There is always someone who understands you and we are always there for each other. To look in a mirror is like looking at yourself and at each other at the same time, so we can see what things look like on us...on each other! That makes shopping for clothes quicker! It has been easier moving schools because we have double friends as we are in different classes.'

Reading through this happy and fascinating encounter, I realise that the words 'same' and 'different' crop up again and again, which leads me appropriately into their description of one of their items of clothing:

'We have T-shirts, which say on the front 'Same, Same', then on the back, 'but different'!

Editor from conversation with twins Pippa and Lottie Brown

**

Joy when something fits straightaway...
On Being Small,

It is far from straightforward being small, especially if you were born with a congenital back deformity that means you can't wear shop bought clothes. Believe me they don't fit, no matter how hard you try!

I envied my friends going out to shop for the latest styles. The only garment bought for me as a child was a school blazer and even that had to be altered. Being short in the body was a definite handicap in my formative years. Nothing fitted properly, I was 3'11 inches when 11 years old, and clothes had to hang from the shoulder, no darts in the back: dresses and skirts looked tiny and they were. School uniform, it was bad enough having to wear one, but it was even worse having to stand for fittings while poor Mrs Hood made and altered it for me.

When I started horse riding again after a spell in hospital, jodhpurs that fitted at the waist were way too long in the leg, a size smaller too short, but elastic kept them down and it did not look too bad. I would have loved to buy a hacking jacket off the peg but again back darts and fitted at the waist was a no no. Even my show jacket had to be made. Getting the material, black, and lining, red, was not too difficult but it had to look right! I was very proud of that jacket and kept it long after its sell-by date, hung up under its protective plastic.

Everything had to accommodate my 'bump on the back' and that was that. 'Can you do anything with the darts at the back?' I asked my mother and Mrs Hood on a regular basis as clothes started to matter when I reached my teenage years. Usually dresses and skirts had to be altered, taken up, trousers were rolled over at the waist if they were not to be too long, otherwise out came the scissors and a huge chunk came off the bottom. On some occasions, especially with skirts, they had to be taken in also so as not to spoil the hang. How nice it still is when I occasionally find something that actually fits and I can put it on straight away.

I was over the moon when 'crops' came into fashion. Never before had I been able to buy trousers that I need not take up! Apart from the fact that they were cheaper, there was none of the cutting down or taking-in, just put them on and go.

Nowadays, fortunately there is an excellent local tailor who is getting to know the 'do you think you just could...'. Nevertheless, having accepted, at an early age, that this is how it would be and we can't all be perfect specimens, I still search in the children's department for something that fits immediately.

Being 4' 3" now, and a size 2 shoe, is not the end of the world. What I wear is who I am, and that's that.

Lesley Bustard

**

In a Jar by the Door...

An unexpected diversion into the enigmatic multi-sensory nature of the fabric which we wear...
Sound, Touch and Smell

At the age of 7, I insisted that my mother buy it. It was a cerise fuscia pink woollen cape, having a black mandarin velvet collar and hat. I can even recall the smell of the new wool immediately. Clothes are a multi-sensory experience.
                                                Jordan... on Woman's Hour – We are What we Wear.

When I consider the loving patience required for creating garments by hand - the use of remnants and the investment in planning, preparation, following instructions, freedom of choice and (precious) time - I think it is a real gift to be able to make an item that will be worn, loved and long treasured. I fondly remember the era when I had things made for me. My own efforts have more of the sixty-minute makeover feel to them because I have difficulty in concentrating on the unseen details. Maybe it is down to my school memories of failed needlework projects, or perhaps the relevant gene is simply missing in the same way that I am also unable to read a map or assemble a piece of flat packed anything!
        Having said that, the excitement at the arrival of the new gingham material (the starchy smell was perfume in comparison to the pervading school odour of mustard and cress and warm milk) was the highlight of the summer term at my junior school. Unfortunately, it was then our challenging task (girls only) to make a dirndl skirt to wear for country dancing. There was a lot of bloodstained gingham!
                                                               Gill Causley

At a Hollywood costume exhibition, from Wizard of Oz, Dorothy's gingham dress, a snip at £140,000. Hollywood costume is not about fancy dress or fashion. It is about telling a story.
        From a Weekend article... If Costumes Could Talk.

One of the favourite smells in all my life occurs when retrieving washing from the line after a good blow, and maybe even better still, when it needs to be prised from the clothes pegs and stands upright in its own strength through having been frozen! Of course, all this delight is lost if instead your clothes have simply been tossed round in a tumble dryer!
                                                               Hilary Vinall

As a retired psychotherapist, I have observed that indeed all sensory modalities can be brought into play when talking about clothes. By this I mean especially sight, sound, touch and, of course, smell. The latter is often neglected despite the fact that often it is emotionally the most poignant ingredient of nostalgia. In terms of sound, perhaps one of the most evocative noises is that of listening to someone with whom you are intimate either dressing or undressing: the alluring prospect of discarding clothes to reveal more than

nakedness, and the contrasting donning of clothing, maybe evoking the opposite fears of rejection or distancing...

Ian Stewart

**

Reluctant medical student encounters the woman of his dreams on a bus...
Beauty in a Fur Coat,

When we reflect on the past, all of us realise that there have been definitive moments. Times when what seemed to be chance, co-incidence, serendipity – call it what you will – has altered our lives in some profound way. So it was for me in my late teens, in my very early days as a medical student, in the mid 1940s. The incident can be recalled with clarity, although time may distort detail.

It was foggy: what we called a Pea Souper. Emerging from the Underground on my way home, visibility was reduced to a few yards. A long queue had formed at the bus stop, but eventually a bus suddenly loomed into sight and we clambered aboard. Heading hopefully to the upper deck, because it was standing room only below, only one seat was vacant. Laden with text books and grateful for my luck, I was about to sit down when I recognised a lady who lived nearby occupying the adjacent seat. This was someone of notoriety in our insular, middle class community. She was a glamorous, ex-chorus girl; a divorced, single mother and, as gossip would indicate, from a somewhat disreputable background. Here, however, is the actual reality of that person...**beauty in a fur coat**. Mention is made of the latter because it seemed to epitomise the lure of this exotic, desirable but unattainable creature. Its sensuous texture was immediately overwhelming. I was in thrall and without the wish or ability to converse. Ironically, soon my ineptitude was challenged.

She turned to me:
'Hello. Don't you live a few houses away?'
"Yes. Yes, I do." Silence.
'I see you are carrying large books.'
"Yes. They are to do with work."
'Oh. What kind of work is this?'
"I'm a medical student."
'Gosh that must be so interesting!'
"No. Not really. Not for me anyway."
'Oh. Why's that?'
"Well, because it's not enjoyable."

Here I must digress to explain. In short, it was already clear to me that Medicine and the prospect of being a doctor had little appeal. Studies in anatomy and physiology were distasteful and largely incomprehensible. The whole ambience of medical school appeared alien, but I was attempting to conform to family expectations.

'Then what would you rather be doing?' she asked.
"Something to do with literature, I suppose."
'Really! That's interesting. Any particular aspect of literature?'

In a Jar by the Door...

"Well, I like poetry."

It was, let it be said, at a time, I suppose, of my delayed maturation, when poets, for example Emily Dickinson or Rupert Brooke, expressed at least some of my adolescent angst.

'Any particular poets?' she continued to question.

It's a measure of my patronising pomposity at the time that I had hitherto assumed this lady to be unintelligent and ill educated, with little familiarity with poetry as a literary genre.

"Well, Rupert Brooke for one," I responded from my superior status.

'Well, give me an example,' she responded.

About that particular time I was enamoured of a Rupert Brooke poem evoking the difficulties youth had in communicating the pain and ecstasy of growing up. My attempts at recall on this vivid landmark impinge on subsequent events. The poem was called The Hill.

I attempted describing a boy and girl on a walk. "One verse begins, 'proud we were who had such wise true things to say'," at which point I seized up, realising the enormity of my self-exposure. However, to my chagrin and surprise, she continued, *'and then you suddenly cried and turned away.'*

Suffice to say there was of course an instant of profound readjustment about my travelling companion, and that moment began a process of integration into a loving family where my aesthetic longings found guidance and companionship.

Ian Stewart

**

The incentive to buy is 'Do they make me smile?'...
Rings and Things

It all started in the summer of 1976 when a lovely friend, who lived in London, went to BIBA in Kensington and bought me a yellow, square plastic ring. To me, as a teenager living in the sleepy Lake District, this was so cool and trendy. Up to that point, the only ring I had worn was a traditional, gold signet ring which belonged to my paternal Grandma but from then on I started looking out for rings of all shapes, sizes, colours and materials.

I have more than 50 rings and wear six of them daily. My favourites are a silver filigree ring bought in Bali, a silver and cubic zirconia, a modern ring from Iceland, a three-armed, diamond and sapphire, gold ring from Thailand and my Edwardian engagement ring, gold with five rose cut diamonds which dates from 1905.

My watch collection is equally large. I wore a traditional, gold link, small faced watch as a teenager and the view then was that you had one gold watch which you 'wore for life'. Not for me! Having always worn bracelets, it occurred to me that if my bracelets matched my outfits, why shouldn't my watches? I have watches of all types now – from a crystal, strapped, rectangular faced DKNY watch to an example of every colour – white with purple spots, pale blue with pink flowers, spring green, forest green, pale yellow,

banana yellow, orange, beige stripes and silver, to name but a few. None of these are expensive and I wear a different watch each day. My favourite has a thin, navy wristband and a large circular face with diamante round the outer edge plus diamante stars on its navy background. It reminds me of the night sky in Kielder Forest.

As for my bag collection, that grows each year too! I have straw baskets bought in French markets, a multi coloured Kipling bag (complete with black gorilla) from a Florida mall, a beautiful, small beaded, pale pink bag from London and numerous work bags. Each season brings a new bag. This year has added a bright orange shoulder bag and a white and pink handbag with large pink flowers on one side. My bags need to make me smile and, as a result, I certainly have no black bags.

Helen Radcliffe

**

Heartbreakingly shameful...
Sally's Rags

I was told this precious story a few years ago. At the time I did not write it down because it felt too sacred to commit to paper. But 'Sally' has assured me that it has been helpful for her finally to share it. She is now a very grounded, self-aware lady, but still experiences excruciating pain and humiliation on recalling one of her mother's 'punishments' for a minor misdemeanour.

Nine year old 'Sally' had a very special dress, which she treasured and loved. A misunderstood and sometimes sadly abused child, she felt beautiful when wearing this dress (on her outside) such that, when wearing it, she could be whom she longed to be... on the inside.

How Sally had upset her mother involved a fairly trivial incident, but her mother in punishment took this dress from her; she tore it and slashed it with scissors until it hung in rags, and then sent her to the shops in it, 'so that people can see how shameful this little girl is'.

It takes my breath away even to recount it for her now, and as I write I am wondering how one woman can do this to another. Yet I am reminded how this anger and fury and envy must be deep in the human psyche, whenever I recall the treatment beautiful Cinderella received from her stepmother and sisters.

'Sally' has carried the trauma of this incident for decades, but she has grown into the woman who has now had the courage to share it, and entrust it to another. In my work, I am time after time overwhelmed by being granted the trust of 'strangers'. Yet then they become no longer strangers but part of my life too...

Editor from a Telephone Conversation with 'Sally'

**

In a Jar by the Door...

Trauma of medical intervention on a mastectomy threshold...
Mastering the Art of Stuffing,

'We recommend a mastectomy, Mrs F,' said the young, slim, dark-haired (newly married) surgeon, looking kindly towards me. I was glad I had a friend with me. All I could think was, 'Do it as soon as possible', and, shocking myself I responded with just those words. The rest is history. My friend said, 'I suppose I should take you home?' I opted for fish 'n chips, mushy peas, a cuppa and bread and butter at the nearby fish and chip, supreme dining establishment of the North!

It was only when I sat down later that I thought, 'What will I WEAR after the 'event'? Will I never wear a T-shirt again or anything strapless or tight fitting over the bust? Opt for the tent line? How elegant is that?'

I imagined nearly all of my wardrobe going to some charity shop. But I didn't want to part with anything. I'm one of those folk who doesn't look for clothes, they look for ME, and are usually very expensive but different. My wardrobe is fully stocked with such items and I love and cherish them all. (It is a small wardrobe!) I went upstairs and looked at those clothes and thought, 'keep them: all of them: you never know'.

I looked down at my bust and couldn't really imagine what it would look like with half of it gone. What do you replace it with? A bra stuffed with cotton wool, like we used to do at school when wishing to show peers in the changing room that we had a bust under the games kit.

A fortnight later, after the op, lying in bed in hospital, I realised the seriousness of it all. I'd had cancer – it had been removed along with my breast and I was VERY FLAT on one side of my body. I just thanked God that I was privileged to be in that state and that life WOULD go on after I'd mastered the art of stuffing !!

I returned home, clutching a bra with pockets in and (as I said) a clump of what looked like cotton wool. I looked at myself in the bathroom mirror and almost wished the surgeon had taken away the other breast too. I decided I quite fancied being flat-chested and wearing Charleston-type clothing and similar vintage stuff which I have always loved. However, he hadn't, so I couldn't!

Later that week, a catalogue arrived called 'Nicola Jane'. This was to let me see that you could wear swim-suits and lovely bras of all types. It even showed me the weird and wonderful types of stuffing and padding, and all that jazz.

As I write this, my lovely clothes are still there and I can wear every one of the pieces in my wardrobe. At this very moment, I am wearing a skinny vest with linen trousers – and I have the confidence to wear the same things I always have. The fear of not looking normal has passed – my clothes and I survive!

PS My greatest challenge? I've just got to make sure I'm not lopsided when I go out!

Rachel Faulks

**

Identity

A clothing inspired smile of joy after a life-changing illness...
'This one' or 'That one'

Recently I travelled to Buckinghamshire to see my longstanding friend Sandra, both of us now in our eighth decade! In earlier times (when I was the 'youngish' old-woman-who-lived-in-the-shoe with five children), I minded her two children after school hours, Sandra having gone back to teaching. So we had very close family connections, and although our lives subsequently went in different directions, we had kept in touch over many years.

I travelled that day with a heavy heart. Shortly after her dear husband Doug had died following a very swift and unexpected illness, Sandra had suffered a severe stroke. She still lives independently but with much help, both professional and from friends and neighbours. Of course Mark and Jenny, her children, visit when they are able as they live in the very distant North! She is amazing to cope with the many difficult challenges, still strong in the spirit of who she has always been; intelligent, engaged, loving company.

But I sat there feeling unable to help much during such a short encounter. Then her physiotherapist knocked at the door, so I knew it was time for me to leave. But, as I left, Sandra's face lit up in a big smile. She pointed to my fuscia-pink silk shrug and said, 'That is what I could do with to wear over this brace.' Oh how exciting! Something I could do! 'I will sort it somehow,' I replied, 'and bring one when I come next time.'

I did not have a clue how I could do that, as this was my all-time-favourite, sale-item of clothing, having been designer made by Manijeh, creator of glorious floaty, silky, velvety, pointy and eccentric garments, this one bought at the Ripley Castle Summer Show. Well, I found a dressmaker nearby and some more glorious linen silk fabric, pink with exotic birds of paradise with feathers of magnificent shape and hue. I wasn't sure whether Sandra would prefer the original plain one, so I took both on a hanger, one on top of the other and offered her the choice.

On we sat chatting as they hung there, while as she tried to decide.
Then, bing bong went the doorbell and I had to go.
'Please could I have them both?' she asked.
'Mm. Yes, of course,' I replied, Yikes!
'My beautiful silk shrugs have been a wonderful addition to my summer wardrobe, instead of my fleece jackets. They cover up my shoulder brace, which, though not very elegant, is essential to keep my arm well supported,' said Sandra in a later thank-you call.

There is an even more lovely sequel to this...I met Manijeh at the next year's Ripley Castle show whilst buying an amazing Donegal Tweed with red velvet slash coat in which I look like an ancient Biblical shepherd, (more anon). I told her the story and she was so moved, she said she would make me another one as a gift as Sandra had received mine as a gift! It hasn't come yet, but that does not matter. The pleasure I have had from the thought of that offer, and from Sandra's joy, and from the enormous smile on her face in a photograph which Jenny sent me of her Mum wearing it, more than compensates for my fuscia-pink silk shrug having prematurely crossed a new threshold! Never ever consider clothes are a frivolous issue!!

Editor from the sofa with Sandra Purrett

Clothes!

God of many guises,
You show yourself to us in so many different ways
Through people, places, events and nature, to mention but a few.

We too each come in many guises,
We dress for different occasions or roles in our lives.

An invitation to rummage through our clothes chests!

God of many guises,
It's quite exciting preparing to lift the lid on our old clothes chests;
To re-discover old favourites,
Re-ignite old memories.
It feels like being a child again
To open up the fancy dress box,
To try them all on,
To laugh and giggle,
To strut and pretend!

But, God of many guises,
There is also a bit of apprehension.
Our lives and our clothes are intimately bound;
Wrapped in each other.
Will the worn out old favourite remind us of what we can no longer do and have had to let go?
When we stand in front of the mirror in what once fitted so well,
Will we see that that particular role in life no longer suits and sits awkwardly now?
Will the anger rise again when we confront the garments we were once compelled to wear by others?
Will a garment remind us of those "halcyon days" long gone,
Or of friends long gone?
Or...

But, actually, God of many guises,
Thank you that we have had clothes.
Thank you that we have memories.
Thank you that we have laughed and giggled.
Thank you for friends and stories shared.
Thank you for our lives
And for the possibility of new clothes, new stories,
New discoveries of you in others
And even new discoveries of you in us!
Amen

Liz Styan

Through the Vestry Door
(editor)

A Reflection

Famous or Infamous?

The conventional image of a Church of England vicar entails certain rules and expectations, established over many centuries. In applying for such a role in three northern rural parishes I am threatening to confound at least three of them. (Maybe in time even more!) I am a potentially mould-breaking appointment. I am lay (a Reader), yet applying for a licensed House for Duty post. I am a woman, when there is still resistance in some sects of Christianity to women's leadership. I am from the South, yet arriving to unfamiliar pastures for interview in 'God's own country'. Not inconsiderable thresholds to cross then.

'Who is this woman?' ponders the Archdeacon of York, one sunny Autumnal morning in his massive study, (huge mahogany table, moulding on the ceiling, auspicious and imposing photographs, various gleaming tureens and the like). He addresses his computer, which tells him that someone has at last responded to his advertisement in The Church Times for a priest to lead his flock in one of his most historically troublesome parishes, right on the very boundary of his diocese, almost in fact falling off the edge. He is intrigued. 'Who is this woman who writes to me and asks, 'I am not a priest, but please can I apply for your post anyway?' I had better see her.'

I find my way to our meeting, apprehensively crossing the threshold of Micklegate Bar, an historic arched and turreted, stone castellated edifice at one entrance to the ancient town of York, which in earlier days was sometimes used to display on spikes the heads of those who had displeased and fallen short! Be warned! And he decides to take a chance. 'Ann, just go and love the people,' he instructs. I did; and I do.

As I was an 'un-ordained minister', one potential conundrum was, 'What shall I be called?' 'How should I be addressed?' Hmm. I wasn't a Reverend, a vicar, a curate, a deacon, in fact few villagers fully understood the designation of Reader anyway. Thus, I became a sort of hybrid, discovering myself on yet another threshold. Some settled on 'Vicar-ess'. One child from school called me the Angel Inspector. Not that it mattered. I was still welcomed in as the Vicar. I did wonder about this, as historically I understand that the term 'vicar' comes from the root, 'vicarious', ie doing the work on behalf of someone else, usually the Rector, or God even! So maybe I was a Vicar after all. Or perhaps a Parson, which sounds a rather pompous description of me. A Pastor then, maybe? What an identity challenge for this unconventional appointee! What, no dog-collar? New 'thresholds', certainly. In church, of course I did wear Reader robes – long blue scarf over clerical vestments. Metaphorically, I would enter the vestry in secular mode, then exit as the personification of a liturgy-friendly, religious leader.

In a Jar by the Door...

But my approach to 'threads' has always been unorthodox anyway. Would that be a hindrance? For some of my old fashioned, new colleagues maybe, but the parishioners were more than comfortable...in the street, in the shop, in the pub, in the school. Similarly, I had been asked by a priest many years ago, whilst I was the manager of an ecumenical hospital chaplaincy team, if I didn't find it a problem, when walking around the wards, not to be visually identifiable by my clothing. My response at the time was, 'No, I don't think so. And at least patients do not need to pretend to be 'asleep' when I arrive at their bedside!'

So, why are my day to day clothes considered eccentric by many? Coats are perhaps representative of my unusual style. One friend's legendary quote is typical, 'That coat is very Ann Bowes, but I wouldn't be seen dead in it!' And another recent one created its own impact too.

This coat, acquired at a Ripley Castle Summer extravaganza, is a bit like a horse-blanket, but made of Donegal Tweed, so it must be all right. Fringes and startling panels of high-quality shades of red/orange velvet nestle in slashed broad panels down front and sleeve edge. Backed by a subsequent Yorkshire G.P. comment, '...amazing. You look like someone famous or infamous', it next made a celebrity appearance at King's Cross Station. Travelling light for an overnight stay in Forest Hill, with only my yellow satchel for luggage, I am unexpectedly greeted by a stranger – a gorgeous young black woman, who says, 'I hope you don't mind me commenting, but I love to see an old lady in distinctive clothing. What a fabulous coat and scarf.' The scarf is bright yellow silk and embroidered in colour of every hue on the other side. Hand stitched and fringed, thought to be part of a sari. (It features Kanthan stitch, I am reliably informed.) We began to converse as she asked me if I was an artist, but I replied that I had written a book on the spirituality of clothing. Whereupon she contacted Amazon on her phone and immediately ordered a copy of 'Naked and You Clothed Me'. Vastly cheered, I went on my way! An unlikely gift to me and a happy, shared, surprise encounter!

The following day, on my return stroll along the concourse and up an escalator from King's Cross, an elegant young woman turned to me on the ascending stair and said, 'You look wonderful in that coat and scarf. The colours together are stunning,' and this sentiment was instantly echoed by an American couple, upwardly gliding behind me, both of them. What is going on, I thought, but happily and giggling to myself as I plunged further along the tunnels of the Underground.

Homilies

Armoured for God

Ephesians 6:10 - 19.
Paul writes to an early church at Ephesus, encouraging its members to metaphorically clothe themselves with God's Armour.

A front page of my Church Times on one occasion featured a full colour picture of two

soldiers in Medieval armour of the sort one sees languishing on marble biers in cathedrals and some churches. It bore the caption '101 ways of using redundant churches'. Slightly incongruous as an inspiration in the modern world.

Today, we rightly take a more sombre view of war and the seriousness of its consequences for those serving in the armed forces and for civilians and women and children on either side of any conflict. As a hospital chaplain I did much work with elderly men nearing the end of their lives, troubled about their wartime experiences and having had no opportunity before to share some of their anguish. Perhaps this is the reason why language which draws on the imagery of spiritual conflict is uncomfortable today. Yet, encouraging us to 'wear God' like a suit of armour to fit us for life, Paul writes of a belt of truth, a breastplate of righteousness, shoes ready to walk in peace, holding before us a shield of faith, and placing on our heads a helmet of salvation. All these clothing items are dressing for defence of our personhood. But importantly we are to carry a sword of the spirit, a metaphor for the word of God.

Actually, the image of armour may be helpful when considering our defence against the danger of attack by spiritual darkness. For an age and culture which is unfamiliar with discomfort, the experience of the battlefield and the stark bloody evidence of the consequences of our choices is something worth confronting as we consider the nature of Christian discipleship. It asks what costs are we prepared to face if we have put on Christ (as armour) in baptism? How does it feel if we make the deliberate choice of commitment to a hidden, mysterious, abiding truth, in preference to the ease of social convention?

Most of these pieces of armour are for defence; only one for offence, the sword ie the word of God, cutting through the change and chance of culture, of time. It reminds us that as baptised people we are part of the new creation in Christ! We are still, as 2,000 years ago, called to serve God in a culture which has by and large turned its back on Him. With our 'politically correct' rulings and pronouncements, it sometimes feels that Christianity is the least tolerated of all religions in this country. Like the early Christians we are called to stand fast against the assaults of spiritual darkness.

The shields of Roman soldiers were designed to overlap together to form a defensive wall to deflect any attack. Don't be discouraged by the statistics around church attendances. Think of us together with our overlapping shields. But nevertheless, the battle is real! Someone once was heard to say, 'We are trying to keep our congregation numbers up so we can pay our parish share.' NO! That is not why we hope our congregations will grow! The battle is real!

The belt of truth; a broad leather apron which went under the heavy armour to prevent the wearer from chafing. A discerning belt which will protect us from lies and deception.

The shoes of peace are very important. 'I wouldn't be in your shoes'. These are the most valuable possession for some peoples of the world. They help us stay upright when others try to knock us off our feet! How beautiful are the feet of them that

In a Jar by the Door...

preach the gospel of peace. A way of living in the world; a society longing for peace. We soon know when we are not wearing the right shoes for the purpose, as my friend told me when she had to walk a mile in an emergency in her 'car to bar' shoes!

The helmet of salvation to protect our thinking and our minds from being led astray down unhelpful and destructive pathways.

The breast-plate of righteousness is a prayer to protect our hearts from temptation to succumb to that which might harm us.

Make no mistake, this passage is a call to prayer. Lord, dress me in your armour that I may stand firm and deliver the good news in the world in which I live. And prayer is not a one off session once a week. If we are to build up the body of the church we are commanded by Jesus Christ to 'pray without ceasing'. To grow in prayer we are to make it a constant and unceasing offering. How do we do that? Like in pastoral work. It is not what we say, but how it feels just to have us alongside as a presence.

C.S. Lewis in his Screwtape Letters rightly says that the general public, even we ourselves possibly, prefer to ignore the existence of forces of spiritual darkness and to pretend they don't exist. Or we feel we can stay comfortable with the caricature of the devil as a little red, horned character with a tail and brandishing a toasting fork. But this passage is a sober and realistic assessment of both the struggle in which we are engaged and the weapons and protection which are at our disposal.

How does it feel if we make the deliberate choice of commitment to hidden, mysterious, abiding truth, in preference to the ease of social convention? Can we creatively use this image of dressing and clothing ourselves in the armour of God, despite it being a slightly unusual component of our wardrobes today?

He is a God of surprises, after all!

**

Shining as Stars

Philippians 2:14-15
Do everything without complaining or arguing, so that you may become blameless and pure, children of God without fault in a crooked...generation, in which you shine like stars in the Universe.'

A Diocesan Advent Workshop day was introduced by these words;
No wonder they say there are four ages of Santa Claus.......
At first we believe in him,
Then we don't believe in him
Next we find we are him
And finally we just look like him

So how do we come to look more like God? How will we ourselves become holy so that, when others see us, they see us like shining stars and long also for that which we have encountered. And I don't think Holy in this sense means being pious and necessarily very goody-two-shoes. But do we

Identity

sometimes find ourselves being critical and judgmental of others whilst omitting to see the plank in our own eye? Or a bit like the Pharisees who pray and fast in the market-place but are not in such self-denial at home. No, we are encouraged to go into a quiet space, where we are prepared to listen to God as well as to speak to him with our myriad requests. And then allow ourselves to be changed by him. By being prepared to cross a new threshold, trying to change the habits, patterns, fixed ideas of a lifetime which are less than life giving now for ourselves and maybe others around us. And that requires humility and that is a tough one. So I invite you to bring this down to earth a little.

However much we may long for our loved ones to go to the doctor, do their home work or take a holiday, we all know from experience that unless they share our concern, they won't get round to doing what to us seems sensible and good for them. We may nag or drop hints or threaten or cajole, but in the end, it is up to them and we can do nothing about that.

Perhaps it is rather like that for God or the Divine spark within us, as he sees what would provide such lasting good for the children he loves, and yet he must watch us often making disastrous choices, never getting round to actually tackling our repeatedly unhelpful patterns of behaviour, wasting opportunities, and by and large ignoring or forgetting to seek all the Christlike teaching, examples and offers of help.

We are each of us only responsible for the choices we ourselves make. It is very important to understand that God will never hold us to blame for any evil committed by our parents or ancestors, and any guilt we may be carrying as a result of another's abuse of us is guilt that belongs to them, not us. It is God's will that we should be freed from such unjust burdens.

The truth is that God promises through his word to teach us how to make good choices. And through Jesus, God is working within us, if we seek it out and allow it. That might mean help from and sharing with others. Not easy to do that, is it? But the promise is here of God through Jesus, inspiring both the will to do good and the act of carrying it out.

So, we are called to be involved in the kind of caring, encouraging relationship with God which really does enable us to tackle those wrong areas in our life. We are never too old, too set in our ways, or too busy to take God up on his offer of live-in help.

God does not call those who are equipped, but he equips those he has chosen. You; me.

We are told very clearly in Paul's letter to the Philippians that it is to Jesus Christ we look for our model. Imitating Christ's humility, (not always knowing best). Look at the fruits of that in these verses: fellowship, tenderness, compassion, in humility consider others better than ourselves. Imagine it! I think connecting with the humility in Philippians is key. By whose authority do you live your life? Your own or that of the one who longs to love us into new being?

First we believe in him. Then we don't believe in him. Then we know we are him. Then eventually we look like him.

**

In a Jar by the Door...

Pray as You Can, and Not as You Can't

James 5: 7-13 Isaiah 35:1-10
'Is any one of you in trouble? He should pray.'

We live in a Pick and Mix society. Choice is allegedly everything; the greater the variety, the better it seems. We are seduced by supermarket shelves and TV advertising. Yet we know that can be more confusing than life enhancing. Thus in terms of spirituality too. We want to know better how to communicate our faith with those outside our congregations, yet we look on in confusion. Much is bewilderingly described as 'spirituality', from lighting incense sticks while soaking in the bath tub to the way we arrange our furniture, through yoga or clairvoyance as well as a myriad ways of traditional prayer via the many faiths in our multicultural society. Where do we begin? Why do we pray at all? What are we seeking through prayer? Why haven't my prayers been answered?

I asked my elder daughter about prayer. She knows what it is to pray and be prayed for, for over 30 years, after radiation damage. She has never 'got better', only steadily worse. This is how she responded...

In a way, for me prayer is as much about feeling God, as words. I pray that he helps me to be the best that I can be – you always taught us that the important thing to God is that we try! When I pray for you all, it is like coming to find you through God and I am as close to you as can be! And importantly, I pray that God helps me to trust in his plan for my life and that I am open enough to him – and brave enough to follow where he guides.

My teenage grandson says he prays anywhere, but often as a *'distress call, if you like'!* Honest!

I have a deeply religious acquaintance who is profoundly depressed and in the darkest place imaginable. He has no words, no love, no feelings of longing to approach God, or no way of knowing how he can even begin. All he can say is *'Here I am'*. (Yet, interestingly, 'I am' is another name for God.)

I was recently privileged to be alongside one of the holiest and jolliest women I have ever known whilst she was dying over several weeks. We spanned prayer in word, music, silence. Eventually she slipped into apparent unconsciousness...So, how to comfort her now? I tentatively slipped my holding cross gently into her hand. After every time when she was turned, washed, injected, she fumbled around for it, restless till she was reunited with it in her palm. I understand it went with her on her journey from life to life.

Four different human beings, in different contexts, praying in different ways. Pray as you can and not as you can't, I heard once. Words, feelings, touch, helplessness, distress, comfort.

To enhance prayer, some people find candlelight helpful, or walking, breathing in a self-aware way. We can be inspired by hymns, scripture, others' words of meditation or poetry. I have recently learned to pray a prayer of examen twice a day; examining the events of that time and being thankful, even for those events which have challenged me or made me disappointed in myself. I am learning to be thankful in adversity as well as joy. How freeing and transforming that has truly been. It reminds me of words I once read in a book about prayer from many different faiths. Prayer does not change God. He is

changeless, but it always changes the pray–er.

There is Celtic prayer, incorporating Trinitarian doctrine in the landscape, season and the sacrament of everyday life. Taize prayer, though one is a bit stuck if one can't read music at a glance and naturally sing harmony. Over the ages and traditions art, architecture, music and the triumph of the human spirit have inspired prayer. For myself, there is the profound value of the Quaker prayer of corporate silence. Once I was prayed for by a woman whom I had known for years without realising that she could pray in tongues. It was like being washed with gentle, cleansing, soft rain.

So, how about us? Many reading this will be in midlife and upwards. But if you are young, still listen, in order to know what is coming. Jung says that most of us are wholly unprepared for the second half of life, as we cross this new threshold.

We take this step with the false assumptions that our truths and ideas will serve us as hitherto. But we cannot live in the afternoon of life according to life's morning.

So how can this shed light on our prayer life?

The first half of our life is about development, establishing our-selves, building work, family, home. And then comes midlife, quite unbidden; the challenge to discover who we really are, what is our relationship with God to become now? We can find ourselves in a place we don't recognise.

The very exciting revelation of being older in Christ can be a coming to awareness that ALL our life is an expression of our relationship with God. The hospitality we offer, the listening ear. All is prayer. Our spiritual life is always in process; there is always the exciting potential for transformation. That is the glorious mystery of it! We may feel sometimes we have mislaid the map, but there are signposts on this threshold, which we can learn to recognise. New ways of meeting God, which may very well look different to the ways which have enriched our relationship with him in the past.

The longest journey of search in prayer is the one from the head to the heart. Be prepared to be surprised by God. Waiting without an agenda of words and expectations sometimes enables us to listen better and the stillness of the listening gives God the space to woo us into an ever more intimate relationship with him.

'The quieter you become, the more you are able to hear.' Rumi.

All are invited in prayer, in silence and stillness to wait for God.

He is waiting for you too.

A Final Musing

'I Didn't Get Where I am Today Without...'

You may remember a sit-com of the Eighties, in which a rather pompous, be-suited and waist-coated executive gentleman used the phrase frequently. This was in order to reinforce his dubious and unlikely success in the face of all the odds stacked against him on his daily commuter line to the metropolis. I find myself using it increasingly, but in a rather more counter-intuitive manner...

'I didn't get where I am today without...

In a Jar by the Door...

...having made a number of mistakes and taken more than a few reckless risks!'

And I am still hoping that if only I could learn by my mistakes, life might be a little more straightforward for me now! Risks of course can be taken, with surprising outcomes...in the genre of another Eighties cliché, 'Feel the Fear and do it anyway'! Here is a time when I did just that and crossed a threshold in an unlikely venue.

A few years ago, late one Saturday evening, I was travelling back by train from London to York. It was crowded, so, just being very thankful for a seat at all, I tentatively sat at a table with three Newcastle United football fans, their team having lost somewhere in London that afternoon, who were working their way steadily through a twelve pack of lager! They were also noisily engaging in a crossword to while away the miles. Later, as the journey progressed and the riotous fun and liquid intake increased, the coach slowly emptied, and I was just considering moving my seat, when, stuck for lexicon inspiration, they began hilariously to involve me in their exercise (the crossword, not the lager). Oh, goodness! Eventually, as the puzzle answers filled up the squares, they asked, 'What are you then? A teacher or something?' 'No,' I replied, 'I am a sort-of vicar.' Silence fell! And then...

'Right,' said one of them. 'The missus wants us to have our Shane christened, but I think we should let 'im grow up to choose for 'imself; what do you think?' Oh, help! I asked if they ever took him to church. 'No, I want 'im to choose for 'imself.' (Oh, my goodness, where can I go with this one on a train with these merry revellers?) Then, an answer to a quick arrow prayer from the unlikely threshold of this journey. Here we go. Drawing not on the resources of my theological training, but on my across-the-generations, male-family-members' football passion, the conversation went something like this.

'When Shane is big enough, will you take him to Newcastle United, so that he can grow to share your faithful and committed passion for your team?'

'Yeah, course I will,' he replied.

'So that would give him the best chance of finally choosing which ground to go to when he grew up, wouldn't it? Because he would be unlikely to just start going, would he, if it was an alien place for him to be? If he didn't know how to 'be' there, what to do, or know any of the people there, or even who the key players were? If he didn't know what it was all about? If he didn't know the songs?'

Silence.

'Yeah. You've really made me think. Thanks!'

We all then proceeded quietly on to York, where I breathed a sigh of relief as I alighted! Too soon alas to relax. What is this? Oh, my! Here is a lady running down the platform after me. And then ensued another conversation...about all the others in the carriage who had been listening and...taking note!

Another story, maybe...

'ee, that's champion…

VILLAGE

A village means that you are not alone, knowing that in the people, the trees, the earth, there is something that belongs to you, wating for you when you are not there. – *Cesane Pavese*

I live in a village where people still care about each other, largely. – *Jan Karon*

There are often village vicars in Midsomer Murders, but the village vicar was killed off years ago. – *John Nettles*

How can anyone be silly enough to think himself better than other people because his clothes are made of finer woollen threads than theirs? After all, those finer clothes were once worn by a sheep, and they never turned into anything better than a sheep. – *Thomas More*

The best fashion show is on the street. Always has been and always will be. – *Bill Cunnningham*

The real leader has no need to lead – he is content to lead the way. – *Henry Miller*

Through the Wardrobe Door
(Contributors)

A new resident steps bravely through a hidden portal known only to the initiated...
Crossing a Threshold in my Lime Green Boiler Suit

It is a warm evening in early September 1983. I am sporting a comfortable, cotton lime green 'boiler suit'. It is casual, generously voluminous, tightly belted at the waist. My hair is captured in an abstract patterned, predominantly green silk scarf and I am wearing canvas pumps of a similar shade. I am comfortable in this relaxed, colourful 'skin' – and my own skin is brown, after a month in Italy.

We are patrolling the principal thoroughfare of Brafferton, in search of a particular Public House. I have been informed of its existence by my 6th Formers at Easingwold School – and that it is un-signed, lacking front door entry and known by locals as The Fox. I am intrigued. It sounds to be a village treasure and has caught my imagination.

We like the village. We think we'd like to live here. We have walked the dogs by the river. We think the main street of Helperby looks almost French on a hot day. There is a Butcher, a Hardware shop, Fish and Chips, an MOT service...and so much more. I would not raise an eyebrow if I were to be told there was also a 'candle-stick maker'. It feels to be 'real' – an authentic community.

'Is there a pub along here?' we ask passers by. We are directed to the Oak Tree.
'Ah yes...but we understand there is another one...The Fox?'
Heads are shaken. We are stared at. Up, down and around.
The lime green outfit is a contradiction to camouflage.
...Tentative exploration through an archway, across some cobbles and a curve into a back door...across the threshold into a dark, but fluorescent-lit backroom....

A pause of silence greets my repetitive refrain, now in tentative, apologetic tone: 'Is this a pub?'

My husband is now silent, uncomfortable. Then comes a slow: 'Aye lass...what are you having?' Chris remains seated. Harry rises. Our eyes slowly adjust to the light.

I feel very bright. Gaudy. Peacock-like in this sombre-toned place. We see the squared configuration of traditional settle seating and newspaper, around a central collaborative table. There is nowhere to hide.

I choose not to ask for a gin and tonic. We have beer, brought from the cellar in a jug. We smile. We know, and more importantly, we feel, that we are in a very special place.

Mutual first impressions and assessments are in the air. These taciturn-looking gentlemen remind me of similar treasures from my Norfolk childhood. I see that they are trying to decipher us, who we are, what we represent – very soon to be evidenced by an amusing miscommunication.

Harry: 'Are you an "Anti"?' (the boiler suit clearly sending a message aligned

'ee, that's champion...

with insurrection against bloodsports). However, allowing for the Yorkshire accent, I heard 'Auntie' – so, whilst mystified by the sudden turn in conversation, I speak loquaciously of my recently born and be-freckled nephew.

Harry is patient. A long pause...then: 'Aye, I love kiddies too...but are you an "Anti"?'

I get it. I smile. I am able to sufficiently reassure him.

We are quiet, respectful, but we engage. We feel like fortunate, almost-accepted guests, despite looking so very 'out of kilter'. And perhaps some measure of our cautious acceptance was the inclusive honour of an invitation to join the collective Fish and Chips order – apparently a habitual, hasty process, before the shop closes.

A 'runner' is sent.

Although we did not buy and start restoring Brafferton Hall until the following spring, this evening was our threshold into Brafferton and our friendship with Chris and Harry Bannister. I think that Dennis Scaife and Arnold Moss were there that night. The old village names.

That lime green boiler suit, so curvaceous, so comfortable, clothed me for diverse and playful outings. It was particularly fine attire for 'forward rolls' on local picnics. It was treasured during pregnancy, gradually loosening, then abandoning the belt, and in October 1985 I sported it into Ripon Cottage Hospital to give birth to our first child, Teddy. I wore it through my pregnancy with Olivia. Later, I decorated in it.

Subsequently. whilst delivering the Parish Magazines, I came to know Harry and Chris and we laughed about that first night, the early connection, the confusing question. They told me stories of the village. They told me their story. Of Harry and the war. Of Chris at home, the brothers divided. Harry only knew Teddy, who he customarily hailed to be 'a fine lad'. Surprisingly, and so very touchingly, they left a small legacy to our children from their Estate.

I hold my lime green boiler suit very dear in my memory, as I do other clothes that are linked to significant events or periods in my life. It feels like a sort of companionable 'bearing witness' to these years. I feel I had 'a relationship' with it.

I can see it vividly, in my 'mind's eye'.

Liz Oldfield-Beechey

**

Pete, the 'garage man' of raconteur fame meets Clare Balding with BBC cameras, in the village...
According to Pete...

April 2012 saw one of the most poignant moments in recent British horseracing.

The sport at the highest level is dominated by multi-millionaire owners, backed by lavishly equipped training establishments and elite jockeys. And no event is more high-profile than the 30 fence Grand National at Aintree – at a million pounds or so, Europe's most valuable steeplechase, with world-wide media and public attention and colossal betting.

But in 2012 a potential 'fairytale' was brewing for a proud but humble, elderly

Helperby garage proprietor, Pete Nelson, with no false expectation of fame or fortune but who now found himself the surprised owner of a National outsider in the diminutive shape of 11 year old According to Pete. A white-faced bay gelding, full of mischief, a Polo mint addict, who had originally lived in a village paddock (behind the workshop, behind the house) and from which as a youngster he had playfully escaped by jumping into next door's garden. Now he was being trained in Ryedale by Malcolm Jefferson and skilfully ridden by young Harry Haynes. Having won 11 races and £200,000 so far, the horse was, however, really still just part of the family whose owner had bred him and was living an unlikely dream in the build up to this, the horse's 50th race.

Pete himself is an archetypal village character, a raconteur of local stories, who knows what is what and who is who, past and present. His family would give a wry smile and raise their eyes when they heard him 'putting folks in the picture', and they would say 'well, according to Pete...'.

Early on, I met this essential character and his wife, Anne, with her soft-furnishing business, plus daughters Louise, with her high-quality catering, and Sandra, with her Parish council expertise. I soon also visited his mother Jean, sometimes taking her Holy Communion at home. Over a cuppa I heard the tragic tale of his little 8 year old brother having been fatally run over, still eliciting tears in the telling, decades later. Pete had been the eldest of seven children – timid, shy, being picked up for school by two girls, Freda and Sheila, but sometimes crying all the way there or running away back home. His beloved Gran always stuck up for him, with perhaps a shilling after his weekend visits to spend on sweets at Nancy's, the little nearby shop. She even gave him a wind-up watch. 'She did spoil me.' Soon an apprentice at Driffields' seed farm earning 25 shillings a week, contributing £1 of it towards mum's housekeeping, with her skills gleaned as a young housemaid at Cundall Manor farm. Weekends might also involve football or cricket on Saturdays and a Wesleyan service on Sundays.

An interest in horses maybe came down from his dad who placed a bet every day from the phone box down the road. Any winnings would be delivered to the house on Sundays! Having married in 1963, Pete bought ponies for his daughters to be kept in two fields (ten acres) that the Bannister brothers had bequeathed to him. Over the years, ten horses came and went. Including a successful filly, Magic Bloom, who won seven races, According to Pete being her second foal. Not a likely prospect, however, because he turned a leg out and had no bone at all. But a fighter, with heart.

What about the Nelson racing silks? Red and mauve with a chevron, and a jockey's hat to match in quarters. A few months before the National, According to Pete carried them to victory in the Rowland Meyrick Chase at Wetherby at 33 to 1. 'I'd dreamt about winning that race,' said Pete, 'but Anne just called me a silly bugger!' However, an even better win followed at Haydock three weeks later. Suddenly, the first Yorkshire-trained National winner since 1960 was a possibility.

Helperby and the villages around were buzzing with excitement. Bets were placed at 40 to 1, then 33 to 1. And Clare Balding arrived with her BBC camera team, all staying at the Oak Tree, a hundred yards from Pete's house, whence he delivered them newspapers on the day. Many locals had indeed been interviewed, but the story had captured the hearts of the nation too. Hopes were high that Pete might soon even be

'ee, that's champion...

leading the horse down the village's main street as a winner.

But tragedy befell this gallant horse.

And there had been a harbinger of doom early in the race. One of the favourites was a 9 year old gelding called Synchronised, winner of the Cheltenham Gold Cup a month before and ridden by champion jockey Tony McCoy. But, spooked before the start, he fell at the sixth fence, the notorious Becher's Brook, first time round, and after running on alone, fell again, broke a hind leg and was put down by lethal injection beside the track.

Meanwhile, According to Pete was running and jumping well. Becher's Brook was made of spruce trees, and notorious because of the size and angle of the 6 feet 9 inches drop on the landing side, which is lower than the take-off. It was the 22nd fence second time around. According to Pete approached it fast, still full of confidence and strength. And all would have been well, but an adjacent horse fell, collided with According to Pete and brought him down. A shoulder broken, the terrible decision was taken to put him down. Trainer Malcolm Jefferson was hit very hard but said, '...it's just a freak accident that could have happened anywhere. Even if the fences had been a foot higher, he would have jumped them.' Nevertheless, only 15 of the 40 runners finished the race. Controversy over the horses' safety inevitably ensued.

Needless to say, Pete and his family were devastated. Still are. Clare Balding and the news team were very caring. Letters and cables came from all over the world. Top trainer Martin Pipe said, 'We all pay tribute to this lovely man. Everything he has ever had he has worked hard for, whilst remaining a humble, gracious man with a gentle sense of humour.' Of course, rallying round Pete, fellow villagers were heartbroken most of all.

The once-in-a-lifetime moment was over. But Pete continued to live a good and simple life. He has done many things he had never envisaged. Going on holiday to Dubai. Owning a historic house in the midst of a village he has long cherished, with a wife and family full of gratitude for every blessing. The village church, with memories of harvest festival and Hidden Gardens fundraising when strawberry teas were served in his garden. And the lifelong love of horses, with that very special According to Pete. A legend, like his owner.

Editor from conversations with Pete Nelson

**

The Pied Piper extraordinaire, for 50 years criss-crosses the thresholds between church, school and playgroup…
If only I had known…

My church life began when I was around ten years old with taking two younger sisters regularly to Sunday school. Other children would follow us, curious to know where we were heading. Eventually they were persuaded to join the lessons, and so it began. Like the Pied Piper, I gathered children along the way.

Once married, my next threshold loomed ahead. My husband and I moved to Brafferton/Helperby when he changed his job to work on a local farm. Our elder daughter began attending the local playgroup but unfortunately it closed down a few months later, so a few mothers took children to a more distant class for pre-schoolers. Then, once our son was old enough to start, I joined forces with another mother to take our children to another excellent playgroup, held three mornings a week. Eventually we were asked to supervise the sessions. By this time we were attracting a range of other local toddlers. (Pied Piper rides again.) Before long, I was elected secretary and then chairman. When our youngest children were old enough to start school, we said, 'farewell', only to be asked to open a playgroup back in our own village. In the absence of an obvious building, the school agreed to our using a classroom which stood alone in the playground.

Thus, Helperby Playgroup, initially with six children, later re-named Brafferton Playmates, started from humble beginnings and grew and grew until thirty years later we were awarded the North Yorkshire Kitemark. For 30 years I went into school each morning to support children who struggled to master the art of reading.

For twenty of these years, as it was a church school, I also served as Clerk to the Governors. Plus helping to set up a 'Sunday School' on a Wednesday evening.

Once again imitating the Pied Piper, I collected up to seventeen children and escorted them to and from the Vicarage. By then, I was also the PCC secretary and Electoral Roll Officer. When people asked what my duties were in Church, I said I did everything but give the sermon. It was easier than explaining yet more roles...verger, cleaner, clock winder, grass cutter with my husband, fund raiser, teacher at messy church and other seasonal activities, 'Open the Book' team member, publicist, purchaser etc, etc.

Another threshold idea came to me one afternoon whilst contemplating how the PCC could encourage more people to utilize the church building, not necessarily to attend the services but to come and enjoy the building in the peace and quiet for a moment with God. A voice came into my head saying, 'People enjoy reading books'. Was it a voice from a higher authority? Who knows? Donated books came in by the hundreds. I appealed for bookcases. Again, they came readily. All books were free to borrow, but a small donation for Church funds would be welcome if they wished. The first year raised £150.00. Unbeknown to me, this coincided with the mobile library ceasing!

By now, the fabric of the church needed some tender loving care. More fund raising. Electrics made safe, decorating afresh, new carpets. The church gradually looked beautiful, fresh and clean again. A few years later the stonework needed attention, so a

'ee, that's champion...

lottery grant was applied for to help pay the enormous cost of up to £150,000. A ramp was installed at the front door for disabled and wheelchair access, and a 'kitchen' in the choir vestry too. Come 2019, everyone was looking forward to the usual joyful Christmas services, but, one stormy night in that November, thieves removed all the lead from the Nave roof. It was still raining the following morning when I went to open the church as usual. What greeted me stopped me in my tracks. Water was pouring in, everything was soaked. I felt sick and angry that someone could do this, but the villagers and schoolchildren rallied round magnificently.

2020 of course saw Covid 19 when much of the nation's life stood still, with churches locked. Though village and church life went on behind the scenes, coincidentally 'retirement' finally beckoned for me. A life-time of service in more ways than one!

Maureen East

**

On the threshold corner between two villages sits an imposing deconsecrated Methodist chapel, subsequently the home of a musical family who share their talents inside and outside St. Cuthberts...
Curds, Whey – Mercifully, no Spiders

The former Wesleyan was not the only such Chapel in Helperby. The other now deconsecrated Methodist church became hugely significant for me personally and for the parish work. That building sits literally on the threshold between Brafferton and Helperby, on the very corner where the one village metamorphoses into the other! Now a domestic dwelling, but what an interesting family dwelt therein! And I met them sooner rather than later. All of them!

While searching for a small, secular job to supplement my pub/restaurant waitressing, and help finance my day to day living, I visited the school. The head asked if I had any experience with children, so I explained about my family of five! 'Well,' she said, 'We have a brilliant mother here who helps with the school music. She has four musical boys and a musical husband, but he has a very busy job and now that she is really poorly and confined to bed, she needs some help. Just someone to be there when the boys come home from school, and to cook a meal for the family until her husband comes home from work and can take over.' Hmm.

Well, I should be able to do that. After all I have had 30 years of child-care experience and cooking for my big family, as well as for all the others who often seemed to end up round our table.

Jess, that mother, no longer even remembers my being there because she was so ill with pneumonia. The house still looked like a chapel actually – even the kitchen, resplendent with royal blue Rayburn, still displayed the old chapel seats, complete with those wooden pockets...spaces for hymn books! Also, the main seating along the wall was a former pew, and the kitchen table had been crafted from another pew. It has a 'Shepherd's' crook engraved on the underside. The worship space was now divided by folding doors which could be opened for large gatherings. The encouraging biblical words of old still graced as a wall-painting, arching over the stairwell as a constant reminder:

With God all things are possible.   Mk. 10 v.27
Just as well, indeed, I discerned, because I was on more of a learning curve than I had thought. Jess was just about conscious enough to say she was glad I was used to cooking on an Aga, and, by the way, the whole family was vegetarian. Oh, my goodness…very unusual then, back in the day. 'The recipe book is on a stand and the sieve and the muslin next to the bowl for making the curds and whey.' Oh, yikes! So, I set off on my Little Miss Muffet tasks with awe and wonder and hoping for no spiders! Another risky threshold for them all, as well as for me. Happily, once she knew that her family would have a good, cooked meal once a day, Jess could let go into the anguish of her suffering and safely stay in bed to slowly recover.

This family came to be a sort of 'causeway' or 'bridge' as I crossed from the South to the North in my pioneering church post. Bridges can be wobbly but still safe. It was as large a chaotic family as the one I had left behind, although my own children were by now grown up. Music was indeed seriously key in this family. Cellos, violins, trombone, piano practices. Even the two-year-old had a sopranino recorder! I came to associate this family with safety, fun, and mutual working.

Still in young adulthood, they recently all joined children from across the county in a concert of river and railway music Jess had organised at Shildon Railway Museum, 'Where the Music Takes us'. On another much earlier memorable occasion, they played a specially composed version of Psalm 150 in all its glory and splendour, including trombone and drums, to celebrate the 50th anniversary of the Myton organist, Douglas Webb. This piece had to be subtly re-written at the last moment because Harry's voice had broken during the time they had been practising! Even more challenging must have been organising an ambitious performance of Spem in Alium for Jess's 40th birthday, with 40 voices singing the 40 different parts, which had happened just before I arrived.

We once shared a conversation about our models of motherhood…and I could see the similarities as her boys grew up. Important that they had a good home-cooked meal as already mentioned, and we were like-minded in allowing them to go their own way, even the wayward ones, and yet drawing them gently, non-judgmentally and safely back when they reached the perimeter. The shepherd's crook, presented to me when I left, had prompted this conversation, as she felt it typified my parenting and ministry alike. 'Like a mother,' she said, 'having an overview of the three parishes, a sort of unconscious consciousness. In the knowing of the people, their situations, personalities and gifts, to see 'possibilities' in taking risks to explore how church and community could work and fit together.' She made a further thoughtful observation. 'Many clergy focus exclusively on the church in the building, and do not look much outwardly from it. Is this because Faith is predominantly an inward and private issue and the calling therefore frequently attracts the introvert?'

Throughout, Jess has helped and encouraged me as I crossed a threshold into working more with children, not only in the village school. Since leaving the parish, I have

'ee, that's champion...

travelled as far as Harrogate and Leeds with the Godly Play stories, working on a BBC project she was coordinating, called 'Ten Pieces'. Schools were given ten classical pieces to enjoy and learn about, of which I performed the Jonah and the Whale story accompanied by 'Storm' – the fourth of Benjamin Britten's Sea interludes from Peter Grimes. A wooden whale ate a little wooden Jonah, then spat him out onto the beach to sit under a green pipe-cleaner tree that actually wilted! Later, in another project, Carnival of the Animals, Noah and his ark inevitably came into its own! An offshoot from these excursions into schools took me to a multi-racial school in Leeds (pupils with 27 languages), using Godly Play to teach The Ten Commandments. One of the classes had no English at all. Except for one little boy who normally could not listen to anything or keep from rolling round and round the room. At the end of this session, I asked the silent children, 'I wonder how Moses felt when God met him and came close to him on the mountain?' I feared receiving no response, but one came from the rolling-round-the-room one. 'He would have felt very blessed!' Both the teacher and I shed a tear!

Jess and I share an approach to life…suck it and see. Whilst encouraging others. 'The truth is Ann, that the church life grew so much while you were here, because you got other people to do most of it!' A good friend indeed. Hallelujah!

Edited from conversations with Jess Hayne

**

From a quiet little village on the river bank boundary, the story of a key historic battle site and crossing place since Roman times…
White Monks in Battle

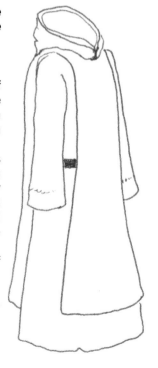

Round a corner at the far end of the lovely little village of Myton-on-Swale lies a commemorative bridge across the river. It marks the threshold to a site of much bloodshed on 20th September 1319, The White Battle. A turning point in the Scottish Wars of Independence.

While Edward 11 and the main English forces were occupied in laying siege to Berwick on Tweed, King Robert the Bruce of Scotland sent a diversionary army of some 15,000 men under his greatest generals – Lord Douglas and the Earl of Moray – to ravage towns and villages in the North of England, and possibly capture Queen Isabella who was in temporary residence in York. However, she fled back south to Nottingham on news of the threat, so the Scots camped in fields outside Myton, pending their next move.

The nearby wooden bridge across the Swale was a crucial consideration. The English feared it could give access to an onward Scottish march to attack York, so an ad hoc fighting force was formed to oppose them, consisting of local people and clergy including the Archbishop of York, abbots, priests and many White Monks. Up to 10,000 men, but with only makeshift weapons and little or no knowledge of warfare, they stood little chance against the superior, battle-hardened Scots. By setting fire to haystacks, the Scottish army caused a confusing smoke diversion and in no time at all the river round the bridge ran red with English blood. By the end of the day 4,000 had perished, whilst others were captured for ransom – the only consolation being that the Scots decided then to return home, with renewed pillaging en route.

The destroyed bridge needed a temporary ferry replacement but was eventually re-built a little closer to Myton. By the 1990s it had fallen into a state of dreadful disrepair, and the village launched a refurbishment fund for the £450,000 required to restore it, before a grand re-opening in 2002, along with two explanatory plaques. This new iron bridge was designed by Gordon Page and overseen by his father, Thomas, who was responsible for the Westminster Bridge in London! In an Easter custom since, the villagers have hosted a guided walk around this historic area, followed by a festive home-baked tea for all-comers!

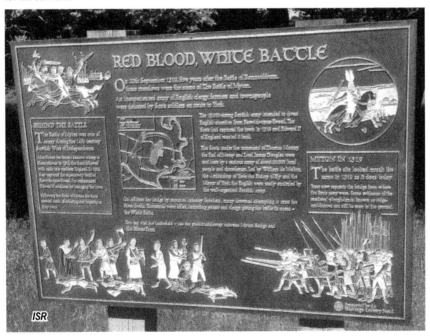

Irene Robinson

**

'ee, that's champion...

A blooming reminder for far and wide...
Flowers: Bright Gems of Earth

I was attending to some flowers in St. Mary's church in Myton-on-Swale when I recalled a favourite text that they had always brought to my mind – 'bright gems of earth by which perchance we see what Eden was – what Paradise may be'. I had dreamed many times of designing a flower festival here; it would bring into play so much of my creative imagination about all things natural. The Millennium was nigh, I realised!

June, the churchwarden, looked doubtful. Then she said, 'Yes, but there will be lots of flower festivals about, how and who would organise it?' 'You and I,' I replied, 'and everyone who wants to help; ours would be different.' Excited, I hurried home to get out paper, pens and plans! We wanted to celebrate, we wanted to raise funds, we wanted to include everyone – but we wanted it to be fun too!

The title of the flower festival was to be *'Aspects of His Love'*. *'O all ye works of the Lord, Bless ye the Lord, Praise him and magnify him for ever'.* Those who wrote this 'Benedicite omnia opera' lived within the rhythm of the seasons in a way which we no longer have to; they lived closer to nature, respected it more, and found a reason for rejoicing in every aspect of it. This canticle reflects this but goes further, it calls for everything to rejoice in its creation and to glorify God for it. Though flowers are just a small part of creation, creativity is a fundamental characteristic implanted in us by God.

We planned a flower decorated arch over the outer gate to attract passers-by to wander in and see what was happening, and also, around the sanctuary wall, a garland of fresh evergreens with pretty silk flowers and ribbons interspersed. Volunteers gradually learned how to wire and tape and bind (and chatter); fun and sore fingers became the norm. By tea time one Saturday their joint effort had produced the best part of the necessary thirty metres – yes thirty metres! Then everyone was surprised when a reporter and photographer arrived. A photo of St. Mary's church appeared in the Evening Press – great marketing for us!

Very soon we had exhibition entries from many local flower arrangers, groups, clubs and societies; Brafferton, New Earswick, York, Ripon, Harrogate, Easingwold, Northallerton, Sowerby, Pickering, Barwick in Elmete, and even from as far as Leeds, resulting in over forty five displays, each telling the story of a particular aspect of God's love and gifts to us.

The celebration weekend began with a preview evening on the Friday. There was to be a short service and official opening by the Archdeacon of York. Music was by the Newton Singers with refreshments to follow in one of the two marquees which the wife of the late Ken Morrison allowed us to erect in their garden at Myton Hall. It was a beautiful summer's evening and the weather remained perfect over all three days. Visitors came from near and far, compliments flowed and the time seemed to fly. It didn't really end there. With the proceeds the village agreed to have a garden seat placed outside the church gate along with a generous donation to the fund for replacing the historic bridge in Myton. Daffodil bulbs for the approach roads and verges were purchased and duly arrived in sacks, which gave us another happy (if somewhat back-aching) morning planting them! Finally, we decided to make a time capsule, in which we placed everything about the festival: minutes, letters, photographs and programmes. We buried the sealed capsule in a very secret place known only to a few! We wondered whether maybe someone, someday, sometime, would find it and say, 'Let's have a flower festival.'

The outcome had been even more than I could have hoped for. All we had planned to do we had done. We had achieved it by sharing our energies, ideas and love for Myton, for St. Mary's, for God. Now every spring we have a 'blooming' reminder as our host of 'golden daffodils' nods gaily in the breezes in and around our beautiful village.

Hilary Porter

**

Another tiny village sees a different form of threshold crossing as a same-sex couple makes the pub 'The Old black Bull' into their home...
The Shawl and the Scarf

The tiny village church of St Mary Magdalen entered our lives very early on after we moved to Thormanby. Rural North Yorkshire is not known for its LGBT Pride marches and most certainly has never had a same sex couple buy a former pub, convert it into a family home and then become Civil partnered. So we arrived at this new destination in life with some trepidation. Would we be tolerated? Would we be scurrying around, attracting knowing glances from the community and living a slightly reclusive life? This was to be a new phenomenon for 'them' and 'us'. The simple answer to that was a big, fat NO.

However, early on, during one evening of 'dancing and partying' in Middlesbrough, a late-night, jovial Peter, my partner, decided to invite a

'ee, that's champion...

dozen or more friends to this new home of ours. He had forgotten (!) until around 11.30am next day, hangover in tow, as I was preparing the roast and vegetables for our original two guests. He had the said flashback and confessed that soon there may be a few more! Well, picture the spectacle. A gaggle of 14 young(ish) gay men sat in the sunshine on our front patio, swigging gin, telling near-to-the-mark jokes and laughing very loudly. I do not think the villagers had seen anything of the sort – ever!! Needless to say, the vegetables and meat per person was limited, to say the least. My excuse at the time involved blaming Peter, yet I felt further justified as gay men do have a propensity to constantly watch their weight.

We both hold a certain faith, Peter a committed Roman Catholic and I being a curious and baptised Protestant. We both agreed it was the same God up there, so wanted to support the only public village facility – our quaint little church. Ann, the 'vicar-ess', arrived on a pastoral visit. The first thing that struck me about this lady in a shawl was her fun, mischievous eyes. She was quirky, not formally stiffly dressed but 'edgy'. She typified my perception of a former feminist activist. I felt comfortable, especially when I met her husband Paul who was a touch more traditional in dress style. Why did I feel like that? I suppose the balance and conflict of how I should dress in our new rural environment was epitomised by our new Minister and her husband. Edgy (think gay urban living) or traditional?? I realised very quickly that this community really would not care. Twenty years ago, I wore a mixture of both, with a third style of compulsory work clothes. Ann and Paul showed that no choice was out of bounds for me nowadays.

Peter and I were approaching a further threshold in our relationship, but when it came to our plans for a Civil partnership, we knew the institution would never allow any sort of ceremony within its building. That still hurts my soul, as we were and still are a big part of the support group at its village church, but equally I respect the formal position. So we planned for two stages. The Saturday was to be the legals at the registry office and the Sunday would see celebrations at home and in a big marquee with all the bells and whistles, in our paddock. Saturday's formalities were limited to close family and friends, then back to ours for an informal lunch. However, we wanted some sort of acceptable religious service as part of our big celebrations for the Sunday, as our spirituality was important to both of us.

This Minister was flexible and approachable. We talked to her. She would be delighted to help us deliberate. We arranged a supper to discuss and decide. Was it to be our last supper with the formal church? I will never forget the evening. She arrived in true style, basket in arm with a pudding, shawl and all. Peter and I could not foresee how this could be. We hoped she would lead us on a suitable path. She did not disappoint. She not only agreed to do something, she embraced it. It cannot have been easy, as there was a conflict between the Church's regulations and her personal support for what we were trying to achieve. She explained that she could not offer anything official but would work on a service that captured all our needs in an informal, rather fun way. She certainly did that, and to boot acted as referee to the inevitable bickering that Peter and I constantly display!

One thing I will always remember was a throwaway thought I offered. I stated that we wanted to be fully accepted, not just tolerated, by the wider community. Ann stroked her scarf, looked at me, understood and agreed. Her scarf to me seemed like a cloth of knowledge, and either that or the shawl wrapped around her offered constant back-up. A sort of fabric of God. She actually used the phrase when speaking, remember no sermon allowed, at the 'service' in the marquee. I do know that the new Vicar, her gaffer so to speak, was uncomfortable with what she was doing but she stood firm and made it clear she was informally officiating at a celebration, not at a service, in her private capacity as a friend.

The ceremony was simply perfect. A mixture of colour, reflection, celebration of our joint faith as well as the commitment we were giving, full of music, hymns and love. As you can imagine, unconventional clothes of all types featured dramatically on this occasion. Ann wore earrings which were magical. Nearly matched by the garments some of our guests wore, jewellery and all!!!

For us as Christians, that very special occasion affirmed life-long commitment to each other and to God. Maybe the scarf and shawl helped, maybe not, but that personal guidance, assistance and support was simply something that no building or institution can ever replicate. It is the type of missionary ministry we hope and believe will introduce others into what should be the everlasting love of God.

Gareth Dadd

P.S. Subsequently, I often saw Peter's ageing mother cared for by his step-father over several years while she lived behind their Old Black Bull under Gareth and Peter's tender care. An impressive lady in spirit still. I visited her too as she lay at a critical stage in the hospital where they were accompanying her in the final moments of her journey from life to life, the ultimate threshold. I took lavender oil, though she had lost consciousness by then, (fragrance is known to be important at this stage), and, for Peter and Gareth's sojourn, some home-made, rough puff butter pastry, corned beef pasties and a couple of cans apiece of gin and tonic. Part of the holistic care of parishioners, as much appreciated and remembered by them as was the special oil.

Editor

**

Speaking of Lemon Meringue Pie, Soup and Stones?

My elder daughter, who, with humour and fortitude, handles a life weakened through ill health unexpectedly once described my Bero-inspired Lemon Meringue Pie as a 'foundation stone in an uncertain world'. So I am now musing on other 'foundation stones'... one such being communal Soup Lunches, of high deliciousness, at reasonable cost. Relaxed occasions where villagers can drop in to meet and chat about news and 'stuff'!

So, in that spirit...

STONE SOUP *(A recipe **not** from the post-war Bero book.)*

A stranger comes to a starving village,

Promising to make stone soup.

He finds some firewood, uses his own pot, puts water on to boil.

As the water heats, he wanders around, selecting, rejecting, cleaning

Stones.

He adds them to the pot, carefully, with strange muttered recipes.

Intrigued, the villagers gather round.

This is the best entertainment their village has had since the famine began.

As they listen, they hear the stranger admit that while stone soup is good,

It does taste better with a pinch of salt.

One of the crazier people (or is she actually more caring?) brings out some salt she has hoarded.

The stranger gets bolder, suggests carrot, and potatoes, and swedes, and dried tomatoes, and herbs.

As each one is added, others remember their own stores and bring them to the common pot.

We have all made something out of nothing

By remembering the old, old blessing, that together we can create opportunities which escape us

When we hide our resources and our skills from others.

Anon

Through the Vestry Door
(editor)

A Reflection

The Poor Relation

At my local interview for the House for Duty appointment, one cold, foggy November morning, I began to realise that no experience hitherto could have prepared me for this moment. It was awe inspiring in the wobbly sense. Maybe I should not have worn my silver-lined, bronze-bar shoes after all. The fog was so dense ('we are known for it here. It's all the water and being flat'), that I barely saw from the outside either the church or the house before I eventually moved in. The St. Paulinus side chapel as I entered for the interview was freezing cold (steamy breath) and it seemed the gas heater was always recalcitrant and resistant to being lit. My future incumbent (should I be considered suitable) was kind, gentlemanly and supportive, escorting me in to encounter the church wardens of the three churches. I shared with them my reflection on what might be possible in this, to me, unfamiliar but exciting landscape.

Thus did I come in my mid-fifties to this new responsibility for a group of parishes which were described by the wider deanery as the 'Poor Relation'. I was shocked at the injustice of that judgement whilst being inspired in some deep part of me. I am a great believer in the wisdom of traditional story-telling and observe that one of the very greatest wisdoms of all is of what happens in the end to the 'poor relation'. In stories of rags to riches, overcoming the monster, on voyage and return, or in tales of the Quest, the lowliest and the least rises to graciously but firmly become the richest in integrity, in beauty, through courage, example and leadership. Maybe we could just possibly become a flagship for the future of the Church of England. There was a long way to go obviously, as remarks about these belittled parishes at deanery meetings included, 'Do you even have an organ in Brafferton?' 'Is there any disability access to any of these three churches?' And 'Can you even get there through the floods in the winter?' Whilst many of the myths abounding were unfounded (St. Peter's church has a magnificent organ!), it is true that it is a watery place. Two of the parishes concerned are bounded by the River Swale which does have a tendency to flood the plains now and again.

At a formal level, the work focused on Church services...leading regular worship certainly, but also celebrating the life of the community more generally. Immersing myself in village life at every opportunity. Being involved with villagers throughout the week, not just on Sundays. A focus for everyone, not just church-goers. Creative events could only effectively happen because village people from beyond the church wall boundaries became involved and offered their considerable gifts and skills, especially musicians of a professional standard, and these occasions were increasingly enriched by a growing

'ee, that's champion...

connection with other village organisations; the School, the Drama Group, the Pumpkin Club, the Reading Group. I began to experience a mysterious movement of 'osmosis' with the village, in part spiritually, back and forth through the church walls.

As an example, I will lead you through the vestry door on to a historic, bridle bridge on the boundary. During my period of service, a significant Centenary anniversary arose, honouring the building of that nearby bridge across the River Swale. The 13th C. church looks out onto the village green and the plain up to the banks of the river, right over to the dales in the far distance. The eye travels in awe across one of the most peaceful and stunning churchyards in the Vale of York. ('The place where all the memories are kept', commented one of the schoolchildren.) A footpath runs alongside the Green to the crossing place of that swing bridge. It marks a special place, deserving of honour, being believed to be a site where St. Paulinus baptised 3,000 in the river on one occasion in the 7th Century. You are invited to join the congregation that sunny celebratory morning as we wander down to the river...

Homilies

Bridge on the Boundary

John 7:38.
Jesus said, 'Whoever believes in me, streams of living water will flow from within him.'

A bridge at Brafferton has stood there over the fast flowing water of the Swale for one hundred years, offering safe crossings for many thousands to and from work, play, trade and refreshment in one or more of the up to 30 drinking hostelries in the two nearby villages in days gone by.

The opening of the Bridle Bridge was described in the parish magazine of that time as a Red-letter day with a 'hot, delicious breeze!' 'Free of debt' thanks to a public subscription of the £344.6sh.6d, cost seemed to be a major factor in the report! Replacing the ford or ferry for foot passengers, this suspension bridge became known as the 'swing bridge' because youngsters used to swing on it from side to side. Although the original bridge was replaced in 1937, it is still colloquially known as the swing bridge. On opening day Mr & Mrs Miles Stapylton of Myton were presented with a silver key to unlock a silver padlock affixed to a chain, enabling them to open the gate and cross a bridge. The presiding vicar warned;

'It must be understood that everyone who crosses the bridge will have to do so at his own risk, as to be bridge repairer and bridge policeman is not the work of the minister of the Gospel.'

Spiritually the bridge has been described as a symbol of encouragement; it helps us to refuse to be stopped in our tracks, a symbol of refusing to take no for an answer. It comes to the brink of the uncrossable, then crosses it...a challenge then, to risk moving into unknown territory. A threshold of invitation. A sacred space. Companion of the life-giving water.

A prayer marks this century occasion:

Creator God,

We scatter the leaves from this bridge,

As the scattering of our fragile love into the River of Life.

Save us from tangling in the weeds of the mud:

From becoming sucked into whirlpools of despair:

From being deflected into tributaries of danger.

Yet, walk alongside on the bank of your shaping.

Sweep us along in the current of your flow,

That at last we may tumble exhilarated

Into the boundless sparkling ocean of your love.

And the 21st century gathering went down from the church as a family congregation to play 'Pooh Sticks', or rather Pooh Leaves, in the sparkling flow.

**

What on Earth am I doing Here Again?

1 Kings.19:1-4 5-7 8-15a.
And the word of the Lord came to him, 'What are you doing here, Elijah?'

What a heartache! And for many people it comes as a relief that the Bible realistically addresses the pains, troubles and heartaches of our life today without resorting to simply telling us these things should not matter; that we should just get on with our lives and put them behind us, or even worse, 'You have to think positively'. Not only by giving us good advice about how to get out of any pit we are in, but also by providing a person who is prepared to climb down into the pit with us. For that is all we need at such times, and all we can cope with.

Elijah is exhausted and worn down, therefore vulnerable to those nagging negatives, which whisper the futility and hopelessness and unfairness of it all. It looks to him as if everything he has lived and worked for has fallen about his ears, and that, as many of us know, is a desolate place to be. God asks, 'What are you doing here Elijah?' We know it well. 'What on earth am I doing here?' Or when we find old patterns repeating over and over in our lives, 'What am I doing here again?'

Firstly, Elijah receives practical sensible caring – sleep, food, more sleep, and

'ee, that's champion...

more food. Thank Heaven for all those practical caring people who act out of this kind of loving without any urgent questions or deliberations or advice. Then he is given time and space to come to God at his own pace. We are in such danger of trying to rush healing, with all the counselling piled on at times of heartache.

He shelters from the storm raging around him outside, reflecting the turmoil in his mind and spirit. But then after the wind, the earthquake and the fire, he discerns the gentle whisper of God calling him to the entrance to the cave, the threshold, the place where change can now take place, and he hears the question, 'What are you doing here, Elijah?'

Then comes the close contact when Elijah is ready for it. Gently God brings him to state the ache (confession?), and that may need to be stated more than once. Now Elijah is ready to move forward. God does the same with us through those who sit alongside, taking us through at a pace we can cope with, using just where we are as a starting point and gently offering a route of hope.

There is much here that we can learn about our encounters with those whose hearts are heavy. Pastorally it is important to just keep in contact through the dark days so that the sufferers do not feel isolated. Cards, short visits possibly, a message left on an answerphone. So why is that care which we can give any different because we are Christians? Well, it helps people to know we are praying for them too.

Or, as Margaret Silf reminds us,

God is the river which connects and flows between all human hearts, because he has made his home amongst us.

That is what Emmanuel means: 'God has moved in'.

**

'There's Always a New Challenge with Sheep.'

John.10: 1-10
The man who enters by the gate is the shepherd of his sheep...and the sheep listen to his voice...his sheep follow him because they know his voice.

Every year, on what is known as Good Shepherd Sunday, we are reminded of the pastoral model, rich in allegory of God's love for his people, set in a culture which fully understood the intimate contact and trust between shepherd and sheep. The shepherds lived with their sheep, knowing them all by name. They recognised his voice, so they followed him. His voice...

We know how important our human exchange is through voice. I have met children coming into the village shop where I have been working in the early hours of

the day saying, 'Mr Barry showed us you being on television.' Help! It concerns a lovely occasion in a garden setting, several years before, when I had asked the programme producers, please not to show my face! 'Oh, it's all right, we recognised your voice,' the children said. In terms of relationship, voice is critical. The sound of a voice you trust gives a wonderful sense of belonging. Through voices, babies and mothers of all created species, humans, birds, animals, recognise each other like a magnetic north. We hear it in the fields all around us in springtime in the call of ewes and their lambs one to another.

For those of us who are 'shepherds' of any sort (including parents, teachers, carers, pastors, friends, etc), voice and tone are very 'powerful'. We need to remember that we have huge responsibility in how we use that voice. So much in terms of respect or regrettably otherwise can be conveyed by tone. Sheep may not be considered to have a very profound capacity for reasoning, but they do know the voice of the shepherd who feeds and cares for them. I recall on my first pastoral visit to a farm, hearing a shepherd assisting at a troublesome birth. The tone of his voice offered reassurance, safety and trust, as she had to surrender to the force of that which held her in its grip, that key threshold to life, and then when she was ready, urging her on to fulfil the task in hand!

So, to be an effective and loving shepherd, and one whose voice is known and heard and trusted, we learn that it is the living in relationship which is key. Sally, a local shepherd, said to me recently, 'There's always a new challenge with sheep.' You who are shepherds know this. I know it too. The institution of the Church of England knows it. It is an institution in crisis. Why? There are many contributory factors of course and it is being very challenged indeed as to how to listen to God's voice more closely. In a rural village I discovered myself working on the boundary of a new understanding of what is or is not 'church'. These are times when ministry questions are confusing. In my final service I recalled the children's words…'We recognized your voice!'

We love it when you read for us in Godly Plays. Your voice is calming, soothing and most of all you make us feel we are in the story.

Churchill said, 'Never doubt that a small, committed group of people can change the world. Indeed, it is the only thing which ever can.'

No one is too small to be heard.

How does it feel to listen to a voice you love? How do you listen to the voice of God?

'ee, that's champion...

A Final Musing

I Wonder...

It is my first Christmas season as a minister in a rural Yorkshire village.

I wonder...

Would they be ready to share in the Wild Goose Adventivity supper? Dare I even suggest it to these people? Its beautiful simple liturgy challenges us to an alternative approach in Advent. It speaks of inclusivity, of welcoming Christ in the marginalised, in the stranger. It encourages the supper to be celebrated in simple, indigenous food, as a contrast to the indulgence of a society of plenty.

I am nervous. I don't want them to feel they've 'got to support it'. I don't know where I'll hold it even if they do. It needs a lot of room. Tentatively, the down to earth, lovely but blunt farmer's wife churchwarden volunteers her farmhouse kitchen, 'although we've never done anything like it here before! I don't know what the dog will make of it. And I don't usually 'do' candles.' Oh, and here comes a potential problem, because 'simple indigenous food' in North Yorkshire at this time of the year may mean venison or pheasant, and of course lamb, (all very fresh, it has to be said), but we manage to compromise on home-made sausages with cheesy leek sauce and jacket potatoes.

The evening comes...

I'm still nervous. I'm tired and have had an awkward phone call before leaving. Will they get the message? Why do I do these things?

I wonder...

I enter the warm gently lit room, filled with the fragrance of the sizzling sausages and jacket potatoes to come. People are gathered expectantly round the table. The evening moves on, and I, the stranger, sit quietly and look and listen. The wine and the conversation are flowing. The candle light reflects on the glasses and in the eyes of those eating and laughing and feasting together. The lesbian couple, the recent widow, the gay couple, the old villager, the new villager, the retired director from Rowntrees, his Scottish Presbyterian wife, the vicar, a Colonel Mustard wife, the farmer's wife ('this dog has never barked in the house before!').

And I wonder...why ever had I worried that they may not get the message?

I am humbled indeed...and full of wonder!

To be Busy...
Or not to be Busy...
WORK

Don't judge each day by the harvest you reap but by the seeds that you plant. – *Robert Louis Stevenson*

If you try and we lose, then it isn't your fault. But if you don't try and we lose, then it's all your fault. – *Orson Scott Card*

I'm a very down to earth person, but it is my job to make that earth more pleasant. – *Karl Lagerfeld*

I don't design clothes. I design dreams. – *Ralph Lauren*

For work I wear art; in real life I wear clothes. – *Meghan Markle*

Normal is getting dressed in clothes that you buy for work, driving through traffic in a car that you are still paying for, in order to get to a job that you need so you can pay for the clothes. – *Ellen Goodman*

Common Sense is genius dressed in its working clothes. – *Ralph Waldo Emerson*

Sometimes people have questioned whether I was making fun of the industry or just of myself... Clothes aren't meant to be worshipped at a church altar. – *Jeremy Scott*

...working in harmony with the earth's rhythms – now you plant, now you relax. Now you work the soil, now you leave it alone. – *Benjamin Hoff*

Through the Wardrobe Door
(Contributors)

Living and working on a Victorian farm, with its railway lines, dominating water tower and historic stables...
Home on the Stud Farm

In recent years the nation, it seemed, became fascinated by the trials and tribulations of farming in the nineteenth century – as compellingly portrayed in the BBC2 series Victorian Farm. Over the festive period, a single episode attracted no fewer than 2.8 million viewers and just one of the tasks undertaken was making and firing thousands of clay bricks to rebuild the old farm forge.

For Yorkshire farmer Nick Ramsden and his brother Nigel, this must have conjured up images of their family's Victorian farm being built back in 1870. Home Farm forms part of the Myton Estate, located midway between Thirsk and York and the seat of the Stapylton family for three centuries from the reign of Charles 1 to 1932.

The largest farm on the estate by far, Home Farm was chosen by Major Henry Miles Stapylton for improvement when he succeeded his father in 1864. What followed was a year of non-stop building, with the bricks made at brickyards near York before being moved first by barge up the rivers Ouse and Ure and then by temporary narrow-gauge railway across the fields. The result was not only a state-of-the-art,  architect-designed model farm based on plans promoted at the Great Exhibition of 1851, but also a stud farm, located a mile nearer the river, where Major Stapylton indulged his passion for trotting ponies.

In many ways, the Victorians' drive to apply 'Practice with Science' to agriculture mirrors the issues we face today: a growing population in need of food but a dwindling rural workforce. As a result, as well as equipping the farm with everything needed for self-sufficiency – from animal housing and grain storage to slaughterhouse, blacksmith shop and dairy – the model farm also sought to harness the latest technological advances. So, while the prospect of installing a railway in a farm building is not one many people would entertain today, for the Victorians it was an obvious thing to do, and the remnants of the two-foot-wide narrow gauge railway installed throughout the new Home Farm building is still in use today, linking Nick's mill and mix machine with the four fold yards that still house 50 head of beef cattle.

The other Victorian passion was steam power, used here to pump water from the River Swale into a huge water tower at the stud, capable of holding 12,000 gallons. From there water was gravity-fed, not just to Home Farm but also to the village of Myton

To be Busy... Or not to be Busy...

on Swale and the Major's residence, Myton Hall. At the farm a further water tower fed a stationary steam engine that was used to provide power throughout the farm buildings and in particular for threshing corn. It was an idea that was eventually abandoned – the steam engine had been taken out by 1900 – mainly because indoor threshing was found to be too dusty!

Nick's family have been farming at Home Farm for three generations, with John Ramsden – Nick's grandfather – farming it first as a tenant before buying it when the whole estate went up for sale in 1932. During that time much of the farm has been used pretty much as originally intended. 'We've always had sheep and cattle and had pigs too until just a few years ago,' says Nick.

'On the arable side we are now reduced to cereals and oil seed rape, having had to give up on sugar beet when the York factory closed. It's only been in the past 15 years or so that we've had to abandon using the extensive granaries provided as part of the farm's original design. While the grain lorries were still at the 15-ton mark we could reverse them under our brick arches and load from the granaries above. Now though, we have had to invest in a separate storage and drying facility.

'As far as the cattle are concerned, we are still using the original fold yards but these days they are certainly not ideal and the cattle take more time to see to as a result. Over the years, some changes have been made to the buildings to make them more workable but there's a limit to how much they can be adapted. There are days when they seem more of a burden than a benefit, but we recognize that part of our role is as custodians of our agricultural heritage. There's always some repair work and at times it feels a bit like painting the Forth Road Bridge, but that's the commitment we have made.'

While restoration and repair work has been ongoing at Home Farm, the situation with the Stud Farm is very different. It has been largely untouched and most of the original features still remain. The site boasts a rich history and as a result it is being extensively refurbished through Natural England's Higher-Level Stewardship Scheme. Shortly after being built, the stud became famous as the home of an exceptional harness horse – Shepherd F Knapp – brought from America by Major Stapylton. The Shepherd (as the stallion became known) was so successful both on the track and at stud that today all Morgan horses can trace their bloodline back to Myton.

The buildings commissioned for the stud included 32 stables, a covered exercise arena, groom accommodation and an impressive coach house. Much of this still survives, albeit in need of remedial work, and this is all the more impressive given that the site was requisitioned during both world wars. Used as a collection and training centre (or remount depot) for horses during World War One, the site saw 9,000 horses pass through on their way to the Front Line in France. By 1918, horses were being brought to Myton from as far away as Canada. During World War Two, the horse boxes were used as secure storage for sugar, which was, of course, rationed. This ultimately proved unsuccessful as the sugar deteriorated so much that it was ultimately unfit for human consumption.

'Renovating the stud is a massive and costly exercise as we are having to replace like for like and use traditional material and skills,' added Nick. 'We will also have a tight timescale as work has to be done around several colonies of bats – particularly Natterer's bats that have taken up residence in the water tower. This is in need of repointing, but work will be timed to minimize disturbance and gaps will be left between some bricks to provide them with the access they need.

'While overall this will be a very expensive project, HLS funding is available to cover 80% of the cost, so we are not facing the daunting challenge of protecting this historic site wholly at our own expense. When it is finished it will be brought back into use, although we are limited in what we can use it for and must reflect the uses to which it has been put during its history. In a nutshell that means equine or storage uses and we could use the covered exercise yard as a fold yard.

'There's no doubt that continuing to use Victorian buildings to run a modern farming business gets increasingly challenging, but we are also very lucky to have this direct link with such a dynamic and inventive period in history.'

Based on an interview with Nick Ramsden by Rachael Gillbanks
(published as an article, 'Living with a Victorian Farm',
NFU: British Farmer and Grower, February 2010)

**

Yesteryear's farmworkers' attire...
Airing the Trilby

When I started work on the farm just after the war, corduroy trousers were very popular, being much stronger and more hard wearing than the type we see today. Jeans did not become popular or universal until a decade later. Most farmworkers (male) possessed three outfits - a very best suit, usually a dark colour, which might have come from Fifty Shilling Tailors and was only to be worn on special occasions like funerals, weddings etc; a tidy outfit which might be the very best suit demoted, or a sports jacket and slacks; and work clothes which might consist of the tidy outfit further demoted and/or the above mentioned cords, because you needed a spare pair for whenever you were frequently wet

through. Nothing was thrown away until it was absolutely worn out. In colder weather a long overcoat with perhaps a trilby hat, or for work a flat cap, was usual. Work boots were usually leather, with the soles heavily studded and with heel and toe caps. Older men wore jackets and waistcoats; in the warmer weather the jacket might be discarded, but the waistcoats hardly ever. Shorts were for young boys and it was regarded nearly as a crime to take your shirt off. During the winter months any clothes which had been in the wardrobe for more than a day had to be aired in front of the fire before being worn or 'you would catch your death'. I suppose it was because the houses were cold and damp. I had an uncle who collected his clothes from in front of the fire when he went to change, but always put his trilby hat there so that it was being aired ready for him when he eventually went out. At that time nobody thought of going out after work without a wash and a change of clothes, even if it was just to the local pub.

There was a lot of ex-forces surplus stuff around at that time and we made good

To be Busy... Or not to be Busy...

use of it. I remember ploughing with a tractor in very cold weather, no cabs or comforts then. I was wearing two pairs of trousers, vest, shirt, wool pullover and tweed jacket. Over that I had an ex-army, 'Arctic' greatcoat, with an extra warm lining and an outer layer of thick waterproof canvas material; the collar came right up over the ears, so I had a scarf and cap on. On my feet were a pair of fleece-lined, knee-length flying boots, with long sleeved, fleecy-lined, rubber flying gloves on my hands and, to add to the sartorial elegance, an empty sugar beet pulp sack tied around my waist to keep the knees warm.

I had always had my clothes bought for me and had no complaints, but at 16 I decided that I should buy my own, with a proper wage instead of an allowance, which was not as financially advantageous but gave me independence. I well remember my first shop, when I had saved up enough money. I went into Harrogate on the train and bought a bright ginger coloured sports jacket, some grey slacks with bell bottoms and a wide pinstripe, a yellow tie with horses' heads on and a pair of light brown, slip-on shoes with a strap and buckle across. Then I went to my aunt's who lived near Harrogate. She said, 'Come on then, show us what you have got.' She enthused over it and said I had done well and shown some flair and imagination. My mother, who was already there and did not share her view, said she was appalled. When, next day, Sunday, I went to get changed in the afternoon, my Mother said, 'Put your new clothes on and show your Dad.' Proud as a peacock, I came downstairs. My father looked up nonchalantly from the Sunday paper he was reading and said 'Clothes look alright, but I never thought I would have a son who was too idle to tie shoe laces,' and went back to reading the paper.

When all the grain and potatoes were moved in sacks, you used your knees a lot to move them round on the trailers etc. This proved very hard on the trouser knees. Knowing that the pairs of slacks I wore for work in the summer were getting worse for wear, I dashed out to buy another pair; not being able to get what I wanted, I settled for a pair of jeans. They were not a posh brand and on the second day that I wore them it was very hot, and working hard, they were soon stuck to my legs with sweat. Bending over to sort out a heap of large sacks which had just been dropped onto the trailer from the combine, I gave a huge heave and RIP, the jeans split from the waistband at the back right down the middle and round to the front as far as the zip. The ribald laughter and jeers from the two combine men I can hear today, if I think about it. I had to wrap an empty sack around my nether regions to get the load home. That was the only pair of jeans I have ever worn.

Some conversations I heard and incidents I remember...

One man usually wore a battered trilby of indeterminate colour because when he hand-milked his cows it became more black with dirt than anything, One day he appeared in a new one. The conversation went like this, 'Nice new hat you have there.' 'Do you think so?' 'Yes, much better than that old brown one.' After a load of expletives, the person was told, "You cross-eyed, colour blind bat, it warn't a b***** brown un, it wor a b***** green un, you stupid b.'

*****

'New trousers?' 'Ay, t' missus gor em for me last night at t' jumble sale.' 'Are they alright?' 'No, I can't bend down in 'em.' 'Why's that?' 'Because they're too caud (cold) and

Work

stiff wi' muck and patches.'
*****

'By, he's worn that top coat for a long time.' Said of a prosperous man wearing a coat which had seen better days; the reply was, 'Ay, an' his father before him.'
*****

I remember my aunt's wedding when I was about five and I was rigged out in new clothes. I can't remember the details, but light beige short trousers and a fancy white shirt, I think. I was told to take care of them and keep them clean. I spent most of the afternoon fighting with the vicar's son, who was about my age; we pulled each other through hedges and wrestled on the lawn and threw soil and muck at each other. My new clothes were torn and stained and filthy and I was not a popular little boy, but my grandma came to my rescue and saved me, until things calmed down.
*****

When it was icy, we used to love sliding, and slid on all the places we could on the way to school and back again. Two of the boys rarely did because they wore very heavy boots and their father made them heavier still by adding more studs to the ones that were already there. Every night he examined their boots and if there was a stud missing they got his belt across their backsides.
*****

There was a man in the village who intimidated a lot of people and loved a fight and bullied a lot of younger people. One day he was on the same bus as me going to York. He got out of his seat and came over to me; I was apprehensive, wondering what was going to happen. He did not sit down, but said, 'You won't fight because you can't fight, so young man, you want to go and buy yourself the biggest hat you can find.' So, I went and bought a great big trilby and wore it. I had no more bother with him and he said to me quite sincerely, 'I respect you when you're wearing your hat.'
*****

After dinner about 12-45 on working days, a goodly number of men used to gather at the end of Back Lane where it meets York Road, and all manner of topics were discussed, together with local gossip. On Thursdays the talk was often about who had had a win on the pools, because that was when the cheques or postal orders were usually received. A lady who lived nearby seemed to be quite lucky with the 3 draws pools and a neighbour of hers said, 'I see She's gotten t'3 draws up again, in fact she's gotten 'em up twice.' Many questions were asked. How much did she win, had she a perm, how many lines? And so on. The man replied, 'Ah don't know, there's 6 pairs on 'em hung on t'washing line at back.' Laughing, everybody dispersed to the fields or outlying farms
*****

Told by a man who was obviously a knicker enthusiast. 'Mrs H went home last night with no knickers on.' When asked how he knew that, he replied, 'Cos I found hers near the hall gates this morning.' On being asked how he knew they were Mrs H's, he replied again, 'Because they had violets embroidered on them.' On being told that still begged the question of how he knew whose they were, he nonchalantly said, 'Oh, they had her initials embroidered on them as well.'
*****

To be Busy... Or not to be Busy...

Another time, the same man said, 'I was very disappointed last night. I went to help Mrs B. load her hay; she was on the trailer loading and I forked the hay up to her; when we were loaded I threw the rope over for her to come down and as she came down the rope her dress ruffled up and she had NO knickers on at all.'

John Reveley

**

Inspired diversity...
The Creative Farm

Farming families are generally reckoned to be practical people; after all they have to turn their hand to many tasks there, not purely agricultural. Both my husband and eldest son, and to some extent my eldest daughter, can mend machinery, fix plumbing, repair and construct buildings, as well as carry out traditional roles in the fields and with livestock. To some extent farmers are credited with being creative – the growing of crops and the husbandry of animals to produce food but not perhaps in the area of conventional arts, crafts and design.

On our farm, creativity sits comfortably alongside the usual activities. Whilst helping his father carry on in the standard farming pattern, our son and two other blacksmith employees he has trained turn out a considerable body of striking bespoke ironwork. And, using some of the willow grown specially on the farm, in another workshop here his wife weaves baskets and other imaginative artefacts, as well as passing on the skills of the craft to others.

Our eldest daughter seemed destined for a creative career from an early age due to her love of cutting up and arranging coloured paper. Now, trained in textile design and after working in London for some years, she has set up her own business here too. She creates, designs and teaches, developing highly imaginative fabric and wallpaper from her studio in a converted, relocated, 1930s cricket pavilion overlooking the sheep paddocks.

However, I left it late to follow my own creative interests, only studying for a degree in Art and Design when all the children were established at school. I developed my particular interest in ceramic sculpture at college and now have my own studio on the farm where I too run regular classes.

The closeness of our studios means much mutual consulting and support. Living together on a farm in a beautiful part of Yorkshire is something we all treasure. It is easy to be in touch with the changing seasons which, in turn, generate our joint creativity, and the landscape also does much to enhance those discussions, and contributes a dynamic influence to our highly distinctive, creative output.

Iris Wilkinson

**

A dressmaking naturist!...
What no clothes...?

Imagine a room in the village hall, kitted out to display a wealth of inspiring craftmanship: dress-rails displaying custom-made creations; a jumble of exciting buttons looking like jewels in colour, shape and shininess; bales of exciting looking fabrics; half-finished garments, pinned and shaped, a mere suggestion of what they would become. The smell of fabric is intoxicating, invoking miracles to come. Colour, design, possibilities rioted everywhere, yet in a controlled and professional context, inspiring respect and confidence all round!! Who is this imaginative lady who claims, 'I sometimes say to people, I can make your dreams come true.'?

Her story...

I was clinically depressed and living with a suffocatingly controlling partner. I was not in 'a good place'. I was living in a remote spot, surrounded by hills and near a small provincial town; I felt tucked and folded away. I was also in the throes of a complicated bereavement. My mother had died. She had always been very unkind to me and I had felt unwanted as a child; my grown-up self thinks now that she was narcissistic...so very confusing and bewildering. . . Here is an example of her diminishing of me...

My sister was getting married and my mother was going to make me a new dress for the occasion. She helped choose the pattern and the fabric and it was beautiful and looked lovely on me. But then forbade me to wear it for fear of outshining the bride. So, I felt obliged to choose an everyday denim skirt and jumper instead.

I have always been 'on the move', anticipating that the 'grass is always greener', and yet discovering that it never was. I can look back now and observe that I have spent much time in my life crossing thresholds! Particularly momentous was the move to Naturism! At first, I was not sure how to receive the invitation to the 'grass' of that particular threshold, but was tempted, 'Just go and try it!' Well, that is history now. Why should this nakedness be so transforming to my lifelong low self- esteem? Well, after only ten minutes I felt OK! Yes, this seemed normal and I felt freer than I had for so long. It is to do with the commonality of it. You see the whole person. The whole personality comes forward; you can't hide anything; there is no visible evidence of wealth or class. I found this especially intriguing because of my interest in psychology.

Sometimes life is funny. As a naturist, my partner at the time and I once met up with another couple who had a lovely German caravan, great big thing with a fixed bed and all mod cons. We had been talking in the jacuzzi and I was told the lady wanted to ask me about something, so I knocked on the caravan door and was invited in. She was a highly educated person working in a University, researching into food intolerances and allergies. There she was, a naturist but cutting out fabric with a pattern, making the beginnings of a costume for a Steampunk parade! The irony of it. Steampunk is gathering steam (!); every year there are more and more events around the country. Some in Whitby, some at a place called The Asylum in Lincolnshire.

I actually managed to get to Whitby one October, with a friend. We both dressed up; he hired a kind of pirate's costume and I found a little fitted black jacket with lace on,

To be Busy... Or not to be Busy...

plus I found a long deep red skirt to go with it and bought a hat at Whitby to top it off. The scenes were incredible in the narrow winding streets; there was every exotic character including Goths, Vampires, Victorians, Witches, Fairies, Mermaids, Spacemen, Magicians, Aliens, even dogs dressed up to go out and about with their owners. Everyone seemed to be posing and standing about chatting. Simply being there became an open invitation to get involved, ask questions of one another and be part of the whole experience. It was brilliant! We even saw a couple of cars which had been adapted to look amazing, all weird and fantastic – as in fantasy.

Today the key to my dressmaking work is in the professional listening. That is how I can get an accurate idea of what the customer is after. I consider what 'style' they are and do drawings for their consideration. So, it is important to offer them the words and the visual and the listening, le beginning to build a trust, which is of course a threshold in itself. In the 80's and 90's my project was entitled Alchemy of Dress. The word alchemy indicates a medieval process seeking to turn basic substance into gold or silver. Miraculous transformation. So, this resonates with Virginia Woolf's challenge that 'sometimes it is clothes which wear us'. Some sewing tasks have been especially memorable. We all know how certain some clothes are very precious to us, but they do eventually WEAR OUT! People are increasingly asking for garments to which they have been sentimentally attached to be re-made into something else. Well, probably they always did, but in more of a make do and mend way. One customer had received a purse from his adored daughter who was subsequently killed in a tragic accident. And being much loved and used, it wore out. So, I was able to refashion it and integrate the original fabric into a new purse, which became very important to him.

Parents decorate throws with memory items from their children's schooling and early life...a tie, a badge, a flag... For re-membering in years to come. People have memory bears or elephants made out of the clothing of a loved one who has died. The word 'remember' means putting together again...these are memories in a visual form to keep forever.

So clothes express who we are, our personality, our mood, and I am in the craft of miraculous transformation! Wonderful! Customers 'light up' when knowing I will take on very unusual projects. It is indeed a joy and a privilege to be able to 'help to make people's dreams come true'.

Editor and Barbara Taylor

**

Avoiding the hallowed turf...
The Village School

I took up post as Headteacher in Sessay on a glorious April morning and, in the same manner as an adult might look back to their childhood days, so many of the memories I have of my time at the school are of long, happy, sunny days.

From the outset the links between school, church and community were evident. There were many established traditions to maintain, most of which were made known to me within a very short time. I did however upset some good church folk when, following my first Harvest Festival Service at the school, I arranged for the gifts of fruit and vegetables to be taken to sick children. I felt that the children delivering the gifts and those who received them gained a great deal from the mutual experience. Unfortunately, what I had not realised was that the usual pattern was for all the gifts to be taken to the village hall, prior to a raffle to raise funds for the church. The Vicar, who was Chairman of Governors, acted as mediator and all was resolved. In future years a compromise was reached whereby some of the donated produce was taken by the school children to those in need and the rest of the produce was given to the church for fund-raising.

The Vicar was certainly not Chairman of Governors in name only; he was actively involved in the life of the school. He knew the children well and was very supportive of the teaching staff. His weekly assemblies were meaningful and fun and were a highlight for pupils and staff. All our special services were held in the village church – Harvest, Christmas, Easter and end of year – and everyone was welcome to attend. The Churchwardens were very accommodating with regard to our use of the church and, fortunately, someone warned me in advance that all donations made at these services were retained by the church!

We held regular open days at the school, and these were well supported by both those who had direct connections with the school and those who were simply interested to see how a primary school operated. Partly stemming from these occasions and also arising from articles about the school in the local newsletter, the relationship between school and community developed further. Members of the community offered to share their time and talents with the children; cooking, chess, handicrafts and a range of sports were just a few of the activities that enriched school life because of these willing volunteers.

When we required space or facilities not available on the school site, the Village Hall Committee generously allowed us use of the village hall and grounds. There was, however, one golden rule to observe; no-one must go near the hallowed turf of the nearby cricket pitch!

Strong bridges existed between school, church and community. We regularly came together in the course of day to day life and also for specific occasions such as times of worship, the celebration of special events, charity fund-raising, making music and playing sports. The ties which bound us together became stronger as we learnt from one another and appreciated the importance of accommodating one another's needs and we were greatly blessed in doing so.

Christine Roddam

**

An ultimate dress-code challenge…
'On the Day'…

As a lady Funeral Director of some 25 years, I have on a daily basis to present myself in formal dress and respectful manner to my client families whilst I arrange the Funeral Service for their loved one. Wearing a jacket at all times, even in summer, I may request

To be Busy... Or not to be Busy...

permission from the family to remove it whilst we discuss their wishes; no one has ever refused, but it is etiquette. Wearing thick, black tights in summer is also not ideal, but then I would never present myself to a family with bare legs; it just wouldn't feel right, let alone look right.

Sitting with a family and helping them through one of the worst times in their lives is not easy. I have to gain their trust, build a rapport and set the agenda whilst looking and sounding professional, but remaining warm and friendly at the same time; after all, this family are entrusting me with one of the most precious things in their lives (their loved one) and every time it is such a privilege.
That is why I say it feels like I possess two heads, because on the funeral day itself my professional head then has to take over.

So now I am putting on my Funeral conducting kit...crisp white shirt and cravat, formal grey striped skirt, black waistcoat, black three-quarter length jacket, my hat and my gloves, shoes polished...ready to go. Today I have to conduct this funeral without a hitch. (No pressure then!) But let me tell you how it makes me feel that when I put on my conducting kit...it makes me feel stronger and more confident as I instruct the staff who will be assisting me, ensuring that all of the family's wishes are followed to the letter. Even my families notice that it is a different 'me' on the day of the service as they all hear me give clear but quiet instructions to the bearers, and give the help and guidance which will assist them through their very difficult day.

A Funeral Director

**

A tradition for man and boy...
Clogs in the Mills

My late brother Graham started school in clogs in 1938 aged five. They had leather uppers and were tied with laces. Rubber strips on the soles and heels were initially sufficient but, as they got older, they had steel strips added, and then, if necessary, even these were repaired by the blacksmith. Our dad put a leather strip between the irons, probably from broken mill belts, but they could still produce a spark!

Snow time produced further complications as the snow got lodged in the insteps and turned very hard, making them wobble. They called them 'cloggy boggies' and wearers had to hit the wall with their toes to remove it.

Clogs were all most children possessed for school days, outing days and play days, football and climbing trees. They were also OK for wet grass and streams alike, as they didn't leak. Youths even rode their motorbikes with them, and my husband-to-be Ken passed his test in them on his bike.

After schooldays ended, Graham went to work on a farm for a couple of years and wore wellies. But on going into the mill to work, back came the clogs, leather uppers, wooden soles and the irons. One time when a bale of shoddy fell on his foot, the clog broke in two at the sole, but that clog saved his foot. His employer bought him another pair and he wore them till he retired. He eventually wore clogs for nearly 60 years, and he used them for his gardening in later times.

Ladies' clogs were more like shoes, with a clasp fastener and could have rubber or steel soles. About 1965 we bought clogs for our two sons. One red ones and the other blue. They each only had leather strips on from when Graham worked in the fettling department of the mill...again using the broken belts.

Clogs made a lot of noise and when the children were running through the chapel mid-service (time for home), my dad used to cringe and threaten to buy them shoes! It didn't happen.

Anne Miller

Editor's comment: these clogs then were the old-fashioned equivalent of the wooden Dr Scholl's sandals which I used to wear for trundling the hospital corridors with heart machines, when a Cardiological Technician. They made a noise too!

**

Making an impression...
Stopping the Traffic

Fifty years ago, I received my first wages as a student nurse. This amounted to the grand total of just over £8. I trotted off to my local Chelsea Girl boutique and bought a sparkling white shirt-waister with an extremely short skirt, which looked pretty good on my 5 feet 8 inches, 8 stone frame. (What a different story nowadays!) Anyway, the dress cost me £7 and the first time I wore it the impact stopped the traffic around the market square in the city centre. I felt wonderful. This was the beginning of my grown-up life away from suburbia and previous parental restraints.

A couple of years later when I was still skinny, I bought a white, one piece bathing costume and wore it to the local swimming baths. Strolling nonchalantly down to the deep end, I was aware I was being noticed, which was pleasing. Having splashed around and swum for a while, I climbed out and strolled nonchalantly back again. This time I was aware of even more attention. When I returned to the changing room, I could see why. I was confronted by a full length mirror which demonstrated that without a doubt my white costume had become completely transparent and I looked virtually naked!

I also recall the deep pleasure of putting on for the first time a new nurse's outfit, complete with butterfly cap and starched apron. I totally looked as though I knew what I was doing. I was a young woman on the threshold of realising just how much I didn't know, but also realised that appearing in

To be Busy... Or not to be Busy...

control and prepared for anything – haemorrhage...perforation...cardiac arrest, was the beginning of the solution. Well, that and knowing my place, which was at the bottom of the food chain and in the sluice with the bedpans!

Hilary Vinall

**

Policing the crowds...
The Intelligent Dapple-Grey

From our first meeting I was drawn to Shirley as she seemed to be a quiet, contemplative lady, and indeed it transpired that she had been a Quaker in earlier times. She and her husband Alistair always went out of their way to make people feel welcome.

Something about Alistair intrigued me. A very elderly gentleman – that is what he personified, a gentleman, and a gentle man. He had a problem walking and looked to be in great pain around his skeleton much of the time, but still remained very distinguished looking and as if he had a quiet sense of humble authority. I was drawn to him too and one day I dared to ask him what he used to do. I sort of knew he had been in the Police, but this was no bobby on the beat. (Oh, how I wish we still had more of those.)

'I was in the mounted police,' he replied. Hm! Yes! I am not surprised to hear this, I think. And I did ask him if he had a photograph. Wow! With others, there he sat on a dapple grey, totally upright and magnificent, sword at his side. Booted, spurred, uniformed and capped. Just appointed to the Mounted Branch, May/June 1954, in a photograph at City Road Stables; he described himself as 'I'm the one in uniform with the most intelligent-looking horse'.

His job had been policing the crowds for official events in London in those times. Repeated auspicious occasions, but none as personally important as the threshold day he met a lovely young nurse who was there also on duty. They fell in love, Shirley and Alistair.

Editor from a conversation with Alistair Calman

Editor's note: Sadly Alistair died a few years ago. He had always wanted to write his story, so it is good to have been able to share this little piece of it.

**

A prioress looks back on her treasured inherited garment...
The Monastic Habit

Today I must repair my winter habit. It is more than twenty years old — patched, darned, with several new panels inserted into it over the years where the girdle (the long leather belt nuns wear) has rubbed against the middle or where my knees have worn holes. It is the work of many hands: the original habit-maker, and successive darners, repairers and general lookers-after, of whom I am the last and least competent. It is, in its way, a collaborative work, rather like community itself. It has adapted itself to the changing shape of my body and the different activities I've undertaken in response to obedience. It is worn and shabby, at the opposite end of the spectrum to the gorgeous vestments some clergy like to wear when officiating at the altar. But it is not just a set of clothes. It is, I would dare to say, my Wedding Garment for the Kingdom, my armour for the battle, a constant reminder of my vows.

Like the vocation it symbolizes, the monastic habit is not something we choose for ourselves or assume at will, it is always *given*, its colour and form determined by the community which confers it. When I was clothed in 1981, I was given the habit by D. Elizabeth Sumner. From her I can trace backwards, by name and date, the way in which such a habit was bestowed and received as far as 31 December 1623, when the first nuns of the Cambrai community were clothed. I can go back further still, though there I would trace a double course, through the English Benedictine Congregation to Dom Sigebert Buckley and beyond, to the pre-Reformation English Benedictine houses, and through the three nuns of Brussels who helped the nascent Cambrai community. There is thus a long chain of being symbolized by my habit.

How romantic, sigh some, but to me there is nothing romantic about the monastic habit. It is too serious for that. From Evagrius onwards, many have attached an allegorical meaning to its several parts, but the real point is the commitment it signifies and the obligations it entails. They are what matter. In the old Clothing Registers we find against many a name, 'She went away'. I often wonder what became of those who had worn the habit for a while, then found that monastic life was not for them. Many, perhaps the majority, took from their brief experience of the cloister something valuable, something that changed the way in which they viewed the world henceforth. Perhaps they learned, more quickly than those of us privileged to wear the habit every day, that the real change takes place underneath.

Maybe I should look on my habit not so much as a Wedding Garment or battle armour but as a school tunic, a sign of my willingness, indeed my need, to learn? That fits the Schola Dominici idea rather better, doesn't it? Life-long learning, here we come!

Sister Catherine Wybourne, prioress
Text taken from iBenedictines © 2013 trustees of Holy Trinity Monastery
**

Why did they keep bringing me a cup of coffee at the Job Centre?...
The Wrong Clothes

In the licensed-retailing business – that's hotels, restaurants and pubs – it's a fact that visitors can be part of a 'boy's night out', a business lunch, a blind date at a wine bar, or just calling in to the local boozer. They can be the same individual at any of these times, but wearing a different 'cap' to suit the occasion and the environment. As the executive involved in these socio-economic machinations, you too know to wear the appropriate gear! Then, market forces alter, job security changes, redundancy looms and eventually cuts you loose, and that sets you adrift into an open-ended and downward slope, to adapt

To be Busy... Or not to be Busy...

and cope.

Such was my fate after 25 years of a marketing career; working in newspapers, regional television and the brewing/retail industry. Two hours' notice, (so you didn't take any secrets or paperwork), no job, no office, no car, no money and too old for a future! It takes a couple of weeks, a few lie-ins, a few cry-ins before the job centre beckons. Be prepared, create a CV, be positive, make an appointment, they say, and I did! So with a good business suit and a small folio and a smile, I headed off to find my way.

The bright, airy, warehouse sized, open plan office looked more like a Spanish Bank at first glance. But there was this enormous queue. I mean enormous! Maybe forty people snaked across the room in an assortment of attire, all seemingly alien to the job in hand – a job search. Denim as smart wear, denim as tat, tight and baggy, blue and bleached...skinheads, long hair, longer hair, and plenty of ear plugs for instant music. Was this where I needed to queue?

I blinked and stepped towards the throng, trying not to look at them while they looked hard and long at me, bemused. Still not sure I was in the right place, and with my confidence waning, I did stand my ground for twenty five minutes, before a clerk came towards me and asked, 'Do you have an appointment?' With an answer in the affirmative, I was ushered to one side and offered a chair (a comfy one) and a coffee and left to my own devices.

After yet another fifteen minutes, I took courage and found a gentleman sitting at his desk, head deep in paper, and asked if he could help me. He promptly asked me which organisation I was from. The question shocked me and my answer shocked him. No, I wasn't from anybody, I was me, unemployed - while he, and they, thought I was a representative from some company or other, waiting to present a host of opportunities for them to dole out to job seekers.

I had worn the wrong clothes. I was utterly ashamed of feeling so conspicuous in unfamiliar surroundings, embarrassed at neither sussing the procedure nor the mood of the unemployed and depressed that I still had to join the queue and shuffle forward for my turn. My business suit felt hideous. Never before had I longed for that proverbial crater to engulf me, and how I wished I had musical earplugs to deafen the mocking in my head of my own indignity.

But my turn came and, with my credentials laid, I explained my predicament. Forms, forms and more forms were completed before I received my own personal 'unemployment number', together with an offer of three job interviews: a van driver, an office cleaner and a pub cleaner. She hadn't seen my business suit, had she; I was now just a number, an 'any-shaped peg' for an 'any-shaped hole'.

And I never did wear a business suit again. And never did sport any particular 'cap' for any specific juncture – rather, I now don whatever makes me feel happy. Clothes are now for me, not for the occasion.

Chrissy Fincham

Editor's Note: Now in her seventies this beautiful woman is the most boldly, creatively dressed woman I know...clothes put together inspirationally, many from the charity shops!

Finding the work/life balance...
Time to Sort the Socks

Employed for 22 years with the same company...
I ponder: What is stress?
One answer could be the demands of juggling full time employment with the problems of trying to develop my own complementary medicine business.

The 'day job' had too much responsibility, not enough authority. It was...No Control, every ball in the air and trying not to drop any. No time, 60 hour weeks, travelling and being away from home. Everything squeezed in: visits to the in-laws, time to see a friend? No time for washing and ironing or even for shopping. Clothes in the laundry basket piling up; more clothes bought on-line of course, delivered by Prime. The garden looks a mess, plants not planted or pruned.

Maintaining any personal life seemed to have become harder over the years. Is it my age or just that the world is changing? Or are my priorities changing?

New Beginnings; **NOW Self-employed finally....**

Treats and more treats. Spa days, massage, sailing. Wonderful times with those nearest and dearest.

Still working but at a slower pace, at my pace, more relaxed. I can choose when or if I work. It was sunny the other day, so time for the garden. I'm sure it's healthier – exercise, diet and definitely less wine.

Spending a morning tidying my shelves feels so rewarding, even sorting out my sock drawer and undies now all in a row, colour coordinated. The charity bag is getting fuller as things un-worn, un-used or just unwanted are shed. De-cluttering is therapeutic, now I gain pleasure in the simplest of things.
Time to develop my skills further and give more time to healing.
Best of all is just having time to...whatever!

Jane Oglesby

Christmas Day Baptism

Religion stops at lunch time: tradition dictates
An afternoon of family, children, gifts. This year, however,
An angel herald planned a change of programme:

Premature baptism in the maternity stable.
Hasten, shepherd, to the manger, bring no gift in hand
But antiseptic gel: walk by star-light
Into a Rembrandt etching of deep shadows,
A bright light where he lies
Glowing on anxious family faces,
While a discreet angelic nursing host
Hovers with quiet caring in the wings.

Incarnation lies in the incubator: a dab of water
On a sterile swab claims for Christ,
He who is already God's gift -
Not what I do, but what Christ's love has done
Beyond the ken of this child in this life:
Not a claim I can make, but a circling of God's arms
Around his church, made wider by this soul.
A Simeon moment, blessed by that bird-thin hand:

Hodie Christus natus est.

For me – for us, I trust – his vulnerable gift
Has made this evening – Christmas Day.

John Lansley

Through the Vestry Door
(editor)

A Reflection

Always Somewhere Else

In a farming, rural community, traditional worship was expected on a weekly basis. As a Reader I could not preside at any sacramental liturgy unless the elements had been pre-blessed by a priest. But one way or another every Sunday I organised, officiated and preached at up to three services over the group, and additionally in the largest village for a weekly Wednesday morning service where sometimes the attendance was greater than on the Sunday. A revived Book of Common Prayer Evensong once a month was in response to being reminded that farmers are not free to attend morning worship as they are caring for their animals, but by the evening their day's work has been completed. This became for a time our consistently best attended Sunday service, supported by a gathered choir of singers and a nearby organist who was delighted at the opportunity to play for a BCP choral service with psalms and canticles.

    Of course, all special times of the church year were celebrated appropriately; Harvest Festival, Easter and Christmas being especially important, when extended family gathered and worshipped together. P.D. James writes: *In the country you lived as a social being and at the evaluation of others. So he had lived in childhood and adolescence in the same country rectory, taking part each Sunday in a familiar liturgy which reflected, interpreted and sanctified the changing seasons of the farming year.*

    An integral part of my work was to continue with further training to assist my own nourishment, development and accountability. I also began encouraging and facilitating worship training for other members of the congregations, as this step was being urgently promoted by the diocese. Parishes were being amalgamated into ever larger groups, such that many people rarely saw their vicar. This mattered in these places, otherwise risking comments like, 'We never see 'im as 'e is always somewhere else.' And 'No one 'as ever been inside the vicarage.'

    In terms of essential secular earning (the church work being non-stipendiary), I began by assisting in the local pub. What a blessing that was in terms of meeting an ever-growing number of parishioners. There were the youngsters with whom I shared waitressing and washing up tasks; the diners, and the supping customers...."Ee, yer'v never bin ter see me yet,' to which I would reply, 'And you've never been to see me either and I am the new person here.' Until one quiet, gentle man replied sheepishly, 'I have, Ann, but you were out.' I was humbled. At another time I even worked in one of the shops as a cleaner in the early hours, serving a different group than the day-time customers – school children awaiting the bus, fishermen coming for their licences.

To be Busy... Or not to be Busy...

And I was delighted to have the support of the PCC to honour in church some of the other secular work going on around me. We prepared one particular Celebration of Local Trade service inviting all our tradespeople to be there, setting up sample stalls (in the market place of the church building) as appropriate, including shopkeeper Nancy's sweets tray, a legend of many decades for the village children. On that day only, they were free of charge! We celebrated with thanksgiving that we still had the blessing of food shops, a post office, a fishmonger in his travelling van, a fish and chip van, a butcher's, a milk delivery van and so on.

But the truth is that, like an iceberg, only about a tenth of the work of a parish minister is actually 'visible', which is why you hear the old cliché...'well, you only work on a Sunday'. Many, many hours in a week are spent in writing and planning, in visiting for baptism, wedding, funeral work, or sitting alongside and careful listening. Some of the following homilies evidence this. It is in the invisible, quiet working of the yeast in the bread or the salt in the food which offers life, energy, flavour, richness and transformation of the whole.

Homilies

Saltiness

Mark 9:38-50 James 5:13-20.
Jesus said, *'Salt is good, but if it loses its saltiness, how can you make it salty again? Have salt in yourselves and be at peace with each other.'*

Salt is an element of purification, preservation and enhancement. It prevents decay. It can be an agent of healing. As cooks know, it transforms bland to startlingly different, bringing out the richness of what was already there, but hidden until flavour is liberated by the salt. Chefs also know that it needs to be in just the right measure to act as such a catalyst. It becomes a threshold agent, moving from one quality to another.

This passage follows the one where Jesus talks to his disciples about true greatness. A passage which is sometimes so hard for us to understand...The last shall be first and the first, last! So Jesus builds now on that teaching in an urgent manner, drawing on the Jewish technique of exaggeration in order to make a point. If you don't keep yourself 'salty', you cease to become a catalyst for others en route to the Kingdom.

Jesus is not talking here about salt being used to preserve food, but to preserve people. If we put salt in a loaf or a big pan of soup, it works in the whole thing, not just for the bit where you put it in. It works throughout. Here we are being called to live as spiritual salt amongst all with whom we live and work, helping to keep the divine purpose in people fresh, alive for ever, preventing ourselves and others from decaying.

So how might we do that? Well, first and foremost, we have to make sure we keep salty ourselves. James tells us that prayer is one way to do this.

Prayer does not change God but changes the pray-er. The prayer of any person of compassion is powerful and effective. What is the source of that power? Not our own status within the church, that is for sure. It is Jesus Christ, the Son of Peace.

When food is salted, it lasts and it still tastes good. We are called to be salt of the earth. If we are to be followers of the Prince of Peace, we must learn to be at peace within ourselves. That peace which is beyond all understanding.

And as a final aside, I can't help remembering that salt also melts ice, so don't give up praying for the melting of even the hardest and iciest of hearts!

**

Yeast is Mysterious.

Exodus 16:2-4, 9-15, John 6:25-35.
Jesus said, 'Do not work for food that spoils, but for food that endures to eternal life.'

Once upon a time, I used to bake all the bread for our family of seven. Every so often, I'd set off with the children to the nearby mill and farm to buy a sack of stone ground flour. Then on to buy a large block of fresh yeast. This we would cut up into portions and freeze until required. The ritual of bread-making was a great source of pleasure to us all. Learning to work together; pounding and kneading and shaping into little rolls and loaves. The joy was in the wonderful fragrance as the mix stood in the warm kitchen on the Aga. The joy was in the yeast working to transform the small flat piece of lifeless dough, so that it grew to fill the enormous mixing bowl. It was in the filling of the whole house with the glorious aroma whilst it baked. Then best of all, in the sharing in the eating of it, around the family table. It was a practical exercise to feed and nourish our children's bodies. But more than that; as such it was an act of love too. Making bread can become a symbol of the relationships we have, one with another.

Jesus said, 'I am the bread of life. Whoever comes to me will never be hungry.' The bread of God comes down from Heaven and gives life to the world. Disciples say, 'Sir, give us this bread always.' Are we sure we really want it? Jesus began to see that people were clinging to his every move but for the wrong reasons. Don't be looking for what is perishable. Jesus is not a restaurant where we indulge ourselves and eventually roll back home to bed; he is the bread of life and supplies us with the food we need in order to live out his risen life (yeast!) among the people we are led to. And of course, it does get rather hot in the oven! 'Give us this bread always.' Do we really mean that? Do we want to be broken too?

The bread that Jesus offers has no sell by date. Jesus was not a new Moses, offering bread from the past, or alternatively bread which needs eating the same day. He tells them that he is offering bread, present, past and future, all at once. 'I am the bread that I bring!' He uses historical language and symbolism to reveal new meaning and life that is not bound by history. So, what does living bread look and feel like? No good just reading about it, we are being invited to taste and see.

To be Busy... Or not to be Busy...

Most of us know the head teaching around the message of this reading. We have all experienced *eating* bread. Many of us have had the experience of *making* it. This account of Jesus' feeding of the multitude links very specifically with the parallel between earth and heaven; with the bread. Maybe we are challenged with the everyday image of bread linking in with our Christian way of living. If we are not, then the yeast of Christ's glorious love is not flourishing in the right conditions for working in us. I heard a complaint on the radio the other day that their Broadband was too slow. It is getting ever outrageously faster, the speed with which most of us try to live our lives, and when I think of bread and the slowness it takes to be beautiful, fragrant and life giving, I am humbled. Are you continuing to allow Jesus to continue to work slowly and quietly in you? Yeast working to life is a mysterious hidden activity. When Jesus is in us and through us, like the yeast in the dough, our lives will be transformed. Others will want it for themselves. Bread is made with love, and for those who love, time is an eternity; a losing of oneself in the larger dream, the larger whole. Eternity can be found in the now.

**

The Cheeseman

Psalm 121
The Lord watches over you – the Lord is your shade at your right hand.

I travel now and again to the Coach House in Kilmuir, near Inverness, as a staging post on my spiritual journey. There I am amongst red squirrels, deer, forests, the Moray Firth and its beach, sighting the occasional dolphin. Woodpeckers frolic on the bird table and a stately, very, ancient cock pheasant, known as Malvolio, struts languidly past. I am told that he changes his collar in the breeding season to a more puffy, startling white. But especially in this place, I can cross the threshold of sound and dwell for just a while in silence.
    I offer you a glimpse into my own alternative to the stress of the 'rat race'. The day begins with half an hour's led meditation in the Octagonal sanctuary, which overlooks the Moray Firth; and ends similarly by the lights of Inverness pricking the water, and stars, the night sky. In between these corporate gatherings of staff and retreatants came the balance of work, rest and pray; walking the beaches or forests, eating delicious home-cooked meals which have been lovingly prepared. For me that was such a joy and release. Each morning I met with a director who encouragingly accompanied me on this journey, offering me scriptural passages and teaching from the writing of St. Ignatius on which to reflect during the day and sometimes through the night too. The silence held without distraction from phone, TV, radio, books or conversation means that the reflection goes on so deeply. It felt to me, as I woke up in the morning fresh with new insights, that it must have gone on in my sleep!
    On a recent visit I spent an hour or so in a small island village nearby, in a very environmentally active and interesting community with art, culture and live music in domestic homes at its heart. Incongruously, I found myself in a Dutch cheese shop, enticingly displaying huge, colourful, round cheeses with figs, cumin and coriander.

Delicious! Small wedges of cheese hand-wrapped in shiny white paper were beautifully arranged, nestling among appropriate chutneys and chocolate. I wondered, how can there be a significant viable market for these in such a tiny place? I heard tell that a customer recently asked incredulously, 'Are you able to make a living here selling this cheese?' And he replied, 'No, but we have made a life!' What a wisdom is that.

Like the Cheeseman, I discovered there an alternative way of living. My experience cannot be sustained in all the hurly burly of work, home and extended family life, but that experience will always now prompt and remind me to stay focused on Jesus Christ as the compass point of my life. I can return to that sacred image of my slender, wobbly pointer, now believing that if he is my true North, then everything else falls into its natural direction and order of things. Easier said than done, especially as I am renowned for having little sense of terrestrial direction!

Henri Nouwen reminds us that prayer, along with being still, silent and waiting... *'is indeed a very radical stance in a world preoccupied with control'.*

And those in this precious place, when my pointer has faltered, have often provided a causeway to keep me safe from the incoming tide until I could swim again.

A Final Musing

Black Horses and Mince Pies

Among my church colleagues recently, it was suggested that we buy a mince-pie at Christmas for our bank ladies (they are usually ladies) to thank them hugely for still being there to greet and help us. They are on the threshold of town, at the edge of the marketplace. Not yet victims of internet banking.

I enter the bifold automatic doors in my local branch to be greeted by pictorial images of glorious, majestic black horses, galloping across the plains, with foals who will follow their streamlined mothers through flood and tempest. This has been my bank since I was sixteen...and I trust it. Therefore, I have indeed decided to buy them a mince pie every Christmas.

Today there is a new lady behind the safety screen...She peers at me from behind a notice which reminds me that abuse to their staff will not be tolerated, and she must have seen an elderly looking lady (me, although I feel I am looking quite 'cool' on this occasion).

She smilingly and graciously asks me, 'Is this cheque your spending money from your husband?' I restrain myself from keeling over in Feminist outrage and make the mistake of replying, 'No, it is my housekeeping.' At this point and giggling, she nearly falls

To be Busy... Or not to be Busy...

off her swivel stool in shock. 'Oh, it is so long since I have heard that old fashioned term.'

At that point I lose the will and, instead of staying calm, I just say, 'Well, in my Brummy working class childhood my Dad, who was a bread roundsman, fresh from the war and saving the nation, gave my Mum all his wages every Friday, and she gave him back some pocket money for himself. The rest she put in a tin in sections to pay rent, gas, electric, food, clothes, coal, etc etc.' I leave, feeling, Goodness, I have in two minutes shared the sociology of working-class finance of seven decades ago. I must be approaching my own 'threshold' too.

However, I will still buy them all mince pies at Christmas time for always being there when I need them, and even this conversation was much more fun than participating in a dialogue with a machine!

Can I Help You?

COMMUNITY

It isn't just a village. The houses aren't just places to live. Everything belongs to everyone else. Even a single person can make a difference. – *Joanne Harris*

Without genuine spiritual community, life becomes a struggle. – *David James Duncan*

Do you not know that God entrusted you with that money to feed the hungry, to clothe the naked, to help the stranger?... How dare you defraud the Lord by applying it to any other purpose. – *John Wesley*

Clothes make the man. Naked people have little or no influence on society. – *Mark Twain*

The church doesn't just take people to Heaven; it feeds, clothes and houses them. It teaches them how to read and gets them jobs. – *Tony Evans*

It doesn't take one person only to achieve your potential. It takes a village, it takes a community, a street, a teacher, a mother. – *Mira Nair*

The best things in life are free. The second best are very expensive. – *Coco Chanel*

Adversity not only draws people together but brings forth that beautiful inward friendship, just as the cold winter forms ice-figures on the windowpanes which the warmth of the sun effaces – *Soren Kierkegaard*

Through the Wardrobe Door
(Contributors)

Garments for looking one's best...
Dressed for Action

Through the eyes of a Catholic girl from a poor family growing up in a deprived area of one of the North of England's biggest cities in the 1950s, Sunday Mass was often a headache for our mother. It was usual, then, to keep a coat, hat, gloves and shoes solely for 'Sunday Best'. We were not fortunate enough to be able to afford such a luxury. Our clothes, though not tattered or torn by any means, were worn on any day of the week as long as they were clean. As we grew they became rather short and tight way before our parents could afford to buy new ones. Then they were replaced by togs which were over long and loose so that we could grow into them. Lost buttons could not always be matched; wool to darn socks and gloves didn't always tone with the original. Hats were beyond our budget, so we did without and went bare headed, except in winter when a knitted scarf or snood kept out the cold. Still, there were so many in the Parish as poor as us, and though we noticed those children whose families were better off dressed in smart well-fitting Sunday outfits, we were too numerous to stand out from the crowd. Besides, we were reminded from time to time by the gospel reading from Matthew 6:28 not to worry about our clothing. Consider the lilies of the field, we were told, which neither toiled nor spun but which were arrayed in a glory greater than Solomon's. In school this message was reinforced often by the nuns, together with the warning to avoid looking in the mirror so as to discourage any latent vanity or envy. That was all very well, but as I grew older I could not help but wonder at the crisp white cottas of the priests, beautifully trimmed with deep bands of hand-made convent lace, and the wonderful turnover of exquisitely embroidered vestments worn on every day in the week. It was also difficult not to notice the generous use of the many yards of soft cotton and wool that made up the nuns' habits. For the most part we accepted with good grace the superior quality and range of attire worn by those in spiritual authority over us as being for the glorification of God in the battle for our souls.

One of the greatest pleasures for us children came on those Sundays when the Salvation Army Band with Officers and Soldiers, and the adherents of the church, marched  into our poor neighbourhood and proclaimed their own faith with short sermons, stirring tunes and rousing hymns. I knew nothing about them other than that I loved the sound of their instruments, the words of their hymns, and most of all their uniforms, complete with officer type caps and old-fashioned close bonnets with perfectly tied bows. As a Catholic child I would never have been allowed – in those days – to enter a Protestant Church

Can I Help You?

or stay within earshot of an outdoor revivalist meeting but as a youngster my mother, whose family went to bed more often than not on growling stomachs, had sneaked off every Sunday to the local Salvation Army Citadel after early Mass had finished. She'd joined in the singing and was more than grateful for the bun and beaker of tea doled out afterwards. Thus, well-disposed as she was towards the Army, she turned a blind eye when my brother and I disappeared when the band struck up on a small piece of ground down the road which had been cleared of bomb debris and levelled.

In times after, I learned more of the Salvation Army. Founded in 1865 by William and Catherine Booth, the idea that its officers and soldiers should wear a uniform began in 1878 when at the Salvation Army's 'War Congress', Elijah Cadman said he would like a suitable set of clothes which would 'let everyone know I mean war to the teeth and salvation to the world'. Since then, although there are different forms throughout the world, their uniform has come to identify anyone who wears it as a Christian and Salvationist. Officers and Soldiers wear a uniform tailored to the country in which they work; this can be white, grey, navy, fawn, and can even be styled like a sari. Wherever it is worn, however, it is a symbol that anyone in need can approach and ask for help. The Army actually has a dress tartan, though I think it's unusual for it to be worn outside Scotland. So, the uniform which attracted me so greatly as a child is indeed the mark of an Army dressed for action while doing such good work among the poor, the afflicted, and the dispossessed, in their battle for both bodies and souls.

Thinking of a Salvation Army uniform adapted in the style of a sari has reminded me forcibly of India. My father was a regular soldier and my first three years were spent in quarters at a Garrison in the North of England where he had been posted in 1946. He had begun his time under fire with the British Expeditionary Force in Belgium and was evacuated at Dunkirk. After the invasion of Malaya, he was posted to India, staying for some time before being sent on the Burma offensive to reoccupy the peninsular. Though he never spoke of his experiences, the few photographs he had of his time in India before and after Burma fired my imagination and desire to learn more of India, even as a child. Though crucially instrumental in the battle for Indian independence from the Raj, my early hero was Mohandas Gandhi, the Mahatma or Great Soul of India. Gandhi had studied law and jurisprudence in London and enrolled at the Inner Temple. After campaigning for the rights of Indians in South Africa where he'd been turned out of a First Class rail carriage simply because he was an Indian, despite being dressed in very smart western clothes and having been allowed to buy the necessary ticket. On returning to India, Gandhi began to campaign for Indian independence through his philosophy of non-violent civil disobedience which had been so successful in South Africa. Significantly, he encouraged his followers to boycott cloth imported from Lancashire cotton mills, and to weave and wear their own homespun cotton (Khadi). He left off western clothes and came to wear the simple homespun loincloth and shawl that became his own battledress as he fought in his own unique way for Indian independence and the tolerance of every Indian towards their fellow Indians of whatever caste or religion.

Everywhere, then, we see there are many ways in which to battle for the good of humankind and, it appears, just as many ways to get kitted out for the struggle.

Chris Kilpatrick

Offering 'official' help...
Encounters in Uniform

Every now and again in the local market town I observe a friend. She is, I discern, often undertaking a community role of one sort or another. Even, in her Ritz cinema tabard, ordering the frantic queue for Mama Mia. I could tell already that not everyone was going to get a seat, and some would for sure have to turn around and go home!! Hmm! Oh dear. How will she deal with that, I ponder?

Mo continues: amongst another uniforms I have worn is that of a Parking Enforcement Officer (wrongly described as 'Traffic Warden' - we work for the district council, not the police) but it'll do.

The Parking Enforcement Officer role has had some rather enjoyable, yet also challenging, situations. Amusingly, one Thirsk race day, I was wandering around in uniform and wearing my hat with the initials HDC on the front. A crowd of (male) 'racegoers' was coming out of one of the pubs and they all looked at me, and one, noticing the HDC on my hat, shouted, 'Hey, lads, she's from the Hitler Defence Corps!'

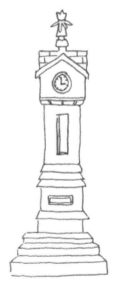

I was often asked to take photos of tourists standing next to the clock in the Market Place, '...to prove I was here'. But one of the less pleasant photos I took was of two racegoers who came out of one of the pubs and then immediately went down the alleyway next to it and used it as a loo (despite my taking their picture), before returning to the pub. I showed the photo to two police officers who were not far away, and they went into the pub and gave them an official warning.

Occasionally I was spoken to rather rudely when I either ticketed someone or gave them a warning. The very rudest person was an able-bodied man sitting in his car on a disabled bay, 'Because it was here, and I couldn't be bothered finding another space.' I said I was sorry, but he would have to move his car, and he then came out with a torrent of abuse like I'd never heard and, hopefully, very few others ever have either. As I stood listening to him, I was also writing down his words and, needless to say, then ticketed him (he refused to take his ticket but did move). I sent a report to my line manager - who wanted to know how I knew how to spell it all!

Then there is the story of the men who were using the cobbles in the town centre to cut up a carpet, '...as it is really convenient for us to spread it out and cut it into the shape and size of the office room we are going to fit.' Eventually, as the Parking Enforcement Officer, and after asking them politely a few times to cut it up elsewhere, I had to ticket them. They soon rolled it up, put it in the van and began to drive away without taking the ticket from me, so I just had time to slap the ticket on the windscreen! Out of the window they yelled, 'what is your name, we are going to report you?' 'What, Mrs P! We can't imagine you're married? Who'd want to marry you?' and drove away.

I also wear a uniform as an Ambassador for Grand Central Train Company

Can I Help You?

which runs trains from Sunderland to London, stopping at only 5 stations on its way.

(*Editor's note...Grand Central ran those exciting big black trains reminiscent of locomotives of old, with Monopoly and Snakes and Ladders boards printed on the tables for commuters' joy and edification! Now gone alas, I am told, as well as the pictures of Marilyn Monroe.*)

My 'helper and information giver role' is a very enjoyable one on Thirsk railway station, by rota with another volunteer. This is a really satisfying job - unless there are travel hiccups, in which case all we can do is pass on the latest information we are given by 'higher-ups' and try to make their situation more bearable.

One particularly unfortunate hiccup wasn't the fault of the railways. On the platform were a lovely young couple, their toddler, two cats in a basket, 1 backpack, 1 large case, 1 medium bag, 1 small buggy for the little one, and 1 handbag. Now, for anyone who doesn't know Thirsk railway station, it is the most difficult station for people with a disability and/or much luggage. There is no lift, only stone steps. This family had driven from London to a village not far from Thirsk for 2 weeks' holiday, which had gone very well. However, when they came to pack the car to return to London, they couldn't find the car key! They had no option but to get a taxi from the village, then the train, then a taxi to their home. Once there, the husband had to do the return journey with their spare car key and retrieve their car. There was very little I could do but sympathise and apologise for the difficulties in dealing with the steps. I took a photo of them and sent it to the rail authorities in order to raise awareness of what an awkward station Thirsk can be for passengers. Fingers crossed, it might help.

Another tale I remember fondly was when I wore less of a uniform, more a badge. I was an interviewer, calling at homes at random and needed just one person (a man) to complete my quota for that day, and then I could go home. A woman came to the next door and I explained who I was, the name of the company I was carrying out research for, and what it was all about. She listened and then I said, 'I'm looking for a man...' and paused momentarily. The woman immediately responded, "Ee luv, tek mine and I'll give yer a bag of sugar!'

Unforgettable!

Editor and Mo Penson

**

Working in and for the community...
Exchange

Over 30 years ago I began training to qualify as a physiotherapist, but a decade ago I felt that my career had reached a threshold – how could I sustain it whilst bringing up two young boys? Could I go freelance, using all that experience to offer private personal care and home support to keep predominantly older people 'happy and safe in their own home'?

My first client had a cruel and severe disability. Gradually, as I visited her every morning to prepare her for the day and maybe take her out, she became not so much a client as a truly close friend. That mutual benefit - practical support and shared wisdom,

plus a listening ear, typified the way in which my business grew.

I now have more work than I can manage, mainly built by word of mouth, such that everyone's a winner in a deep and impactful way. The fulfilling part of community generally is that exchange – in reaching out to help others and accepting it back, maybe in a different form but richly rewarding nonetheless.

And one of my sons typified that thread and weave of community life recently by clearing the churchyard paths as part of his Duke of Edinburgh volunteering, and now ongoing!

Micky Wood

**

A special garment meets the Queen in York Minster...
Maundy and Majesty

The Maundy ceremony began in the reign of Charles II in 1662 and continues to this day. In a UK cathedral or abbey, the reigning monarch presents specially minted royal coins to local pensioners in honour and recognition of their service to church or community. I believe that in times past the monarch used to wash the feet of the poor and humble as well. But of course, this practice no longer takes place. It was to her delight and surprise that Olive's invitation arrived, inviting her to attend the annual Maundy Service in York Minster. She accepted and then thought, 'What shall I wear?' So, a few days later a friend took her shopping and she bought what she now calls, 'My Maundy jacket'.

She explains, 'I had to find out a bit more about the word Maundy. On the day before Jesus was crucified, he hosted a supper for his disciples, surprised them all by washing their feet and then tried to prepare them for what he knew was to happen. He said, 'I command you to love one another as I have loved you.' The next day he was crucified. So Olive learnt that the word Maundy is adapted from 'command'.

On the day she wore the special jacket, feeling both humbled yet elated, she remembers that command, 'Love one another'. When she wears the jacket occasionally now, she is always prompted to recall those words of Jesus, and she says, 'For a while I love and like everybody I see. Perhaps I should pretend that I'm wearing it all the time.'

Adapted from a conversation with Olive Davey

**

Two 'homeless' men in two different doorways...
His Home is a Doorway

I was recently reminded of this moving account, when stumbling upon two men huddled in sleeping bags, on a mattress of newspaper, on a filthy staircase in a railway station. For the rest of my journey, I thought about them and took them some food on my return, but they

had gone. I went home and discovered this story which I knew I had once encountered and saved.

The balmy halcyon days of summer are but a distant memory of the past – and equally distant dream for the future. The mustiness of the wet autumn leaves is fading and now we can taste Christmas, smell the warmth, envelop ourselves in the glow that comes from being safe indoors with friends and families during the long dark days, well supplied with chocolate and cake and other creature comforts. And thank our lucky stars that we do not live on the streets.

I recently met a young man inhabiting a doorway. He was reading the Times. Really??? I dared a second glance. Normally, I look away. Avert my eyes. Pretend to be absorbed in my phone or shopping list. Hurry by and avoid eye contact. I don't think of such people reading The Times, so this time I looked again and stopped to talk. Of course, his physical appearance and raggedy clothes were part of the confusing paradox.

The doorway was, to my eyes, just a doorway, much like any other, but in homeless-land, he told me, it was considered a prime spot. Number 1 in doorway terms, sandwiched as it is between a Costa coffee shop and a newsagent's.

His road to the doorway had involved no sin or crime on his part, and came as a complete surprise to him. White, middle-class, normal happy family life with a decent job, wife, two young children, car, TV and tumble dryer. But, mortgaged to the hilt, when he was made redundant his world disintegrated. The job gone, his home soon followed. His marriage couldn't survive the harsh reality of poverty. His wife was living in the family home, but had moved another man in who could better provide for her and the children. He didn't blame them, but he was now alone in his doorway.

A kind waitress in the coffee shop brought him a warming cardboard cup each morning; and the newsagent delivered (free) a copy of The Times. This intriguing man quipped that he might ask for The Telegraph in future – the bigger pages would make better bedding.

Not for him, this year, those warm smells of cloves and Christmas tree; the dry, fluffy slippers and tinselly decorations; the glow of the fire, the laughter of the children teasing over their presents. For warmth, he might get on a bus and spend all day going nowhere, for as long as the bus driver will let him.

He – and thousands like him – will be spending Christmas in their doorways, reaching for the drugs and drink which provide relief from the cold and boredom, despair and throbbing ache of 'What if' of the streets, dreaming of better times ahead. This man could never have imagined that his Christmas could ever be like this.

So dare a second look, consider being a friend, and share the experience of sleeping as did he, every night, for one night only – take part in a 'Sleep-out for the homeless' event or sponsor someone who is. Or just take a few minutes out to talk to someone who does it all the time. Five minutes which – I promise – will be quite illuminating and might change your life.

Anon

**

His Home is a Font

One Christmas day in our village church, we were looking forward very much to the Archdeacon coming to take our service. In the anticipatory spirit of the day generally, we assembled, but most soon felt too uncomfortable to encounter fully because, lounging on the steps of the font near the door, was a very smelly tramp, looking somewhat the worse for wear, and obviously 'sleeping it off'. Most of us felt uneasy; churchwardens began to get uncomfortable (what shall we do with him before the Archdeacon arrives?), children seemed interested.

The time of the service drew nearer and the anxiety increased, with no sign of the preacher either! Eventually, as the church clock struck, the 'tramp' slowly arose and taking off a few garments revealed the Archdeacon!

That of course became his sermon, that Christmas morning.

Eileen Bennett

**

The locked church door...
Two Swallows Don't Make a Summer

'Well, we've shut God out for another week,' I say, looking up at the vicar who holds the big iron key in his hand. No access to crossing that threshold today then! But this to me is God's house where he lives and where he oversees our christenings, weddings and funerals, as well as the other services and sacraments.

Having lived longer than my allotted three score years and ten, having worshipped in many churches, and attended many meetings of an Evangelical nature, I know that the church is a vital part of rural community life.

Unfortunately, the church has been pushed aside by the pressures of 'the world'. People in general are too busy shopping on Sundays, or at car boot sales, or simply at home with their families, or out to Sunday lunches, to consider attending church. To convince them otherwise is down to one person – a leader who really cares and is joyful and loving and who follows Christ's example...ministry of Presence is a God-given gift – an ordinary person who is genuinely concerned for the spiritual well-being of people – and who can help them out in any situation (like Jesus did).

Regrettably, I have witnessed in my Christian journey many people connected to the church who were lazy, unconcerned, pompous, didn't know people, never met them! Sadly, one vicar even refused me entry to a church on Good Friday because he wasn't holding a service. When I said, 'There's someone else coming,' the reply was 'Two swallows don't make a summer,' and with that the vicar went home! So much for some of the hierarchy! Fortunately, however, there

Can I Help You?

are also many who are like martyrs, who are the real life of Christianity – they are almost saint-like in what they give. Thank the Lord for them. The Christian church is needed by all. There are millions who couldn't live without it – and neither could I.

Rachel Faulks

**

Meeting pastoral expectations?...
'Come in.'

In recent years, congregations in some of our churches have decreased rapidly. With some regular worshippers it is because of old age, becoming infirm and being unable to cross the church threshold any longer. It is these people who concern me, because not attending church certainly does not mean they no longer believe.

Some have quietly given their offerings and more for many years, but because they have not been on committees or the various church rotas, their faces have not become familiar to the vicar, who now has so many churches to serve that it must be very hard for him (or her) to remember faces and names. This is where regular church members can help, by recalling to the vicar, new or old, that 'George Brown' or 'Jane Grey' are rarely able to attend church and very much miss taking Holy Communion. Because the parishes are now so large, the vicar has much more to do – travelling further and taking extra services - but if he or she could just go over these people's thresholds to spare time for a chat, they would feel that they are still remembered.

Yes, we have church members who try to visit the lonely, but to have a vicar call in once every two or three months would really make their day. And their own front door would become the threshold! The church crossing it to them...a reversal of the 'norm'.

Julia Barker

**

Coachloads enjoy a summer treat, stepping over village garden thresholds...
Around and About Hidden Gardens

We had lived in the village for about six months prior to our first Hidden Gardens.

It was always held in early July and as the day drew nearer signs would go up on all the approach roads to the village advertising 'The Hidden Gardens of Helperby'. The week before the event, leaflets came through the letter box asking for donations of books, bottles, plants, bric-a-brac and home-made cakes. There was also a request for cars to be removed from the cobbles on the Saturday evening to make way for the various stalls

to be set out next day on either side of Main Street.

Hidden Gardens mornings were nearly always fine and dry - much to the relief of all concerned! Throughout the morning the sense of anticipation and excitement grew. The sounds of stalls going up and people getting ready could be heard from about 8.30am. Stall holders arrived soon afterwards and began setting out their wares. Everything was beginning to come together and there was a definite air of festivity.

At each end of the village two huge columns were put up - these were at the entrance to 'Hidden Gardens' where visitors purchased their tickets and received a card giving information about each open garden and its location. The organisers, who had worked tirelessly to get everything ready, were conspicuous in their pale green Hidden Gardens T-shirts.

The whole of Main Street was closed off for the day and cars were directed to car parks at either end of the village. Visitors from far and wide, some in coaches, usually started arriving in good time, especially if it was nice weather, and were happy to amble along at their leisure to see what the various stalls had on offer.

The gardens opened at mid-day. There were usually around 10 to visit - varying in size, design and content. In latter years poetry reading and singing took place in some of them. The entertainments on Main Street also began at 12. There were Morris dancers, street dancers, a jazz band, reggae music, to name but a few. All took it in turn to perform in this happy open-air setting. Often the church also hosted a choral, folk or classical music concert.

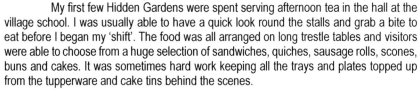

Hidden Gardens was very much a community event. Everyone in the village pitched in and played their part. The list of jobs was endless - organising the event and stalls, opening gardens, manning stalls, serving at one of the many refreshment areas, marshalling in the car parks - it was all hands on deck!!

My first few Hidden Gardens were spent serving afternoon tea in the hall at the village school. I was usually able to have a quick look round the stalls and grab a bite to eat before I began my 'shift'. The food was all arranged on long trestle tables and visitors were able to choose from a huge selection of sandwiches, quiches, sausage rolls, scones, buns and cakes. It was sometimes hard work keeping all the trays and plates topped up from the tupperware and cake tins behind the scenes.

One year I was asked to host strawberry teas in our garden - living on Main Street we were in a good location to attract visitors and we had a big enough garden to accommodate all the necessary tables and chairs. It did mean that the garden had to be presentable - quite a challenge with three young children and two boisterous Labradors, but we managed. Scones aplenty had to be baked - many of these were made ahead of time and frozen. Chairs and tables came from the village hall and were set up on the morning. Crockery was borrowed from a local WI. The strawberries were donated from a local farm and had been freshly picked that morning. Once people started arriving, it got very busy but there was always a jolly atmosphere, with people just wanting to sit down and enjoy some refreshments! We were exhausted by the time the last visitors left and

Can I Help You?

were glad to sit down ourselves.

In 2011 my son was serving in Afghanistan with the Rifles, so my daughter and I organised a bric-a-brac stall outside our house to raise funds for Help for Heroes. People were very generous, both in donating items for sale and in their purchases. We were delighted with the amount we were able to pass on to the charity, and the support we received.

At the end of the afternoon, around 5.30, the visitors started drifting back to their cars, usually laden with plants, cakes and other sundry purchases. A few visitors lingered at the pub to enjoy a drink and the late afternoon sunshine. Gradually, the peace and quiet returned to the village, cars could be returned to their places outside the houses and life settled back to normal. The stalls were usually dismantled the following morning.

The final part of Hidden Gardens took place a few days later when all the "helpers" were invited to go and view the gardens that had been open to the public. It was always a jolly evening and culminated with a glass of wine in one garden and the announcement of the funds raised by Hidden Gardens. Everyone gave a huge sigh of relief - all the hard work had paid off. Hidden Gardens was over until the next year!

Louise Denison

PS. A tribute...every year, the curator of the village archive, David Bottomley, could be observed tirelessly walking the main street for the duration of the festival, selling his legendary quizzes. Typifying the village, this was his personal contribution to this annual fundraising event towards the upkeep of St.Peter's Church, Brafferton.

Editor

**

Natural well-being for body, mind and spirit in the heart of town...
Stepping Into a Secret Garden

The initial seed was planted in my heart many years ago during a time of prayer. I shared the vague idea with the Elders at church, but I was too busy with work, so the seed just lay dormant; largely forgotten, even by me. The intended garden plot became overgrown with brambles, nettles and self-seeded trees; accessible only to wildlife and those determined to drink, shoot up drugs and smash the church hall windows which overlooked the dereliction.

But slowly and quietly things were changing, until a critical threshold was reached. My retirement from General Practice came earlier than expected, and a chance conversation between the owner of the plot and a 'retired' church elder resulted in the possibility of 'someone doing something useful with this mess'. Yet, despite that flash of recognition and excitement on hearing the news, knowing that 'this was it', it still took another six months to take the leap of faith to actually commit. I was assailed with a sense

Community

of inadequacy, the aims were 'fuzzy'; I doubted that I had the skills, who would help me, how would it work? Perhaps even bigger; what would it 'cost me', would it swallow me up? I fought valiantly, despite knowing this to be from God, and despite the Church being more than happy to financially support this hare-brained, ill-planned scheme. The tipping point came from a farming ex-patient, cross that I had abandoned her, but for ever practical – 'What's happening with this gardening project? My cows are busy filling the shed for you!' I crossed the threshold and, oddly enough, God came with me!

As five of us started to clear away the overgrowth, we didn't just discover a patio, a path and an air raid shelter, but we also discovered that the aims became clearer and a steady stream of 'God-co-incidences' opened up new possibilities, allowing each next step to happen. The Secret Garden was growing organically; it had a life of its own, and all I needed to do was facilitate and mediate. For the first time in my life I finally discovered that I could indeed trust God. Inevitably there have been times when I have felt overwhelmed, but I am gradually learning to 'hold the garden lightly', to share my visions and hopes, burdens and fears with others and to trust that help will come or a way forward will be found.

It seems to be a liminal place, a thin place, where the sense of God ('the Other' or 'the More') seems more real and more tangible in some way, both to those of faith and no faith. There is a sense of peace and acceptance; all are welcome, all will be respected. Healing is gently offered by all elements of the garden, whether through food, friendship, silence, stillness, activity or giving, beauty, scent, colour and more. A small taste of heaven perhaps?

One real joy is witnessing the positive impact that daring to cross the garden threshold can have on others too:

- Meaning and purpose – providing a reason to get out of bed
- Acceptance and welcome, activity, social contact, friendship and laughter
- Opportunity to give and not just receive
- Peace, refreshment, breathing space and sanctuary whether sitting or wandering round the garden alone or as part of a quiet retreat day or outdoor service
- Play and creativity, learning and discovery for children and adults
- Sense of pride in belonging to something bigger, that is generous and open-handed
- Awe and wonder at the beauty, abundance and interconnectedness of nature from the smallest minibeasts to our biggest trees
- Taste and see discovery; potatoes from the ground and peas straight from a pod are sweet

Can I Help You?

The delights of The Secret Garden are accessed through a small gateway alongside the United Reformed Church in Northallerton. It is a garden for sharing, run by volunteers from our community. The aims are to:
- Provide a therapeutic space for groups or individuals who may find it a helpful place.
- Provide a haven for wildlife
- Share sustainably grown produce with Hambleton Food Share, Women's Refuge and our volunteers

Crossing the threshold, trusting the process, walking into the unknown: this is the stuff of 'God's Kingdom' where the hungry are fed, the outcasts are welcomed, burdens are eased, healing is found and we learn to love and live respectfully with all God's creation on this earth.

Why do we ever doubt God's topsy turvey ways?

In due course we were so delighted to achieve the URC and Congregational Insurance Community Award and we didn't think it could get any better. How wrong we were!

Right from the start we had been encouraged to enter the RHS Yorkshire in Bloom 'It's Your Neighbourhood' competition. The aim is to encourage projects which engage with the community, take environmental responsibility seriously and use appropriate good gardening practices. Being novices in this field, we did as we were told!

The first year's assessment was particularly helpful. We were surrounded by weeds, piles of logs and debris, with only a small patch of ground cleared to grow veg with the help of the local guides. Yet the lady who came to assess us was really enthusiastic, encouraging and full of good practical suggestions and ideas. We were so engrossed in conversation and shared vision that she forgot about meeting up with her daughter and granddaughter; so they came and joined us too. The granddaughter promptly skipped her way up and over and round the air raid shelter, revealing all sorts of new possibilities – what a gift that has proven to be.

For the next two years we were considered to be 'Thriving' by our assessors. That felt very gratifying and comfortable; recognising the work that been done, and our journey onwards. We applied again the following year in a casual way, with no great expectations of change. However, the gentleman who visited came in and said 'Wow!' He had positively chosen to be our assessor and had been wanting to visit for a while. He just 'got it'. His enthusiasm was infectious; he provided specific advice around 'light–touch' management of our wilder area. It was a really encouraging meeting but we certainly did not expect to be awarded "OUTSTANDING!"

He particularly noted that 'the space is seen as having a positive benefit for the wellbeing, mental and spiritual, of the wide range of people who use the garden on a regular basis. An oasis in the centre of town, with a wide range of wildlife, bird song and environmental habitats'. We have all just grown a little bit more!

Liz Styan

**

An unconditional invitation to ...
Enter

It had been a vision in the town of Northallerton for a long time, I learned, and for the last year or so a colleague of mine had been meeting with other church leaders in planning a fresh way to widen their support for the vulnerable. Would I be a backup for future meetings?
   The aim was to create a safe space, a hub, in neutral premises (not a church) in the centre of town where people struggling to thrive, or even survive, could be supported. With representation from churches, charities, voluntary bodies and local authorities, an expanded, one-off meeting was called to discuss the findings of a specially commissioned survey (via the Cinnamon Project). Yes, there was clearly huge potential demand for help with isolation, trauma, distress, mental well-being. So much so that the five main churches in Northallerton next agreed to create a steering group to explore further. A project, faith-based but not faith-biased, offering practical support to all, without discrimination. Now feeling called to a more committed engagement, I became one of the five trustees in an ever more deeply rewarding involvement.

It was time to put the theory to a public test by hiring the very large main space at the Forum centre for a day. An open invitation was extended to anyone, with either a professional or personal interest, to experience a mock-up of the 'living rooms' concept. A large table for crafts and shared learning; sofa-style seating; café-style seating; relaxing lighting and, equally important, private space for personal contemplation if that was felt helpful and healing. The founder of the Renew Wellbeing network added her insights into the value of such a safe place, where it was 'OK not to be OK'. And by the end of the day, the number of attendees had been impressive. 250 people, full of enthusiasm to spread the word, and many of them potential volunteers if it could be brought into being.
   The trustees formed further sub-groups for the detailed planning required. Suitable premises were identified in a central but peaceful location adjacent to various retailers – an ideal ground floor, plus a separate entrance leading up to meeting rooms or offices above. Financial seeding was provided by the churches, along with separate grant funding and future pledges – all backed by training for the volunteers. A year on, an enthusiastic and prayerful official opening would happen! We would be very busy came the predication. Correct. From day one onwards.
   Fundamental was the offer of caring, simple support for the many and varied people who would bring their needs – hundreds of them. One in particular springs to mind though, a lady who had obviously plucked up courage to walk through the door but felt unable to speak or join in conversation with others. The hosts that day made her a coffee and let her sit apart from everyone else, in her own space. She watched on as some joined together to complete a jigsaw puzzle and others carried out some craft work on the large open table. She did not speak to anyone that day. As the second session was about

Can I Help You?

to open two days later a host noticed the same lady hesitatingly walking up and down outside, but unsure about coming in. Eventually, however, she did and joined a small group with their craft work. Over the weeks she became a regular attender and so much so that eventually she ended up leading a demonstration of her own craftworking skills!

Partnerships were quickly formed with Hambleton Foodshare, Jubilee Debt, The Secret Garden, Men's Sheds, while various professionals and voluntary organisations are on standby to provide more specialised advice. The Living Rooms is still at a flexible, early stage of its development. Basic hospitality, a listening ear, signposting to experts. People can visit as often as they wish, but, if they no longer feel the need, we are equally happy, in the hope they have found a renewed, confident way forward in their lives.

Roger Tucker

In the Silence of God's Garden

Lord, I thank you for this quiet time.
A period for reflection in the beauty of our Secret Garden,
For all the richness of nature's many colours.
Just being still and silent,
Or noting the faint sound under our feet
As I walk the gravel path,
Accompanied by the bleating sound of lambs,
Gathered in the mart nearby.

Lord, I thank you for all the birds singing,
Flying in and out of the trees on this peaceful day.
And for our blackbird's nest with her eggs,
Bringing new life into the Secret Garden.

I thank you Lord for the stillness,
The calm and the warm sunshine trying to break through the clouds,
And twinkling through the leaves on the trees,
Accompanied by the wafting smell of home-made pork-pies,
Crafted in the butcher's shop nearby.
Thank you for the gift of all those who made this beauty possible,
A new oasis for the benefit of all in this busy town.

Lord, I thank you for all your gifts,
For this fellowship of being at oneness and quietness
With you, my Saviour and Lord.

Audrey Wilson

Through the Vestry Door
(editor)

A Reflection

We See 'er About

After prayer and preparing to conduct worship, my next priority was being a conspicuously visible presence for those of any faith or none, in all three of my allocated villages. They came to see me as simply Ann and to know where to find me and to experience me as being accessible and approachable when they really needed me. That might even be in the fish and chip van queue!

       The work of a pastor is holistic at every level, especially in a rural context. The ecclesiastical word 'curate' comes from the Latin word 'curare'…cure of souls. Caring for the whole person, not just spiritually. Caring for the whole community, not just the church-goers. Attending village events, village hall coffee mornings, soup lunches, barbecues etc.

Community

Using the local shops.

On my visiting homes, the door would be opened in response to my tentative knock. I didn't need to introduce myself, "Ee, cum in. Yer welcome.' One elderly gentleman to another at a village barbecue was overheard to remark, ''Er over there with the shoppin' basket's t'vicar. She looks just like an 'ousewife, but she's reet clever really.' (Raffle tickets in my basket!) Or I would visit the middle aged farm worker who cares for his blind and deaf mother, doing everything for her, dressing and bathing her and enabling her to stay in her own home, who takes me in and says, 'Ee, this is champion. 'Ere's t' vicar ter see yer, mother.'

'Meet and Eat' suppers, held in my home, brought villagers together who did not necessarily attend church on a regular basis, for conversation, community and companionship; a safe place to share their stories. Food was locally grown and bought, supporting local production and trade. Guests crossed social, intellectual and married status boundaries. I had at these times an insight into what 'take, eat' could really mean, as I observed the sense of fun, equality and the honouring of one another as guests, around a table. Maybe only in a rural setting would you find those who have served sitting alongside those who have employed them in the past; reflecting an important Christian teaching of Jesus, of our challenge not so much to be served as to serve. (The 'grandest' lady of all took home all the washing and ironing of table linen and napkins.)

This all gives credence to one of the more accurate pictures the Church of England has of itself, that it is a club which also exists largely for the benefit of those who are not of its membership. This is especially important in a rural community where all villagers feel they 'own' the village church building, but rarely attend regular worship. Community groups annually raise money to support their church's Parish Share, even if they only ever use the church for family celebration, ritual or support. In one, the village contributes by opening their gardens, having a street market and fair, Morris Dancing, live music and choral entertainment in the gardens etc. In another, the fishing club twice a year holds a fund-raising fishing match. In the third there is an annual Party in the Paddock. It is unlikely that these little churches could continue to pay their parish share without these events. I am reminded of pitfalls and dangers for the institutional Church, as hinted at in this prayer by Nicola Slee...

> *Snipping this way and that,*
> *They mould the bushy green growth*
> *Into ever more ingenious designs:*
> *In their tending of theological topiary, they fail to notice*
> *God popping on her walking gear*
> *And slipping out the back garden gate,*
> *Heading for the hills, quietly whistling.*

In the years since my retirement, I have been intrigued to note both similarities and contrasts as I became part of a Christian outreach to the large county town of Northallerton. For historical reasons, Zion United Reformed Church is more secure financially than most churches today, of whatever denomination. It owns property, including

Can I Help You?

a cottage alongside its approach drive...on the cultural threshold, such that it has almost got a shop window on the High Street. What do people see through the window looking in? What can be seen through it looking out? As with any 'shop' it is part of a huge offering of hospitality to its town. In worship, Tiny Time. Market day, Way In, music, coffee time fellowship, soup lunch, Food Bank, a Secret Garden for community use, a green and other special interest groups, plus work with issues of justice, peace, and climate change, pastoral and bereavement care, free or subsidised use of its facilities, etc. etc. Here others from the town are welcomed where they 'belong', and find a place where their needs can be met and nurtured in the exchange, resourcing one another. Good News for thousands over the 200 years of its history.

Such is another model of mission, without anyone needing to speak in an 'evangelistic' way to the guests of these groups. It offers an incarnational model. You may know the words which St. Francis of Assissi used to his disciples, 'Preach the gospel at all times, using words if necessary.' God is out there in his creation and in people's lives. In this post-modern world, it is in the honouring of others that we recognise that everyone has a story to tell.

Homilies

Gone Fishing

Matthew 4:12-23
I will make you fishers of men?

Fishing was certainly one of the new challenges I came to know a little about in the parishes on the boundaries of the River Swale. Sacred were the two annual Fishing Matches in Myton. Money raised from the entrants' 'pegs' was a large contributor to the funding of the little church there. We were all on board for helping where we could, from providing the generous sausage sandwich and scones and jam and cream lunch for the helpers and participants to providing raffle prizes, and then my very scary personal responsibility for drawing the raffle and giving a speech of thanks to these taciturn Yorkshire fishermen. Nothing in my hitherto ministry training and experience had prepared me for this. The Golden Ticket was the supreme peg to have drawn.

And in reciprocal generosity, freshly caught fish frequently appeared on my doorstep from zealous trout anglers, all wrapped in newspaper, cleaned and gutted with love! The first contribution to a donation appeal for new hymn books came from the Brafferton Fishing Club. Extra generous, at the initiation of a donor who had thought I usually chose 'terrible 'ymns'.

Years ago, I worked as a hospital chaplain. Not ministering formally, nor expecting to catch 'fish'. Mostly I worked alongside non churchgoers, virtually none of

Community

whom in a million years would have asked to see a chaplain. And yet, in the visiting and walking alongside in that context where life is fragile and mortality is evident all around, once people began to know and trust someone listening to **their** story, very often the conversation turned naturally to issues of faith. It was there that I learnt never ever to go in with a script or agenda of what I ought or ought not to be **saying**. I learnt to trust and be led by them. They knew I was there alongside them in the name of Christ. More than one said to me, 'I can't believe in God myself, but I feel safer now that I have met you who does.' It was in that place that I learnt that sometimes our 'vanity' is in thinking it is we who are to do the 'mission', instead of being simply part of something which Christ does through us and sometimes despite us. What a relief!

I mentioned in my reflection that I latterly spent several years worshipping in a United Reformed Church. The elders and congregation there have an exceptional gift of hospitality. If the question were asked about these faithful disciples, 'Do their lives speak authentically about the presence of Christ within them? then the fruits of their time, commitment and discipleship clearly evidence a big YES! If, like them, in humility we can offer up our own story, not in proclamatory style from a pulpit or megaphone but round the table in conversation, people will get it! It is an essential precursor to understanding the waters we are fishing into. We are a mix of disciples, as in any worshipping community, all adding our own gifts, serving, living and loving as a team and sharing Christ's mission as best as we can, where we are.

From a book of women's sermons, we read more about Going Fishing...

Some of us are flying fish, flashy performers who show God's glory for all to see. Some of us are very old and grey and have swum the great depths that life has to offer. Some of us are catfish, scavenging for God's realm, and helping to keep the waters clear. Some are eels who dart through a few times a year. Some are kind and gentle dolphins... Some are sardines labouring so hard just to avoid being eaten...shy, determined and slow turtles, or sharks darting around and scaring the others.

Some of us may be Evangelists, and can do 'mission' by words, but look at the team Jesus began to assemble, several of them actually fishermen, some very unpromising everyday people like us. Andrew who brought others to Jesus; John, thoughtful and reflective, Simon Peter who said what he thought and loved Jesus passionately, and James, chosen by Jesus to experience the Transfiguration, thought to be the first martyr who died for his Christian faith. He even chose Judas who betrayed him.

Johnny Baker, Anglican Missioner, wrote, 'In the past we have had a welcoming 'come to us policy', but now we must get out there, to better understand the 'tribes' of the UK and realise it cannot be a one size fits all approach'. He continues, 'Stepping outside a church building is crossing a cultural boundary, as people don't 'get' the church anymore'.

Today's churchgoing communities are not there because their members are wonderful people, but because God can continue to use ordinary people to do wonderful

Can I Help You?

things for him! And people in our communities certainly did know about all kinds of fishing! And about the joy of winning the prize of the Golden Ticket which takes them to new possibilities!

**

Water, Wine and Transformation

John 2: 1-11
When the wine was gone, Jesus' mother said to him, 'They have no more wine.'

One of the rich symbols of Epiphany is hospitality. Epiphany, meaning God is about to do something new. A new threshold is to be crossed. Many of us welcome guests at Christmas and the New Year. Some will have been more welcome than others. All will have made an impact of one sort or another by the time they have left.

In this reading we have an account of a wedding at which Jesus and his mother are guests. It opens with a lovely human conversation, whose dynamics those of you with older sons will recognise. Mary, a middle-aged lady by now, is anxious for her host who had run out of wine. A very serious breach of hospitality in those times. For some reason she expects Jesus to do something about it, and what is more important knows that he can. And she instructs the servants, 'Do whatever he tells you.'

At this point, let's think realistically about these jars. 20-30 gallons each. 6 of them. Perhaps about 2,400 bottles of the best, saved until last. The precise numbers are not important, but it indicates the tremendous abundance, free and richly flowing. A gift, more than enough for this particular feast. Interestingly, wine is a symbol of the old law of Moses, so here again maybe is an allusion to the transforming of the old law to the new. No longer under law but under grace.

But what about the wine itself? The qualities of good wine are fragrance, taste, appearance, but above all it is intoxicating. That has implications for the gospel message too. We can become transformed by it. Steeped in it and prepared to take risks for it. It is yeast that transforms the water and fruit into wine. I am the new life. The new energy, the new law. I am the gift which I bring. How can we be the gift ourselves which we bring to others? That which can transform, energise, renew?

Anything can happen when he is around! Everywhere Jesus went, the old became the new. The unexpected of Epiphany? How can we offer more gracious hospitality to him in our lives? It may feel we are ok and going along nicely, so how can he use ordinary everyday material, like 'water' in us to make us into the best wine? How can we cross that threshold?

As with all our guests, relationship is the key! We meet him in the scriptures, in prayer. In silence. I read recently regarding silence in this noisy world: 'Silence is the workshop of the Holy Spirit'. If we grow in the spirit, our work will also grow. Like a garden, we will not grow individually, nor as a church community, if we do not nourish the soil. So what are you going to do about that? It is easy to make personal resolutions about growing

spiritually, but the first step is to acknowledge a need.

Jesus was not sent by God to be a safe pair of hands to hold his people where they feel comfortable. He challenged the status quo, offering wine such as had never been tasted before. Dare we allow the yeast to work in us anew?

'Christians again must learn to be the new life bubbling up and intoxicating all around it with the new life of Christ.'

'I have called **you** by name!'

To offer Jesus true hospitality is to encounter him, and when we encounter him we will be changed! We will certainly feel the impact! Our prayer life will change. Our giving will change. Our communities will change. In a marriage service I sometimes offer the image of the diamond in the engagement ring. I encourage the couple to imagine the contrast between the light that reflects from a diamond and that from a stone made of glass.

This marriage involved Jesus in the feast. God bless us and disturb us as we dare to move away from familiar ground, to cross the threshold, in order to have our eyes opened. It may be unsettling, but it will also be full of unforeseen delight and grace.

**

Weeds and Plants

Matthew:13 24-30. Romans:8 12-25
'Hope that is seen is no hope at all'. Who hopes for what he already has?

So, when we speak of the Christian 'hope', we mean 'in faith'. And that is the trusting bit, where we are out on a limb in a culture that says 'what you see is what you get'. Everything must be open to scrutiny; be rational and even reasonable. But what do we have here? For as long as the weeds cannot be distinguished from the plants, let them grow together.

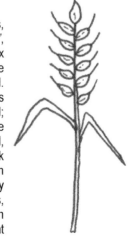

From the famous hymn we know well the words, *'Wheat and tares together sown, unto joy or sorrow grown'*, suggesting a much broader understanding of the complex mystery of good and evil, both in ourselves as well as in all the mix of society and culture. We ourselves are God's own field. The soil into which the mix of wheat and tares grows. In this story there are no panic measures to separate good from evil; an approach very different from that of the purist sects of the time, the Pharisees and Essenes. The saved and the unsaved, echoed in some Christian teaching today also. But let's look at the band of Jesus' followers and disciples? Were they an exclusive bunch? No. They did not particularly show any aptitude for the life they were to lead. Some, eg Bartimaeus, 'followed him along the way'. Others tagged along. Women stayed around to help look after him. And it has to be said that

Can I Help You?

amongst them were quite a few of the reprobates and rejected of the day.

No one had to join a preparation class to belong to this group, or do a course, or pass a test, all these being reasons why the established religious of the day could not cope with Jesus. He infuriated them. The group around Jesus of Nazareth had no name, no organization, no hierarchy. It was all wonderfully ad hoc, unsystematic and light years distant from the ever more managed institution which has developed to represent him now. I am sure it does not tell us how to farm. This scheme sounds as crazy as a shepherd leaving all his sheep to find the one lost one which got away, but it tells us of how God puts up with us all. This is how God works in his kingdom here and now, and it is not a way which makes sense. John Pridmore writes, 'The mad way God works is that he does not weed out anyone. That is how crazily hospitable the company of Jesus is'. That it is also a tale for our times need hardly to be stressed. It contains two questions. The first goes unanswered. 'Where did these weeds come from?', the servants ask. We ask this about what we grow in our gardens, fields and allotments, and we can ask it about our beautiful world, fashioned and created, so finely tuned. The servants have a second question; not, 'Why is it becoming a choked and stifled world?' but, 'What should we do about it?'

There is a psychological test which involves listing anything you most dislike discovering in others. What are the traits which most irritate you, get under your skin? Pause for a moment and reflect. We then review our answers and usually discover these traits within ourselves, dormant and often unacknowledged and recognised.

We are a mixture of the wheat and the tares and mercifully God embraces us in all our mix. Pridmore continues, 'Repeatedly, sickeningly across the centuries the church, wonderfully confident that it knows which are the weeds and which is the wheat, has sought to incinerate the former, so as to maintain the purity of the latter'.

Plants or weeds? It is not for us to take God's judgment into our own hands, but to recognize with humility that we would all be condemned, were it not for the amazing merciful love of God, who has dropped the charges and set us free. That is our hope. The weeds growing with wheat is a note of patience. God's patience with us, and thus our own in our dawning faith. This is not a passive threshold of people waiting in a dark room, hoping someone will come with a lighted candle, but people in the early morning who know the sun has arisen and are now waiting for the brightness of midday.

Community

A Final Musing

True Sharing

This story comes from a black township in South Africa, where the weary parish priest found that he had to attend the final part of a school play during the last week in Advent.

After the gloriously attired Wise Men had come and gone, three unexpected arrivals appeared - really strange characters. One was dressed in rags, hobbling along with the aid of a stick. The second wore only a tattered pair of shorts, and was bound in chains. The third was even weirder – his whitened face topped by an unkempt grey wig, wearing an unlikely Afro shirt.

As they approached, a general warning rang out, 'Close the door, Joseph, they are probably thieves and vagabonds hoping to steal all we have.'

But Joseph said, 'Everyone is entitled to share this child – the poor, the rich, the sad, the dubious. We cannot claim this child exclusively for ourselves. Let them enter.'

The new visitors stood staring at the child. Joseph picked up the gifts left behind by the Wise Men. To the first strange man he said: 'You are poor: take this gold and buy whatever you need. We will not go hungry without it.'

To the second he said, 'I am helpless to unbind your chains. Take this myrrh – it will help to heal the sore wounds on your wrists and ankles.'

To the third he said, 'Your mind is in turmoil. Maybe the aroma of this frankincense will soothe your troubled soul.'

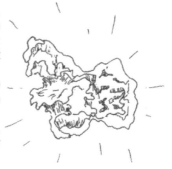

But the first man replied. 'I don't think this gift is appropriate for me. Anyone who finds me with gold will think I have stolen it. And, sadly, in due course this child of yours will be judged a criminal too.'

The second man said, 'I think you should keep this ointment. One day this child will be wearing chains similar to mine.'

And the third man said, 'My anguished mind has no spiritual hope. So keep the incense for the child. He will lose faith in his heavenly father too.'

In confusion, Mary and Joseph covered their faces; the three men addressed the child. 'Little one, you are not from favoured lands of gold and frankincense. You belong to the country of want and disease. Our world. Let us share. We want you to accept our gifts.'

Can I Help You?

The first man took off his ragged shirt. 'Take these rags. One day you may need them when they tear your own garments off your back.'

The second man said, 'When I remove these chains, they can be for your use. On that day you will really feel and carry the pain of humanity.'

The third man said, 'I give you my despair in life. Carry my grief and loss along with your own.'

The three men turned and walked back out into the night. But the darkness was subtly different. Something had happened in the stable. Their pain was slowly diminishing. There had been a kind of epiphany. They looked up.

They were even noticing the stars now.

Anon

Stop, Look, Listen...

DRAMA

All the world's a stage, and most of us are desperately unrehearsed. – *Sean O'Casey*

Your story is what you have, what you will always have. It is something to own. – *Michelle Obama*

Playing dressing up begins at age five and never truly ends. – *Kate Spade*

I had no idea of the character. But the moment I was dressed, the clothes and the make-up made me feel the person he was. I began to know him, and by the time I walked onto the stage, he was fully born. – *Charlie Chaplin*

People will stare. Make it worth their while. – *Harry Winston*

Drama is life with the dull bits cut out. – *Alfred Hitchcock*

All good drama has two movements; first the making of the mistake, then the discovery that it was a mistake. – *W.H.Auden*

Drama is very important in life. You have to come on with a bang. You never want to go out with a whimper. – *Julia Child*

Religion enabled society to organise itself to debate goodness, just as Greek drama had once done. – *Edward Bond*

Through the Wardrobe Door
(Contributors)

From little girl to principal boy to pantomime dame...
On Dressing Up

Even as a very little girl I wrote plays, starred in them, directed them, and promoted them. The joy of creating the tickets, curtains, stage and seating still makes me smile. The even deeper response of simple childhood pleasures, adults' tolerance and encouragement I still honour today.

My first really vivid experience of audience reaction was in my second year at school when I entertained the class with a ten-minute sketch about using a telephone box in the character of Marlene as created by Beryl Reid. Where did that come from? It is deeply embedded in my psyche.

I moved on to secondary school where I continued acting, producing and added dancing to my repertoire. I had succeeded in getting to grammar school and house competitions were a thrill. Also working at our local theatre, helping with costume making, lighting and front of house. The whole atmosphere excited me and watching productions maybe five or ten times was wonderful – observing nuances of performance, mistakes turned to triumph and seeing first-hand how important interaction with an audience could be.

On to university and more productions and dancing. The ability to shed one's own skin, step into a costume and take on another persona, scary but amazing. Alec Guinness said that he couldn't find his way into a part until he found that character's shoes, really proving the old saying 'I walk a mile in another man's shoes'. Then came teaching and throwing myself into passing on my passion to the next generation – watching from the side of the stage this time as young performers blossomed and found confidence. There really isn't anything more inspiring than art/music/dance to develop character and commitment.

We moved abroad and had our two absorbing children, so life took over for a while, but when we returned to a small North Yorkshire village, I really hit my stride. Our village had an active Drama Society and it was a wonderful way to get to know people and enjoy myself.

The village Panto was an institution – acting and dressing up – what more could I want! My first role was as the Queen of Hearts – beautiful dress and long blond wig – a small part, perfect. I then moved on to Principal Boy which was to be my forte for nearly 25 years. A girl playing a boy in jacket, leggings, frilly cravats and fabulous boots. I still find it hard to wear long boots without adopting a wide stance and putting my hands on my hips and slapping my thigh. I always feel sick before a performance, but with makeup, costume and then onto the stage with lights up, a metamorphosis happens – you stand

Stop, Look, Listen...

taller, you smile and you step into the role. The great thing about Panto is that the audience is another member of the cast, willing you on, and with experience it is like riding a wave. A good performance is an incredible high and I'm only an amateur. No wonder it takes professionals ages to 'come down'. I continued being a 'goodie' for ages until I was given the role of the Wicked Stepmother in Sleeping Beauty – brilliant, I loved it. The costume was amazing, a huge black cloak with a collar of peacock feathers; no matter that I always had to come on sideways as I couldn't fit through the stage flats, it felt incredible. I even wore it to a school assembly, I loved it so much. Again, the transformation once it was on, raising an arched eyebrow and swishing that cape! I think I was pretty scary but I'll leave that to my audience to decide.

My biggest challenge was as the Dame in that well-known Panto, 'Santa in Space'! The Dame (a woman now playing a man playing a woman...keep up) was a real challenge. It was only after I saw an old episode of 'I Love Lucy' that it all fell into place. I found my mannerisms, slapstick. At last I could relax and enjoy, and finally the costumes made sense.

I have always been a Drama Queen and I am glad to report this has passed on to Ella and Martha {my granddaughters}. They love dressing up, creating plays and performing for us from our dressing up box; the younger, in particular, is her own woman, most often choosing the 'wicked role' rather than the traditional fairy! Very famously, Marilyn Monroe was once walking with a friend in a busy New York, hiding her identity in a simple dress, headscarf and glasses. Her friend said how amazing it was that she wasn't recognised. Marilyn asked if she wanted her to do it. 'Do what?' her friend asked. 'Be Marilyn,' she replied. 'Watch.' She removed her glasses, headscarf, stood tall and sashayed across the square. Everyone turned and they were surrounded. 'See,' she said. We can all do it on a good day and the stage has been my good day, on a good day.

Sue Thorne

**

Casting a spell...
A Fairy? Me?

An invitation to be The Fairy in the annual pantomime. An honour but...

Now, I'm not a fairy type person and doubted myself as someone sparkly, beautiful, gentle, kind and good. In my real life I'm too old and cynical, well, most of the time. However, I do like to dress up and become someone else occasionally, so there I was, decision made, offer accepted, I was Cast!

The panto was entitled 'The Magnificent 6.75' and I was one of the 6.75, a campaigner for justice and rights for all. Someone who could cast the odd magic spell if good deeds were not working to plan.

The era was the 1850s and the setting was a North Yorkshire version of the American Wild West. Trumper, the US President, has invaded Britain and appointed Blojo

Drama

as his British President. War had been declared and had raged on in the village since Mexit! The villagers have been left destitute and occupied by banditos from what had become known as The East Coast Mainline in Mexican North Yorkshire.

How on earth does one decide how to present one's character, given such a brief!

In supporting my new I.D. I enlisted the help of a professional theatrical dresser, who happily remembered me from previous years' costume challenges. I told her I wanted to be an 'Annie get your gun' cowgirl type Fairy, with Mexican undertones.

Whilst she disappeared, searching for inspiration, into the catacombs of the wardrobe store, I set myself about too, looking for the threads I needed to wear to become Airy Mary Fairy! The Mexican waistcoat, the peasant blouse, the pink cowboy hat. A great start!

Then, as if by magic, the dresser appeared with white cowboy boots and a magnificent red tutu. Time to try it all out. I built up the outfit - skirt first; 'cause I'm a Fairy, the waistcoat to set the tone, the boots...and I'm ready to strut my stuff... The hat being the icing on the cake. I looked in the mirror...that is exactly who I wanted to be!

I left with pride...Outfit bagged and wand in hand.

First night, and I am nervously awaiting curtain call in the dressing room.

The lights are on, the stage is set, curtain up, I'm on!!

From backstage to front stage I step across that threshold, with nerves on edge.

First line delivered; and audience reaction helps me believe that they believe I am who I believe I am. I am the feisty Fairy in our made-up land.

Pam Jackson-Vickers

**

A scarf with a hidden note...
Mystery Music

My friend once shared a flat with a girl in London in the late 60s. She was given an old silk scarf by her godmother. Every time she wore it, she believed in some way she could hear music. She mentioned this to her mother with a smile on one occasion. Her mother knew that the scarf had originally belonged to an opera singer, who had given it to her godmother as a gift in recognition of their mutual friendship. What do you think? I like to think there are mysteries we can enjoy by entering into them as just that! I have recently seen on a greeting card in a shop a picture of a scared and bowed down looking man with a briefcase. He is peering apprehensively at a notice in his path on a wall. It reads;

'If you see anything mysterious or unusual, just enjoy it while you can!'

Heather Shone

**

Stop, Look, Listen...

Never late for a parade...
Infanterie du 21ème la France

John brought two beautiful coats to show me...one for action and one for relaxation. Hand made, natural fibres...wool and lined with cotton. French colours and designs of early 19th C, eg Battle of Waterloo. Leisure coat...cream. Action coat...black, white, red. Brass buttons, hooks and eyes. Hat...dark blue with red 21. Flaps for keeping head warm.

English equivalent uniforms of the time would include a stock at the neck. The French wore a scarf. John explained the difference to illustrate that a tight, high stock made the soldier walk more upright and stiffly, but the French scarf enabled a more relaxed walk which was considered to be beneficial. In pursuit of 'upright and stiff', British officers wore corsets under their uniforms.

'When I put on these clothes, I feel a different person from my everyday self... and yet that is who I am also, deep down inside me wanting to get out. Dressing is a process. I sometimes even need help doing up the top hook and eye. It is such a serious business getting dressed in time and not being late for drill practice that it even frequently manifests in my dreams...that is how deep is the significance of dressing correctly and on time.' Terrified he would be late for parade! Once dressed he 'becomes a French soldier'. He takes instructions in the French language. He feels 'patriotic' in the uniform. They almost 'worshipped' Napoleon and his ideals.

'As a French soldier it is initially difficult to feel that I am fighting the English, but I soon get into character. When I am in France with 'the regiment', the French locals love to engage with me, especially as I speak to them in French. They appreciate that I have taken the trouble to dress up as if I were on their side. I am often offered free wine as a sign of their appreciation!'

Here is a gentle, gracious, Yorkshire man, quietly spoken and with a twinkle of eye! I asked him how he felt with the uniform on in battle...'really bloodthirsty' was the response! Whilst conventionally appearing as a Northallerton gentleman, he said that with the uniform on, he loved to be out in a re-enactment town 'showing it off'. (Apparent change of character-type) 'C'est vrai que je deviens mes vêtements.'

I didn't see his musket. Locked in a gun cupboard. At night the soldiers camp in an authentic manner, sleeping on straw or sitting round a camp fire making cartridges for the next day. Sometimes he is asked about the morality of re-enacting war. He responds tactfully without trying to excuse himself.

A major feature of his love for these special and valuable clothes is in the caring of them and treasuring of them. Cleaning, maintaining, eg darns, polishing of buttons. These clothes are not dispensable or allowed to 'wear out' or be thrown away. As I listened, it felt as if this tender caring for them is an act of love. The fact that they had to keep as clean as possible affects the way the 'soldiers' move around and sit, especially in camp when they may get muddy. For the same reason John usually takes his coat off when eating and drinking wine!

With his uniform on and with his fellow infantry, he forgets about the modern

Drama

world with its events and habits and thoughts for those few days. He recognises that as part of his personality he likes to escape to a fantasy world, exercising his imagination.

Editor from a conversation with John Henderson

**

Leaving the modern world behind...
The Drummer Boy

Little did I realise at the time but there have been some significant outfits in my life in which I have subsequently found new meaning. My little party frocks bought for me by my mum (a lot of my clothes came then from jumble sales, so having a new one was very exciting), my oversized, gabardine mac bought for when I went to 'big school' ('Don't worry, you'll soon grow into it!'); my black suede waistcoat with the long tassels, together with the pink grandad shirt bought on an exciting trip with my pal to Carnaby Street.

At the age of fourteen, I enjoyed the only childhood holiday ever with my parents; we toured Kent in dad's Robin Reliant and had a day trip to London where I bought beads and a bell to hang around my neck. Onto a pair of flared trousers in a gorgeous shade of purple I sewed some bright pink ribbon around the leg bottoms. I listened to music by the band, Cream, and loved the psychedelic colours that were around in the 1960s. I was desperate to be a hippie, go to music festivals and maybe join a commune but I hadn't the courage to rebel and break away from the apron strings which bound me to my parents, especially my mother!

But here comes 'Bob' into this. At the grand old age of 50, my husband, Barry, introduced me to the Sealed Knot Society which is an English Civil War re-enactment group. He had been a member some years before he knew me and was keen to re-join, so, anything for a bit of fun, I agreed to go along with him. The local group in our area is Sir Thomas Glemham's Regiment of Foote, part of the Marquess of Newcastle's Northern Royalist army. I was immediately encouraged to join as a drummer. As I didn't have any kit, I was able to borrow from the store and was put in charge of the huge regimental drum. As a 17th century drummer, I was more 'up-market' than the common soldier and carried out an important role. My job was to convey the orders from the officer in charge of the battle to the troops. As can be imagined, there would be so much noise and shouting on the battlefield that the officer's voice would not be heard and so the message had to be passed along the field in an alternative way. Different drum beats meant different things from launching an attack to the order to retreat. There were also many marching beats which were great fun to play and, hopefully, they instilled fear into the opposing army, the dreaded Parliamentarians, as we arrived at the battleground. An added role was to act as a 'go-between' when officers of the opposing sides were required to communicate with each other.

Getting changed into my drummer's kit was interesting as we originally only had a 'two-man' tent on the camp-site, so there wasn't a lot of room. However, it didn't take

Stop, Look, Listen...

too long to lose all modesty and just get into my kit outside the tent; after all, we were all friends. The first item of uniform was my shirt – long enough to wear as a nightshirt, should it deem necessary, cuffs tied with ribbons of cotton, as was the collar. Next, the socks, yellow cotton, ill-fitting, designed to be pulled over the knees. A pair of woollen socks worn over the cotton meant that they (the woollen socks) could be turned down to cover the inauthentic 20th century desert boots, as to get the real handmade leather boots was way beyond my budget. Now, the woollen, black, baggy knee breeches, fastened with buttons, no zips in those days. The legs stopped just below the knee and were fastened with 'drawstrings', in my case, red ribbons.

The jacket came next. As a drummer, it could be as flamboyant as the individual desired. However, mine was made for me by another SK member and was quite basic. Sadly, I never did make it as elaborate as I would have liked. I did once borrow a jacket which was beautiful with embroidered leaves adorning the sleeves and further stitching down either side of the buttons.

My hat, oh how I loved that hat, black, wide-brimmed, a relic from my teenage, frustrated hippie days. They say that if you hang on to your clothes long enough, they come back into fashion. That 1960s floppy hat was not out of place in the 17th century. I tarted it up a bit with a couple of ostrich feathers and pinned one side of the brim up with a pewter brooch in the shape of a lizard.

Finally, the bag. A simple, satchel style bag, made from rough sack-cloth, somewhere to keep the essentials, handkerchief and mobile phone. (Er! Not quite 17th century but carried just in case of emergencies, which did happen occasionally.) Also attached was the 'bottle' carrier made from the same rough sack-cloth. Water was always needed on the battlefield and this disguised the plastic bottle.

Once dressed, I left behind the 20th century (apart from the mobile phone) and became a 17th century drummer, set to go into battle. As I marched to the field with the other drummers, beating a steady rhythm to keep the men on an even step, the adrenalin would begin to flow. Once there, we would wait with bated breath whilst the officers took stock. A shout would be heard, 'Have a care', which was the signal that cannon would be firing and the battle was underway. At most re-enactments, the cavalry would be involved. That was when it would get really interesting. Whilst drumming, not only was I listening for the orders to convey to the troops, but I was always looking around to make sure I knew where the opposition cavalry was situated. It was quite daunting to find half a dozen or more horses charging towards us and, as I was unarmed and had to be protected, I was ordered in no uncertain terms to get into the pike-block. It was no place for wimps!! Many of the horses were trained to deal with riotous crowds and had learned to cope with cannon fire, marauding men, shouting etc. I remember one instance when a horse actually was moving us as a group with its flanks – it obviously saw us as a 'riotous crowd'.

Unfortunately, my life as a drummer was relatively short-lived. After only about three years, I suffered my 'war wound'. It was at a re-enactment of the Battle of Naseby (14 June 1645) which was a decisive battle of the first English Civil War. The Royalist army was under the command of Sir Thomas Fairfax and we were ordered to run for our lives as we were being outnumbered and pursued by the Parliamentarians under the command of Oliver Cromwell. I made it safely off the battlefield but not before pulling a tendon in my

Drama

knee. It didn't hurt too much at first but the following day I was in agony. It resulted in my having to take a few days' sick leave from work and undergo a course of physiotherapy. I made the sad decision to retire from my role as a drummer.

Finally, why 'Bob'? Well, it wouldn't have been appropriate to have women on the battlefield, at least not while the battle was raging. The victors would go afterwards to pillage whatever they could find from the bodies strewn all over the place. Therefore I had to take on a male persona. When wondering what to call myself, I immediately remembered the Blackadder II episode when Kate goes into Blackadder's service dressed as a boy. When asked her name, she replies, 'Bob.' So, that became my name. 'Bob' by day and 'Sue' by night (I had a lady's outfit for night-time, but that's another story!).

Sue Thorn

**

On playing the same character at 70 as she had played at 14...
A Very Large Nose

Every girl likes to dress up, doesn't she? Well, this girl carried her childhood fun into adult fun! During my time in Bournemouth I took part in various productions, but particularly remember the first in 1962 playing a housemaid in 'The Paper Chain'.

Whilst in Southampton, my drama life involved roles in various productions, including dressing as a 'flapper' in 'Maiden Ladies'. That was particularly jolly, and the Roaring Twenties would certainly have been a time when dressing up was a permanent delight! Whilst with the Bitterne Park Players I took part in a play set in Egypt and I was a secretary with very large dimensions and a very large nose. The clothes I wore weren't particularly glamorous, but it was entertaining all the same, even though I felt as if I was walking around in a bell tent!

Moving on to Sunderland in 1987, I joined a group who used to perform two three act plays and one pantomime per year. My love of dressing up really came to the fore in a variety of ways, including as a drunken down-and-out who found sanctuary in a church hall. A very taxing part with pretty ghastly costumes. At the other end of the spectrum, I had great fun dressing up as the Crystal Fairy in one pantomime and as one of the Spice Girls in another.

The pantos I refer to were performed in a local church hall, with ample space provided back-stage for costumes and props. The drama group had been formed many years before I joined and therefore a lot of costumes had been accumulated. The faces of the young girls when they were presented with their costumes for a show was a picture of sheer delight. They could dress up for four nights and one afternoon of the show and let themselves go!

The final time I was on stage was in Verwood, Dorset, when I played a maid who aged from 20 to 70 over the course of a ten-minute sketch. Looking back, I find it uncanny that the first time I was on stage aged fourteen I played a maid and the last time, aged 70, I was playing the same character, wearing very similar costumes.

Stop, Look, Listen...

Since leaving there (the ageing maid), I haven't had the pleasure of donning a costume, but I have equally enjoyed the challenge of dressing others up. For a Panto at Zion (URC church) recently, how fascinating it was raking through my old curtains in the roof looking for suitable Kings' costumes etc. And so this strange phenomenon of transforming a personality via the 'threads' of different clothes and crossing the 'threshold' to the stage has followed me all my life...what fun it has all been, whilst hopefully bringing enjoyment to other people!

Gillian Tucker

**

Hooked or...
'Nailed'

Cross-dressing and gender reassignment may seem quite modern preoccupations, but I knew about such things back in the early Fifties, when my early acting career flowered at a single-sex boys' secondary school. Here it was the fate of juniors with treble voices and 'pretty' faces to take on the female roles in the school plays. I drew this short straw for three years before a baritone voice released me, and even then I only progressed to playing Puck in *Midsummer Night's Dream* — a fairy, for goodness sake!

After parts in *'Love and Friendship' (sic)* by Jane Austen, and *The Merchant of Venice*, I was cast as Beatrice in *Much Ado About Nothing*, opposite the headmaster's son as Benedick. There was the usual palaver of dressing up in an Elizabethan lady's gear, being made up with powder, rouge and lipstick, discreetly padded, and taught how to sit down elegantly and to curtsey without falling over. These moves I usually managed quite successfully — including negotiating a passionate kiss with Benedick — until one alarming evening in mid-performance...

The Maddermarket Theatre in Norwich, where the school plays were performed, was constructed in the early twentieth century in the likeness of Shakespeare's Globe; its history is interesting to explore, and it remains intact to this day. The roof is supported, as at the Globe, by two substantial wooden pillars, and you need to imagine a seat built, on this occasion, around the base of each one.

So there I am (she is), alone on the left-hand seat, delivering the soliloquy at the end of Act III, Scene 1, ready to sweep determinedly off stage – Beatrice was very determined. The speech ends, Beatrice stands, turns on her heels and departs – or rather tries to... Unfortunately, the seat had a nail sticking out; I was caught on it and couldn't budge. So I sat down again.

What to do? Stay there and invent some timeless blank verse? Strip off to my (masculine) underpants? No choice, really, as Beatrice was required to exit at this point. So up I stood once more, turned on my heels, and tugged... The next three events, in

Drama

order, were (1) a nasty ripping sound, (2) a revealing split in my skirt, and (3), as I left the stage, a loud four-letter expletive not often heard in the school plays. I understand the audience loved it, but for me it remains a seriously red-faced moment.
Moral: If in drag, don't drag!

Geoff Oxley

**

Twilight, firelight, starlight and angel light...
No Tea Towels

As I am a parent and a primary school teacher, nativity plays have always meant learning repetitive songs with children, desperately trying to find a suitable outfit for my child to be an angel (complete with wings which don't droop), and comforting the child (or her parent!) who desperately wanted to be Mary and ended up being a sheep. In the past, nativity plays have never really moved me or made me think more deeply about the Christmas story, but this year was different.

Imaginative ways were being sought to use the church's Secret Garden' more. A group of people came up with the idea of a 'walking nativity'. Loosely (very loosely) inspired by the classic episode of The Vicar of Dibley when their nativity took place on Owen's farm, our nativity was to be acted out in various places around our church – starting in the hall, moving to our small back garden, into the secret garden, out to the front to our small fenced garden and finally into the church building itself. The strolling congregation was witness to young Mary being visited by a disembodied angelic voice and then breaking the news to Joseph. We visited the wise men's palace, only to hear that the little family had left to follow a star. We shared the angel visitation to the shocked shepherds and heard King Herod discussing events with the Wise Men. Finally, everyone gathered together at the birth in Bethlehem.

I will confess that, originally, I had my doubts. I have witnessed too many cringe-worthy attempts at drama in various settings and dreaded the thought of adults with tea-towels and neck ties for headdresses. I truly dislike the mindset that because it is church and open to all, we have to lower our standards to be inclusive. How could this project be any different? We are a small congregation with few younger members. How could such an ambitious project be carried out well? What a doubting Thomas I was. In God's hands, anything can happen, as I would discover!

Along with some very experienced direction and a genuine desire to make the Christmas story relevant and accessible, an extremely thoughtful script was put together. It was no rushed undertaking. The worship group diligently planned for over eleven months, and a number of people created original costumes (many of the headdresses came from Bethlehem itself and there wasn't a tea towel in sight). Another expert member put together a lighting system which was perfect for the winter dusk in which the performances

Stop, Look, Listen...

took place.
 So, after only a few rehearsals, we were ready for our audience. At the last moment, due to illness, I was promoted to 'walking narrator', accompanying people around the various tableaux, and was honoured to borrow a long black cassock. I cannot tell you the difference that made. Suddenly I felt the responsibility of passing on the good news of Christmas in a way I never had before. The twilight, the fires, the fairy lights, and the emotion expressed by the actors all combined to make this an almost magical afternoon. The words I was reading, making connections between this long-ago experience and our current world had never had such an effect on me. When we all finally gathered in the church, at 'Bethlehem', singing 'Silent Night', it took a great deal of control not to shed a tear.

Alexa Barber

**

Making a statement...
Clothes 'what i wore'!

Being a war baby I don't remember a great deal except that my sister and I seemed to be dressed more like twins – kilts and mohair jumpers. Sadly, I was a *big girl* and, as a result of rationing, I was made to wear my maiden aunt's cast-off, wrap-round brown tweed coat with a brown hat, which all made me look very old for my age of about eleven – admittedly I was 5'4"
 The next item of interest was my school green gymslip which we still had to wear, even in the sixth form. Playing hockey in green bloomers wasn't much fun either. Later on, being large and fulsome, I always had trouble finding clothes suitable for a twenty year old until the arrival of the Evans Outsize shop on the high street. Clothes were designed for 'large ladies' and yet were still stylish, even if the shop name was embarrassing!
 After my first husband died far too young, I returned to my home town where I had been known as a young musician, and decided to go to a local orchestral/choral concert. Quite why I wore a bright orange tunic and trousers set I don't know, but the effect among an older audience in greys, blues and blacks, was to put it mildly, startling. I loved that set but it was very orange!
 When I started singing solos as a semi-professional, I really was given no advice about what to wear and for one performance of the Messiah (contralto solos) I wore a high neck, long sleeved white blouse with red and blue spots under a red velvet full length pinafore dress. I thought it was great but looking back it must have looked dreadful.
 Trying to find coats to go over evening dresses was difficult, but I had seen a soloist on television walking to a venue in a beautiful full length cape which I wouldn't be able to afford, so I made one. It had a big hood and slits for the arms to poke out, but I made it in a black, woollen fabric with a purple lining. I wore it a number of times and felt very glamorous in it. I no longer sing professionally, so my beautiful cape has become a witch's cape for my grand-children's Halloween party.
 I seem to have a penchant for capes. As a young mum I used to like it when I could wear my Welsh woven black, white and orange cape which was a short one with a

Drama

high neck. It had a three button fastening across one corner and a belt that went round the body but popped out through slits and was buckled in the front so that the back swung as you walked. That has gone, but I now have a beautiful Scottish black cape with red lining and an attached matching scarf.

Over the years I have had a number of very bright jackets – emerald green, cobalt blue, multi coloured rather like Jacob's coat and my favourite red. My daughters always say that when they couldn't spot me in shops they could always see the red blazer.

I haven't mentioned shoes. I always loved to have a red pair and was distraught one day when I tripped and scraped the toes of my beautiful red kitten heeled shoes. At the moment I have a tapestry pair of blue shoes and also a black pair with white line in a check pattern, as well as the usual 'sensible' shoes!

Hazel Sumsion

**

Adding an artistic touch...
Shoes on the Wall

Some years ago, I was working at the Theatre Royal in London on the oldest paint frame in the country, painting backcloths for a variety of pantomimes. This was a very interesting place, one of history and tradition. People trained at RADA to enjoy this type of work; and yet here was I, very appreciative to be accepted through word of mouth, and hoping that my work ethic and painting skills were up to decorating these magnificent pieces of art. I was fascinated by the wall. On it was a collection of shoes, a dedication to the hard work and sheer amount of paint that was used to decorate these huge cloths, because many shoes had got covered in paint during this task. The floor was also highly colourful, after splattering, spraying and glittering. In fact, after each job the head painter on one side of the paint frame would paint his current shoes, all the furniture and the floor black…the start of a new page after the canvas was finished and before he moved to the next job. When shoes became very crispy and uncomfortable to wear, hanging them on the wall had become a tradition. They weren't identifiable; it wasn't about them, more the work that was put into each cloth and the volume of paint used.

I had come to work in London after a relationship split; my fiancé at the time had a cancerous tumour in his back. This changed his life tremendously and we separated. This was a painful time for me, having looked after him shortly after my father also died of cancer, in addition to his alcoholism. But I could then concentrate on my love of art, so I did.

I lived and breathed being a freelance artist, and my clothes represented my role. They were often splattered with paint, but that was ok with me. When I wasn't working, I enjoyed an artistic flair in my appearance, placing disparate items together but then adding a scarf or a brooch to connect the pieces. I had some long boots with big buckles, a long khaki green coat from Fat-Face and a hat/cap. I looked like I was going shooting, but I

Stop, Look, Listen...

think I was just missing home, North Yorkshire. As a reminder of home, I had sometimes collected acorns from Guisborough woods in my large coat pockets (you could fit all sorts in them, they were deep enough to hold my brushes as well) to place in my London house.

Meanwhile, I opened my home to care for another loved one. Then the next summer, a new relationship broke down. This left my world broken, financially and spiritually. I moved back home and spent time recovering from that, whilst waitressing in traditional uniform of white shirt, black skirt, black shoes and black waistcoat. I didn't care so much about my personal clothes at that time, though I still had my big boots and long coat, jeans and plain tops. But I then qualified in a totally different profession of Occupational Therapist, where I also wore appropriate uniform, and was accountable for my professional standards, quite daunting really and in huge contrast to my previous life!

I got married around this time, with a son born the following year. When he was three, I made a quilt out of his old shirts; he even got involved and helped me choose the pattern, with guidance and support from my grandmother. I hadn't sewn since my previous life. My grandad's old army shirt was brought in one day and grandma mentioned throwing it out. 'E'ee, no don't do that, you can make a cushion out of it.' Nothing more was said. Until the scary task eventually fell to me! I procrastinated and stared for ages. But after a lot of thought, I began, then added a little pocket showing grandad's details and role in the RAF, signed 'made by me'. The process of doing that was utterly moving. And equally so when it was finally returned to my stewardship. It came back to me in a carrier bag from my mum. Grandma told me, 'It's for you, my dear!' I cried.

For three years I worked for a mental health charity, without too much red tape. I could wear my own clothes again. But then came redundancy, before a fresh start with a drug and alcohol charity as an OT and group worker, teaching resilience, anxiety management and how to build a new life after substance misuse. I am also using my artistic flair to create an environment that promotes relaxation and its importance for health and wellbeing, along with being true to myself.

And I can still wear what I like!

Kerry Bass

The Drama of Night

Dark clouds, drawn like curtains at the end of the day,
They signal finale at the close of a play.
Sceneshifters are waiting, they lurk in the wings,
Dramatically changing the pattern of things.

From fiery red sunset to clouds dull and grey,
These dark clouds have gathered, daylight scurries away.
It seems just as quickly the stars appear bright,
Transforming the heavens to a clear magic night.

The pale moon translucent through wispy like haze
Seems to draw like a magnet – as upwards we gaze.
Enchantingly still, casting light far and wide,
Breath-taking and awesome – put day's cares aside.

The darkness returns before morning's light breaks.
It's just a few hours till the whole world awakes.
Whilst most were still sleeping, these changes occurred.
The drama of night went unnoticed – unheard.

Jan Portlock-Barker

Through the Vestry Door
(editor)

A Reflection

As the Bishop said to the...

The churchwarden looked at me quizzically. I had quietly slipped in through the vestry door, about to preach that morning in her little rural church. I had been there before, taking the service for this small, welcoming congregation. I always arrived early in order to get myself robed and sorted out before the visiting priest would come in. He would be presiding at the altar for Holy Communion. The warden took a deep breath and was about to speak to me when the door opened again and a very tall, ascetic-looking gentleman stepped in. He carried a small suitcase. He did look a bit familiar. We were introduced... Oh my goodness...it was the recently retired Archbishop of Canterbury. 'This is Ann who will be preaching.' Flashing through my panicky mind were these words of wisdom I was offered once when I was unexpectedly promoted at work, 'Some are born great, some achieve greatness, and some have greatness thrust upon them'. Recovering swiftly from this potentially terrifying challenge ahead, I met his smile as he placed his suitcase on the table and lifted the lid. Graciously he asked me, 'What would you like me to wear?' Whereupon another ancient quote came to me, 'As the bishop said to the actress...' He went on to explain that he had brought with him two alternatives of outfit and the choice was mine.

Well, I can't remember the subtleties of it all now, but it illustrates that the Church of England takes dressing up for the drama about to unfold very seriously indeed, as much in little country chapels as in the great cathedrals. And the worship liturgy is a drama involving costume, props, some of the finest music, movement, 'a dance', specific language, the nuance of the illuminating and the extinguishing, and lines to be learnt; sometimes there is even smoke! It needs to happen as a seamless garment so that it ebbs and flows and at some points will involve audience/congregation participation. Each movement and garment worn will reflect the spiritual invitation to experience the awe and wonder of the occasion. The bishop will have a tall hat (making him reach a little nearer to God than the rest of us). He will carry a crozier, a sort of shepherd's crook denoting his pastoral care of us, his flock. Choir members wear a distinctive cassock and white surplice. A verger will wear a long black cassock and carry a long stick called a virge. (The provenance of this is that they were to head a procession of clergy and use it to sweep away the riff raff before them.)

The furniture of a church is part of the drama and movement around the 'stage'. Bible readings will happen at a lectern, preaching from a pulpit, presiding at the Eucharist from behind the distant altar, baptism at a font, rails at which to kneel to receive a sacrament, the choir on display beyond a rood screen in the chancel. Everyone knows their place. There are no tickets, such as on entry to a theatre, but a small bag or plate collects what people choose to give in thanksgiving for what they have received from God. It is called a free will offering. Curtains do not close on the proceedings usually these days, neither do people generally applaud, other than occasionally after a particularly fine recessional organ piece has been performed. Unlike in a concert performance, people rarely sit quietly and listen to that rendering of exquisitely executed, inspiring music, but more likely get up and wander about and chat to their friends or move to the coffee room. Then finally they go to the main door where the priest, or even an archbishop, will offer a valedictory hand.

But a church doorway is not just for use on Sundays. On weekdays one of the first jobs in my church on the boundary was to unlock it so that everyone had access to the quiet, sacred and safe space beyond, soaked in the prayer of centuries. Available as the setting for their own personal, spiritual dramas!

Homilies

Through a Locked Door

John20:19-31.
A challenge to move beyond doubt into faith and peace.

I am in a retreat house specifically to write in the peace and quiet whilst everyone else is on a fully silent retreat. The doorbell rings loudly, bing bong. So I go to the door, as the others are doing Holy things at that moment. There, standing hopefully is a bulky, jolly white van delivery man who is waiting on the threshold with a large, floaty, Happy Birthday helium balloon, a profuse wicker basket of flowers and an enormous box of designer chocolates. Reading the card of greeting, I whisper, 'Please bring them in and I will give them to her later.' He replies, also in a whisper, 'Well, I need her signature.' To my whispering, 'I am sorry, but I cannot disturb her at this moment,' he responds, also whispering, 'Well, will you sign then?' 'Yes,' I whisper in return. Then he booms out with a chuckle in surprised realisation, 'Why are we bloody whispering to each other?' I say quietly, 'Because this is a retreat house and today it is in complete silence.' He looks horrified and turns to bolt out of the door…but oh help, he is unable to turn the handle because it has a special safety lock. He can't get out! Is he locked into this mad place? He turns to me, shocked and hopeful… and mercifully for him, in compassion I kindly enable his speedy escape.

Wells, springs, washbasins, mirrors, windows, and hearths…The threshold was the most significant place in the home, as it represented the crossing place from one life to another, from public to private and from community to family. It required special protection.
Claire Hunter

Stop, Look, Listen...

A doorway then, a sacred space. But in the passage from John the threshold was crossed without using the door!

On the evening of that first day of the week, when the disciples were together, with the doors locked for fear of the Jews, Jesus came and stood among them, and said, 'Peace be with you.' With that he breathed on them and said, 'Receive the Holy Spirit.'

Except Thomas. They had all been there, astonishingly meeting with the risen Jesus except Thomas. When he heard that Jesus had been with them all, he just could not believe it! No, absolutely not, unless I can see and touch him for myself...

A week later his disciples were in the house again, and Thomas was with them. Though the doors were locked. Jesus came and stood among them and said, 'Peace be with you.' Then he said to Thomas, 'Put your finger here; see my hands. Reach out your hand and put it into my side. Stop doubting and believe.'

Jesus came back for Thomas. The most dramatic moment in Thomas' life.

Forever, he is now known as doubting Thomas. He was very fearful about what would happen to himself and the disciples next. Had everything he has lived for and hoped for died along with Jesus? If ever we find ourselves behaving in an inappropriate way towards others, being oversensitive, unforgiving, untrusting, the underlying emotion is frequently fear. There are not many of us who live entirely without it. Fear of other people maybe; fear of being inadequate, of unemployment, of ageing, of ill-health, of financial debt; the consequences of mistakes or judgements which we now maybe regret. So let us enter that upper room with Thomas today, to see what hope this encounter might offer for us, in our fears.

Jesus came back for Thomas, for the one who was not so sure.

Like him, we were not present on the extraordinary occasion when Jesus appeared to the rest of the disciples after the Resurrection. And so, what does Jesus say to all these men, locked up in their fear? And thus likewise, to us? He does not say, 'I promise to take away all that troubles you in your life. All that of which you are afraid.' No. He says, 'Peace be with you. Peace be with you within your fears.' And we are not commissioned to go unequipped, ill prepared to leave our comfort zones.

With this peace comes a commission to 'go'. To go in his name to share that peace. 'As the father has sent me, so I am sending *you*.' He did not say, 'You have served me well. You can see I am all right, so now you can go off and live a quiet life. You can return to where you were before you met me.'

Those men took up the challenge, often to their death. For them, there was no going back. Jesus' scars speak not of a sanitised and bloodless faith. His wounds bear witness to a statement of profound self giving. And of course, scars themselves carry the evidence of the whole uncertainty of life.

As it was for Thomas, how about for us?

When people meet us at work, at home, at the shops, at school; our neighbours and friends in the village, will they sense that we have been touched, breathed on by

Jesus? Will there be something about our demeanour, our kindness, or even our faces, which gives us away? And which others long to share? Or will we be like the many people who do brush against something special in church week by week, but remain the same once they exit through the door?

The freedom of true peace draws others into it. It attracts wherever it appears, where others feel safe and want to dwell. Is that an invitation for you to cross the threshold, and long to offer what is life-giving on the other side of the door?

**

Rebirth in the Garden

John 20:10-18
'...and she, supposing him to be the gardener...'

An award from my local drama group. Sounds impressive, but actually it was a humbling award in the extreme. I had become ill and unable to take my part in the village pantomime, after having been learning lines and practising for months. I had won the award as The Most Promising Absentee!

I wasn't there when it mattered.

Mary was there. Outside the tomb entrance, crying. As she bent over to look into the tomb, she saw two angels...where had the angels come from? They hadn't been there moments before when Peter and John had been inside the tomb.

Angels in all world religions are messengers from God. On Easter Day we hear that they bring the message that Jesus transforms his relationship with Mary and all humanity into a new love, a new life, a new message of hope for the world. So what is the message of the angels for us today? When they appear in the Bible, they are offering hospitality, protection, frequently new birth, always leading and guiding. Here they are inviting Mary over a new threshold. Preparing her for her subsequent encounter with the risen Jesus in the garden.

How would we respond to an invitation to cross a new threshold in our faith?

You will know the words from the Bible, 'entertaining angels unawares'. They remind us that at any given instant, all people we meet may be for that moment angels in our lives, calling us to cross a new threshold. These words are both a prompting to treat and honour all our human encounters with love and respect and also a reminder to keep our eyes and ears open for whoever those angels might be.

Children have an instinctive knowing of angels. They can draw them at a very early age. They can be an inspiration to us as adults to learn to recognise the angels and be thankful. Until we are prepared to be transformed as Mary was that morning. The ultimate drama for her, Mary was the first person to see Jesus alive again. It rings true,

Stop, Look, Listen...

as no writer of those days would have made a woman the centre of this earth-shattering account otherwise. She had this encounter because she was moved to be there. Not just a devoted and promising absentee. She was there, becoming the apostle to the apostles.

An angel, then. How do we recognise them when they appear? They come in a variety of disguises. Desmond Tutu reminds us that God says to you, to me, 'There is nothing you can do to make me love you less. I take you. I take you very seriously. I take you – body and soul. You, the visible and the...invisible of you. I love you.'

**

Kings Crossing the Threshold

Matthew 2: 1-12
Then they opened their treasures and presented him with gifts of gold and of incense and of myrrh.

This is the image on one of my Christmas cards. We see the three Wise Men in their house with their pinnies on. They have just finished cooking the Christmas dinner. The table is all beautifully and festively laid. Candles lit, glasses sparkling. All is ready. Through the arched window you can see a little family coming down the path towards the lit and welcoming house. Mary and Joseph pushing a toddler-sized Jesus in his buggy. One wise man says to another,
'*Last year we went to their place. This year they are coming to ours.*'
Well, yes. It is only a fun card. But let's look again at its message.
Hospitality. Something most of us experience often, either giving or receiving. We have come to regard these wise men as representing the grand and comfortable in the Christmas story. But behind the façade lurked political dynamite. Herod pretended to make these Kings welcome, but his hospitality was false. Jesus, Matthew is saying, is the true king. Old Herod is the false one; the impostor; a usurper. Wise men? Though deceitful Herod too can at least be applauded for his wisdom too. Keeping his cruel intention up his royal sleeve, he asked to be informed of the child's exact whereabouts, because he was bright enough to foresee the risk to himself. We are still exposed to that risk, our mask uncovered.
Yes, a warning: we may discover that the baby will grow to question our assumptions, challenge our prejudices, reorder our priorities, temper our ambitions, alter our expectations, thwart our selfishness and ultimately claim our life. The welcome and hospitality in the stable was genuine but costly.
T.S Eliot interprets that for us in some poetic words of the magi ...
'*Were we led all that way for birth or death? There was a birth, certainly. We had evidence and no doubt. I had seen birth and death but had thought they were different; this birth was hard and bitter agony for us, like death, our death.*'
These men seemed to return home with as many questions as they brought with them. Their journey, it seems, is not done. Neither is ours. Are we, wise men and wise women, prepared to move away from familiar ground? Think about what it meant for Jesus

Drama

to be the true King. And then come to him, by whichever route you can, and with the best gifts that you can find. And they may well be costly.

In fact it would be to no avail if Jesus Christ was born in a stable in Bethlehem all those years ago, yet not born again and given hospitality in our hearts today. He will knock in a variety of disguises.

Will we recognise him when he comes?

A Final Musing

Liability or an Asset?

It is Rush Hour in Central London. 'Grab my arm, Mum. You see that train over there? We have three minutes to get along the platform, up those stairs, over the bridge and down the other side. That is the first of our trains if we are to make it on time.'

Am I now still an asset, or more of a liability to my family?

We are off to the theatre. 'Restricted view, Mum, but your eyes are better than mine.' I begin to sense that this theatre outing is not going to be much akin to my usual sedate Yorkshire expeditions, which are relaxed, dignified and predictable in the main. I should have realised the possibly intrepid nature of this outing when my son first suggested we go on his scooter, an offer firmly turned down by myself, much to the disappointment of my grandsons whom I had gone to look after for Half Term. 'You can borrow my helmet, Grandma...'

The second train was the underground, heaving with the homebound crowds. Jeremy pushed me on; the doors closed, trapping us both as he shoved me into the arms of a large, florid gentleman. I apologised profusely saying, 'I am sorry. I am from Yorkshire.' Whereupon young men and women alike stood up for me to offer their seat, not I hasten to add because I was from Yorkshire but because I had GREY HAIR! (Anyway, I certainly don't need to apologise for being from Yorkshire!)

At this point I want to pay tribute to the fact that in recent years I have never yet walked across the London travel stations and undergrounds, up and down stairs and escalators, whilst having had to carry my own suitcase. Every single time, youngsters of either gender lift up my luggage with a smile and off they go! It is the grey hair, I think!

I digress.

Ten minutes to go. We walk at a great pace ('I'm not 100% sure exactly where it is.'), dodging traffic, cabs, scooters, skipping lights. On we go across Westminster Bridge spanning the heaving black, black waters of the Thames, with the Houses of Parliament on the right, and on the left, the huge brightly lit, red London Eye. (Made me realise I had been in exactly this same place the day before to visit St. Thomas' emergency Eye Clinic with my own huge red eye, but on that occasion, escorted in a civilised cab by a glorious Nigerian by the name of Julius, 'as of Caesar'.) Am I

Stop, Look, Listen...

now a liability rather than an asset?

Jeremy says, 'Hang onto my arm, Mum, more steps.' But we are here, albeit breathless. Where? At the most magnificent Old Law Courts of the City of London, where will see Witness for the Prosecution by Agatha Christie as if it were a real trial. We were in the public gallery and yes, it was a restricted view behind a colossal pillar, but we could just see the resplendent judge by peering around it.

A memorable and unique occasion, but once back at my own home, the whole week's experience had left me asking Jeremy the question, 'Please tell me, am I now more of a liability than an asset for these looking-after-the-boys situations?' He burst out laughing and said that he remembered my mother asking me exactly that same question, thirty years ago! Oh well, that reminds me of the T.S. Eliot circle about going back to the beginning and knowing it for the first time!

After all, I don't think assets and liabilities come into it really. It is all part of the journey of loving family life in its widest sense, and we celebrate it with thanksgiving!

Hither and Thither…

TRAVEL

Tell me, what is it you plan to do with your one wild and precious life? – *Mary Oliver*

Let the world change you, and you can change the world. – *Che Guevara*

I like Cinderella, she has a good work ethic…and she likes shoes. – *Amy Adams*

Wherever the wind takes me, I travel as a visitor. – *Horace*

If we are smart, we will choose the way of Pooh. As if from far away it calls us with the voice of a child's mind. It may be hard to hear at times… but without it we will never find our way through the forest. – *Benjamin Hoff*

Believe in a love that is being stored up for you like an inheritance…a blessing so large that you can travel as far as you wish without having to step outside it. – *Rainer Maria Rilke*

A happy life is not built up of tours abroad and pleasant holidays, but of little clumps of violets noticed by the roadside… – *Edward Wilson*

A tree that can fill the span of a man's arms grows from a downy tip; a journey of a thousand miles starts from beneath one's feet. – *Lao-Tzu*

Through the Wardrobe Door
(Contributors)

Another climate, another life style, other clothes...
Browsing the Bend Down Boutique

A couple of decades ago, I went to Ghana for two years as a volunteer with the VSO (Voluntary Service Overseas) – to live and work as a 'local', earning a small wage and providing labour and training to foster sustainability after I left. As I had worked prior to this adventure as a hotel manager, I was employed as a Hotel and Catering Lecturer at a polytechnic in the small town of Ho, two hours from the capital. A challenging new threshold to cross in my life's journey.

This was a West Africa without mobile phones, supermarkets, Sky television; in fact, little Western influence at all, and TVs were only to be found in maybe one loosely titled bar in town. Bars were known as 'Drinking Spots' and could usually be found in a dark, walled off area behind someone's house. Restaurants were more organised; there were one or two in Ho which would elaborately advertise extensive menus, including offering a variety of rice, chips and stew dishes. However, when it came to the crunch of ordering from the lovely, polite and kitted out in full, black and white, waiter regalia garçon, the only thing available from said menu was boiled rice, which we usually had with an accompaniment of salt. Very nice it was too.

My English dresses just could not stand up to the constant rounds of hand washing and bleach drying under the scorching African sun. Moreover, local department stores or shops specialising in the art of selling clothes were as rare as chicken on a restaurant menu. Most people wore the local cloth made into their chosen garment, by their very own tailor, from whichever brightly coloured and elaborately patterned batik cloth would suit you and for which circumstance. For example, weddings were as big as funerals, and yards and yards of cloth were required for the entire outfit of 'up and downs', plus head dress and over the top sash.

I myself succumbed to securing the services of a tailor once my British bought clothes began to show signs of wear and tear. In addition, I was losing weight rapidly as I was no longer 'swanning' around Britain enjoying farewell dinners and copious pints of Yorkshire ale. Plus, now I had to sweep my house, bent double, with an 18 inch twig brush, wash everything I wore or slept in, and on, by hand, and walk to work, to the shops or to anywhere, in fact.

In the end I took my favourite British clothes to a very nice man who was a tailor working from his shop along the main street just off the only roundabout (known in Ghana logically as Circles) in Ho. My tailor's six foot by six foot shop with brick walls, a concrete floor and a tin roof meant that he was established and successful; others simply sat under a tree with their ancient Singers, just like the one my Grandma used. He was able to copy

Hither and Thither...

and recreate all my clothes into a whole new wardrobe of vibrant African clothes.

The dresses were made from cotton and therefore didn't cling, which was better for the soaring temperatures. The trousers, baggy, with an elasticated waist, I named 'my happy trousers', as they were brightly coloured and cheerfully patterned. I had managed to achieve a look somewhere between a child in a colourful romper suit and a clown with baggy trousers; only I didn't wear the big bulbous shoes to match!

As an alternative to African-made, British clothes, I had the option of visiting what is locally known as a 'Bend Down Boutique'. This is merely 'Western' clothes unceremoniously dumped on a large piece of plastic sheeting on the orange African earth at the roadside. Nobody knew where these had come from, the price was made up on the spot, and the standard of the clothes varied, as did the smell. I spent many an hour shamelessly grovelling around. How my life had changed.

But every Friday I put on my jeans; I didn't care if I was too hot or not, I wanted to feel like the 'normal me', as the rest of the time I was 'going native'. I'd heard that there were 'white folk' who went to a bar aptly named 'The White House'. I think they were as happy to meet a new face as I was to enjoy banter and laughter in my own language and many, many, perhaps too many, hours later my bike was stuffed into the back of their pickup truck and I was given my first of many Friday night lifts home.

One day I met up with VSO friends from other towns to complete what is known as 'the ridge walk', through thick rainforest up a hill, down a hill and along some very long African dirt roads. It rained of course, it had to, we were walking through the rain forest. Completely sodden, our clothes finally rubbing, we were invited to shelter in a genuine, African mud hut. The kind of adventure I used to dream of as a child. After some time, the rain stopped lashing down; we thanked the family and repaid their hospitality with a packet of biscuits and continued our walk in the now bright and lovely warm sunlight. My so-called friends, plus a man I had just met (and was destined to become my husband), were walking behind me in hysterics. My pants could apparently be seen clearly through the almost white, very thin material of my very favourite, sodden, 'Western' shorts. 'Star Knickers' became my new nickname, which was quite funny, especially when I confessed that my Dad had chosen them!

I took the same route to work every single day for two years, and children would run from their houses, chanting 'Ya Vu,' meaning 'white woman'. I was like the Pied Piper until thankfully parents or older siblings called them back. Talk about being a black sheep, it was roles reversed. My walk then left the estate and crossed a road through a maize field, with plants higher than myself, towards the polytechnic. I used to march and stomp through that field, as I had then, and still have, a massive snake (hereafter known as 'S' as I even hate to type the word) phobia.

One Saturday morning, I opened my front door to sweep the veranda and 'Oh my goodness', or words to that effect, what is that long, black, skinny thing draped across my outdoor furniture? 'Oh, my goodness', or words to that effect, 'Oh my goodness', or words to that effect, 'Oh my goodness', or words to that effect, get the idea? I was clearly experiencing the sudden onset of Tourette's Syndrome. It was only a sunbathing Black Mamba! You can imagine my shock; heart racing, red in the face, hyperventilating, am I going to faint? I ran, at near enough the speed of a hungry cheetah, to the small wooden shop just down my road. Ignoring the queue and shouting at the top of my voice, 'Help me please, somebody help me, there is an 'S' on my veranda!' Then I suddenly realised I had run out on a peaceful Saturday morning, in my very best and very comfortable but very faded tartan pyjamas. They must still remember the time the 'Ya Vu' made a scene...

You may recall that I had been instructed to take a pair of sensible sandals for work; but the remainder of my time I lived in what had become affectionately knowns as 'Challey Whatees'. Flip flops. 'Charlie' was maybe a term for anything familiar and 'whatee' meant 'let's go'. Others say a 'chale' is a friendly expletive used for sentences such as, 'ah chale, that's too much' during the ever- popular market bargaining affairs. An activity so loved by the Ghanaians they are almost disappointed if one agrees to pay the first price quoted.

During my last two months, I spent three days sitting and sleeping on sacks of cement on a barge travelling up the River Niger to Timbuktu, saw sacred and scary fish that eat live chickens sacrificed to them in Burkina Faso, and spent a week in a nunnery in Mali waiting for the train to Senegal which would never arrive.

But by then I did realise that I could not fly back to the UK without some proper shoes, even simple pumps from the local market. I spent time practising walking normally again in this stiff and clumsy footwear!

On arriving at Heathrow airport, clearly unable to drive owing to the aeroplane gin, I optimistically decided to book into the Hilton Hotel, deserving some luxury after two years roughing it in West Africa, but alas, I did not even get past the first hurdle: the front desk. The receptionist took one look at this person standing before her, wearing happy trousers, an off white, baggy, 'Bend Down Boutique' T-shirt, and crisp new pumps, with a metre long, carved wooden boat under her arm, and suddenly all the rooms were full!

Nicky Coope

**

One disaster leads to another...
Dave's Dreadful BIG Birthday

'Poor Dave' is an oft-quoted epithet for my husband because married to me. Originally the words of a lovely French family friend. Unreasonable? Not in this instance, as you may shortly agree. 'Poor Dave' indeed.

The Birth of a Great Plan
Rainy season in Dar es Salaam would pose problems for us in planning a trip for Dave's big birthday. I said we should go to Egypt, being a sun lover and dreamy archaeologist, but it was Dave's birthday, and he should get to choose. He chose a safari in Northern Tanzania. It could be very expensive, but his theory was that the out-of-season rates would be lower for accommodation, the crowds less, and after all it was his BIG birthday; he works hard, 'poor Dave', and it was his time for a treat, and mine too, even though I don't work as hard. We had dozens of complex planning meetings and set out on an eight-day road trip to some of the most outstanding safari lands in the world. We did deals with accommodation owners and compiled a full packing list. Not long to go now!

Hither and Thither...

The Cat Among the Pigeons
Meanwhile, I was out running one day, enjoying a wonderful sunrise over the Indian Ocean and on a bit of an off-road adventure. I looked up to greet a fellow, early morning runner, when I should have been looking at my feet. I went down like a ton of bricks. The man I'd waved at stared with a horrified look on his face. Unfortunately, rather than lying there to await and receive his concerned help, I yelled that it was his fault that I had fallen and waved him away. I leapt to my feet, Tourette's syndrome kicking, before noticing a rather large skin flap in my knee. I ran the mile or so home, fuelled by adrenaline or more probably embarrassment.

Assessing the Damage
Once home, I jumped in the shower and assessed my injuries whilst trying to wash off the wee and poo which had been populating the ground that I had been running over. I finally realised that this gash really did hurt and was very deep indeed. It wasn't really bleeding though, which concerned me rather. I decided sticking a plaster over it this time just wouldn't do.

Visit to London Health Clinic, Dar Es Salaam
I had to take a tuk tuk, which was a bit awkward as I couldn't fit my now erect leg into the back where the passengers sit. I spent a good forty five minutes on the treatment table, begging for more pain killing injections which, although excruciatingly painful, was a better option than the doubly excruciating pain of anyone being remotely near the wound. Plus, the previous pain killing injections were wearing off. Leaving the clinic with a bandage, five stitches and a promise, that I wasn't sure I was going to keep, to re visit the sadistic doctor three days later to check for infection. Another tuk tuk home, this time with bandaged knee sticking out of the side.

And you thought this story was going to be about Dave...

That Afternoon
After all the initially wonderful, pain killing injections had worn off, I was in additional and very real pain. I could hardly walk and I'm not exaggerating. I couldn't stand and weight bear. I couldn't sit straight on the toilet and ended up weeing down my leg. My right arm was extensively bruised and now I had a new pain, my ribs. I have no idea what I fell on, but my ribs were in agony. But not as much agony as my knee. My knee by this stage couldn't be seen. I just had one long sausage for a leg. I had developed elephantiasis, as my good friend pointed out. Going to bed was difficult as the weight of the bed covers hurt my leg, my foot, and I couldn't turn my knee to lie on my side because my knee and ribs hurt. No sleep. The beginning of grumpy me.

The Return Visit to the London Health Clinic, Dar Es Salaam
This time Dave drove there. Dressing off, let's squeeze the wound until it hurts so much that the patient grabs hold of the doctor's arm to make him stop, and voila, what a surprise, some puss came out; it was infected. Antibiotics mean only one thing to me... no beer. A big increase in grumpy me.

Back to Dave's Dreadful Birthday
Nicola can't drive, she can't bend her leg. We were about to embark on a twelve hour road trip up t' North of Tanzania for Dave's special and much planned birthday. What shall we do? Wait to see if there is a miraculous recovery?...no, not happening. Decided to cancel each of the accommodation options which had been researched so painstakingly. Dave's big birthday treat cancelled. 'Poor Dave'.

Another Visit to London Health Clinic, Dar Es Salaam
Visit, begrudgingly, the sadist who actually gives me a kind of good news; infection gone, need an x ray; x ray ok but wound not healed, more stitches...blah blah blah.

New Dave's Birthday Plan
Dave cancels his full week off work, and we make a reservation for a very posh and plush hotel, the kind we wouldn't usually stay in, for two nights, by the beach, two hours south of Dar. Ok, now we have something to look forward to.

Tanzanian Weather
Rain, rain, rain and storms, and on the morning we were due to leave for the posh hotel, we receive an email cancelling our reservation as the hotel had been hit by a massive electrical storm. Dumbstruck.

What Now?
Decide to book a hotel two hours north of Dar. This is a quirky hotel, a bit bohemian and hippyish. We actually go. We drive through the pouring rain, Nicola seated like Lady Penelope sideways on the back seat as it's too painful to sit like a normal human being.

Evening at Hotel
Cold beer...at last. Had a nice evening reflecting on Dave's life and preparing him for his big day. Go to bedroom, just getting ready for bed when we were nearly hit by a massive fruit bat, obviously scared and looking for an exit back to Batland. All of a sudden there was nothing wrong with my knee as I broke the land speed record and dived onto the bed under the mosquito net. Having never had a bat in his bedroom up to the eve of his fiftieth birthday, Dave went to find help and returned with a Masai man. Now, for those of you who don't know it, Masai men are everywhere in Tanzania, usually employed as security people. They dress traditionally in a colourful cloth wrap, often showing off plenty of muscular torso. They wear a very large dagger attached to their waist and carry

Hither and Thither...

a short stick, traditionally used to herd cattle. So, there we are, a partially naked Nicola cowering in her bed, watching a Masai man chase a very scared bat who was splattering the whitewash walls with poo around our bedroom, whilst Dave stood there, probably wondering if this is the most exciting thing that's going to happen to him this birthday. The lovely Masai man managed to stun the bat with his stick and remove it from our room, but guess what, I didn't sleep a wink...that's normal, right?

The BIG Day
Still raining and we're still at the hippy hotel where we spend all of the day sheltering from the rain (it's an outside-only hotel, apart from your bat bedroom) and alone as there were no other guests. Dave opened his presents in the bat bedroom, and we put some balloons up, but it wasn't what we had planned. He was supposed to be sitting in a safari vehicle cruising around viewing vast quantities of lions and elephants in the Ngorongoro crater. 'Poor Dave'. We tried to make the best of it with help from some vodka, my bad influence, of course; and umpteen beers, until we met an interesting guy called Rob who arrived in his big truck. Rob is sixty two years old and is spending five years travelling the world in his big overlander. He was quite a talker and I'm sure it made a change for Dave to hear another voice, but 'poor Dave'. We had some lovely cake though, which his wife didn't bake for him, and he was probably quite relieved about that. Plus, I did sing to him in the bat bedroom, which he probably wasn't that chuffed about either, and I forgot the candles. I'm a terrible wife.

Yet Another Visit to the London Health Clinic, Dar Es Salaam
By this stage, the receptionist knows my name, which I'm not happy about. Wound still not healed, so one more stitch. Swelling going down, so beginning to bend it but may need an MRI as I may have damaged the knee properly. Dave and I are both in denial about this and have refused the scan as I can't go through being out of action again and he can't face putting up with me being out of action again, which is fair enough.
Next visit to the London Health Clinic, Dar Es Salaam, is tomorrow...fingers crossed.

For the 'Poor Dave' foundation, please send any donations to our DFID Tanzania address or I can provide our bank account details if necessary.

Nicky Coope

**

A problem shared, a problem solved...
WIZI to Ghana

Charity may 'begin at home', but world-wide spread is important too. Every Christmas the congregation at Zion United Reformed Church in Northallerton donate to a Christmas Appeal for a good cause in lieu of sending cards to one another... one seasonal appeal recently reaching an impressive £500 for an "Ashanti Project" in Ghana. Little did they realise what they had let themselves in for!

The charity's prime focus is to provide sanitation and clean water to villages there, but it also works with the local health and education services, and provides microfinance to establish small businesses and encourages farm diversification.

Visiting Ghana in a personal follow-up, I unexpectedly discovered some girls had difficulties accessing or being able to afford adequate sanitary wear as they prepared to cross the threshold to womanhood. Was there a solution? Because they either dropped out of school altogether when they started their periods, or missed a significant amount, resulting in only 75% of girls completing their schooling and gaining lower results on average than the boys. They also had little or no education about family planning or even how to access it, as sex education was not allowed at school. Teenage pregnancies were the frequent result. As there was no organised method of waste disposal in the villages, this meant that single use sanitary towels were an environmental hazard too.

A big personal and community problem. The charity decided to carry out an initial trial with a basic, re-usable sanitary towel which the girls could (largely) construct themselves. The style of the sessions proved to be a great success in terms of producing towels, improving self-esteem and knowledge around menstrual health, but also in terms of allowing more relaxed conversations between teachers and peers rather than the usual didactic teaching methods. Some of the sessions also involved a family planning nurse. The charity wanted to expand and develop this project.

On my return, the Women's group at Zion were true to their name 'WIZI' (Women In Zion Investigate) and wanted to take this further.

A talk by 'Days for Girls' (an international organisation providing re-usable sanitary wear to developing countries, refugee camps and natural disaster zones) proved to be a very inspirational evening! The towels were of a much better design, much more flexible to girls' varying needs, and more robust, possibly lasting 3-4 years if looked after well. They are also very colourful, attractive and didn't look like sanitary towels if hung on a washing line to dry – all very important factors.

Thus arose the challenge of making 70 packs of towels for me to take out to Ghana the following year.

As always, the benefits extended way beyond the end product. The crafting sessions became a real social event, leading to conversations about sanitary towels and period poverty with anyone and everyone, including those working with the food bank or with girls at the local senior school. The waterproof backing layer and larger sized option also inspired conversations around incontinence and dignity for both men and women. In due course the packs were blessed at a service where re-usable sanitary towels were hung as bunting on a washing line around the pulpit! Next stop, Ghana!

Triggered by our example, the charity is now working to establish a sustainable way of producing these locally in Ghana for the schools and for sale. You never know where something small and seemingly insignificant will lead, not to mention what a lot of fun and laughter can be had along the way!

Liz Styan

Hither and Thither...

Enjoy a magical evening...
Cindy at the Thai Banquet

I looked at the clock. Five minutes to six. Under an hour to transform myself from an unkempt slob into a dazzling beauty. Wishing I could simply wave a magic wand, I stepped into the shower with an armful of shampoos, conditioner exfoliants, moisturizers, scents and pedicure paraphernalia, and set to work. Miraculously, just over an hour later I stepped out of the house in a new wine-red velvet evening dress with matching choker, high heels, diamante earrings and my grandmother's fur stole, feeling like a princess with a secret rendezvous with a forbidden prince.

'See you later,' I called out, remembering the babysitter watching a pantomime video with my twin four-year olds. 'I'll be back just after midnight.' The taxi driver opened the door of the back seat of the Mercedes and I slid into a new world.

*Hockliffe House in Bedfordshire had been transformed into a Thai Palace for a New Year's Eve banquet. A life-size, wooden statue of a Thai princess swathed in red and gold greeted people at the door, her eyes demurely focused on her tiny, immaculate feet. A photograph of the Thai king and queen had replaced the floral decoupage. I looked closer. Both were young: he, tense and unsure of himself, uncomfortable in Western clothes; she relaxed, calm, charm personified. The tables, set to welcome twenty groomed and glittering guests, were decorated with baskets of exotic fruits: mangoes, kumquats, lychees, passion and kiwi fruit. Somewhere Ann had found spring flowers, yellow tulips swelling slightly in the heat, deep blue/purple irises, crisp greens. The room was bathed in candlelight which bounced off the china and echoed round the walls. I saw my reflection in a tiny bowl: a squashed, rubbery, egg-shaped face. I turned away.

'Would you like a drink?' A mousy-haired young man hovered discreetly at my elbow. 'Yes please,' I replied, smiling at two elegantly dressed women – one in white and one in black – standing next to me.

'Cindy, there you are! I was beginning to think you weren't going to make it.' Ann, barely recognizable in a rustling red silk outfit, took me by the arm.

'These are my great friends Pat and Kate who lead the storytelling workshops we run. And this,' she continued, squeezing my arm, 'is my friend Cindy who is – well, you'll find out.' She threw me a look, part mischievous, part conspiratorial as she went to greet her next guest.

'Have you been in the kitchen?' asked Pat. 'The chef's only just arrived. Have a look while there's still room to get in there. You'll hardly recognize it.'

I knew Ann's kitchen well: a huge wooden table in the centre, an Aga, lots of warm-hearted clutter, comings and goings. This evening it looked as if the Chiang Mai night market had moved in. The chef, eschewing the Aga in favour of a row of calor gas burners, waved a greeting as he briskly heated a small charred wok to steam a mountain of assorted greens. On the table I saw catering-sized bottles of chilli, soy, and, surprisingly, tomato sauce. He had it in hand, despite his Thai time-keeping. It struck me that there were as many people in the kitchen as there were seated at the banqueting tables. The bustle and steam of preparation filled the air. The banquet was an event we had looked forward to for months.

I returned to my place at the table to find myself sitting next to the storytellers. As the first dishes began to arrive – tiny crisp parcels with soft vegetable centres, red curry, green curry, chicken with cashews, chicken with prawns, sweet and sour chicken – I learned they were not just storytellers but also successful and knowledgeable dieters.

'If you have slimline tonic, you can have two gins,' said Kate. 'With an ordinary tonic, it's only one.'

As the continual supply of food finally slowed gently to a trickle and we were toying with the passion fruit, Pat started to tell me about her research on the Cinderella story.

'Every culture has a Cinderella story, every nation its version of the wicked stepmother, the ugly sisters. Everyone wonders aloud, at some time in their lives, whether they'll turn into a pumpkin at midnight.' She fingered one of the long, silver pearl earrings that set off her white dress. I was glad she had not noticed that she had lost the other.

Simultaneously, we laughed and looked at the clock: a quarter to twelve. Around us, other guests were beginning to flag; bow ties had been removed, belts loosened. The buzz of excitement had quietened to a low hum, punctuated with full stops of silence. I looked round. The Thai princess's gold jewels, I could see now, were only brass, tarnished in places. The flower which had been tucked behind her ear had slipped and been trampled underfoot. The flowers on the table too were beginning to wilt, the heads of the tulips drooping. The baskets of fruit had been plundered and the table was in disarray: spots of red sauce soiling the crisp white cloth; grains of rice and scraps of meat spilled amongst the pips and peelings of passion and kiwi fruit. Out of the corner of my eye I saw a mouse scoot into the skirting as if on wheels. I looked round for the waiter to ask if he could bring some more water, but he had disappeared.

There was a knock at the door. I turned to look out. The taxi had come ten minutes early.

As I went to follow the other guests into the drawing room, I caught my dress on a splinter of wood under the table, and tore a strip of velvet from my thigh to my knee, revealing over a foot of dimpled white flesh. Swearing under my breath, I joined the chef and kitchen helpers who were pressing into the drawing room. Most of them had changed into evening dress. Relieved of their aprons, they now shone like diamonds.

As Big Ben struck twelve, there was pandemonium in the banqueting hall. I arrived back there to find the heavy front door wide open, creaking on its hinges as it swung gently to and fro. Although there was no wind, the candles had been blown out and the moon had flooded the room with its shadow of light. The Thai princess had been knocked flat on her back, where she lay with her legs apart. A dirty, white cat with half its tail missing sniffed through the leftovers on the table. I slowly picked my way through the debris to the open door. Outside on the driveway I could just about make out the shape of a pumpkin, soft and rotting, where the Mercedes had been waiting.

Janet Stow
Hockliffe House, the editor's home to her former Wellsprings Retreat Centre
**

Hither and Thither...

The 'missionary message'...
'Laura Ashley' goes to Thailand

Leaving the family home to spend up to two years as a volunteer with VSO in Thailand is a major threshold in a young life. In the months leading up to my departure I had managed to locate the mysterious destination on a world map and had attended a week's course to prepare me, meeting London based staff, returned volunteers and other outgoing volunteers. It was terrifying.

During this week some time was spent explaining how we were to behave in the expected ways of polite and acceptable behaviour in our host countries. As a young, single woman, certain dress codes must be followed. Extremely modest clothing, so as not to cause offence - which meant that I must not expose my shoulders, whilst skirts should be of a generous length. No sleeveless tops, no shorts and certainly no bikinis on the local beach! Well, knowing that the temperature was going to be very high all year long, this posed a bit of a dilemma. Long sleeves and covered legs in the evening were to be expected in a country that still had a problem with malaria, but at work and in the heat of daytime?

What did I pack? Naturally my usual Laura Ashley summer dresses of thick floral cotton, ballooning gathered sleeves and subtle colours. Modest? Yes. Blending in with my new community? No. Cool enough for 36 degree days? No again. The only time I ventured onto a Bangkok bus wearing my Laura Ashley smock, a young man immediately offered me a seat, assuming I was pregnant. What about swimming in my mum's substantial swimsuit? I must, in the words of another local young man, be a missionary.

My work placement was in the laboratory of a large general hospital. An environment where I had been used to covering my everyday clothes with a protective, poppers-down-the-side lab coat, but now I'd need a simple dress. So...I had to adapt and do it Thai style. I was taken to a dressmaker in a shop in one of the main streets. The panacea for so many. Here numerous body measurements were taken and within a day or two several smart, perfectly fitting, white dresses were made available for me in a light fabric that I could wash through, in a bowl of cold water, at the end of each working day.

That dressmaker was the saving grace really. From then on all my clothes were made for me. Brighter and more colourful than I was used to, lighter in fabric and really, I have to say, rather more stylish. Somehow, it didn't matter that the shirts had little sleeves, high necks or collars and skirts that skimmed the bottom of my knees. They fitted, of course, perfectly, in more than one sense of the word. They fitted me and I fitted in. One of the volunteers likened Thai women to the French in their sense of style. I think she was right.

At the end of my stay the dressmaker had an important assignment when, secretly, hospital staff organized, as my leaving present, a traditional Thai silk outfit. Made to measure and to treasure. Long narrow sleeves, high neck, short fitted blouse, with an ankle length, narrow skirt. It was striking in colour; beautiful deep green silk with peacock blue and silver broad stripes at the border.

However, the tough Levi jeans I'd carried with me and which had proved so unsuitable in the steamy heat of Thailand became unexpected and welcome currency on my way home through India. There I could branch out and buy an embroidered, fine silk Kaftan top in Delhi and an Afghan jacket in Nepal. It was the '70s after all.

Jane Price

**

Shimmering like a rainbow...
Buying Silk in Jaipur

Before my visit to India, I had promised to buy a piece of silk for my sister. In my innocence I had thought this would be quite a simple exercise – however, on arriving in Jaipur it soon became apparent that I wouldn't just be able to nip to the market to buy a piece of silk. It was going to require some local knowledge. Our guide was very helpful and suggested we meet up with him in the early evening and he would drive us to the shops.

We left our hotel at 6pm, the night heavy and warm. Already it was quite dark but with no reduction in the volume of traffic or people. We drove for about 30 minutes before parking the car and finding our way to the main shopping area, passing various animals in the streets - quite a few cows rummaging in the bins (not quite like the green fields of the UK), several dogs trotting along scavenging on scraps, and a few goats meandering about. We approached the main road and nervously took our lives into our own hands whilst negotiating a constant stream of cars whose drivers were constantly honking their horns! In addition, many motor bikes were whizzing along, weaving in and out of the lanes. It was a common sight to see whole families on the same motor bike, a small child in front of the father driving the bike, another child behind him, the mother behind that child and a further one behind her! Interestingly, the only person to wear a crash helmet was the dad.

The shops were 'bursting at the seams' with clothes, or leather goods, or sweets etc., with the shopkeepers sitting outside, leisurely drinking tea and encouraging you to view their wares. Once you had been enticed inside, nothing was too much trouble for them. They would take any number of items from the floor to ceiling shelves, extracting beautifully folded garments from the packaging, shaking them out, all the time displaying them with a proposition to buy not one but, by negotiating a special deal, three or more! And while you were mulling this thought over, along came cups of tea infused with ginger, further delaying your departure! The little shops were just buzzing with activity and banter, all being run by men! The temptation to buy was overwhelming and, without realising how, you were finally walking out of the shop with a bulging bag of unplanned goodies. In the UK, the items looked somewhat out of place in our climate and environment.

Jaipur is renowned for its silk and fabrics, so our guide

Hither and Thither...

had also arranged for us to visit a small specialist store/factory - again staffed entirely by men. The walls of the building were lined with silk in the most beautiful rainbow colours that shimmered in the artificial lighting. Large wooden counters facilitated the best possible display for you to touch and feel the quality of the silk of your choice. Perfect English was spoken by the member of staff serving me. Unhurriedly, he discussed my intentions in order to recommend the most appropriate quality of material and combination of colours. At this stage, not being comfortable with haggling, I would gladly have accepted whatever price was quoted, but our guide discreetly negotiated on my behalf and the deal was done. My silk was cut, folded and carefully placed into a cotton carrier bag. An occasion so wonderful and yet so different from anything else I had experienced before.

After our stay in Jaipur, we moved further south to Kerala where I enjoyed another 'silk shopping' encounter. On the recommendation of fellow hotel guests, we hired a guide to escort us to a large department store, also renowned for its quality silks, in Trivandrum. Every year en route home, this couple takes large quantities of fabric/silk to Dubai, where one of the many tailoring businesses creates lovely garments for several of their family members. The department store had no less than 7 or 8 floors, each totally filled with bolts of silk in differing qualities. Again, we were dazzled by the walls of colourful shelves and noted the long wooden display counters, manned by dozens of staff waiting to serve. It was fascinating to observe wedding parties choosing appropriate wedding silk, and smaller parties examining fabric to be fashioned into other no doubt imaginative garments...

Totally intriguing, but without the excitement of that evening shopping experience in Jaipur. All heightened there by the knowledge that my silk purchase – once carefully repackaged in the UK and forwarded by Royal Mail – was destined to be created into a beautiful bolero/shrug to replace one that my sister had very kindly given to a special friend.

Sue Gibson

**

Encountering an entrepreneur...
Shopping on a Goan Beach.

In Goa for our annual visit, each day we wended our way to our local beach shack to claim sunbeds under the palms. Then Ratuja squeezed through the gap in the fence from the beach shack next door. With all sorts of vibrant textiles on her head, she had that grace all sari clad Indian women possess whatever their caste, however heavy their burden. With her glorious smile, she was beautiful, and she instantly became my personal shopper. Laying out her bundle of beach wraps, 'umbrella' dresses, harem pants, cotton shirts, and more, we discussed sizes, colours, styles. I was in shopper heaven, an unusual place for me. There was a style I liked but doubted the colour. There was a style and colour I liked but doubted the size. Embracing the Goan ethos of 'Susegad' (the relaxed easy going attitude found there), I threw aside my reticence. Wearing a swimsuit, it was easy to try on and take off almost anything in several blinks of an eye. With quick reference to Ratuja and guided by her, decisions were made sans looking-glass. Haggling is customary and a necessity for beach-sellers who must get the best price for their goods. I didn't bargain hard. Later, at our accommodation, those decisions didn't look half bad in front of the mirror.

While we were there we learned Ratuja's story. She became a beach-seller in Goa when she fled her home in neighbouring Maharastra. Her husband was violent, and due to his chronic alcoholism couldn't hold down any work. Her family was unsupportive; her in-laws were very abusive. With three daughters and two sons, she moved to a small town nearby, found a safe place to live, and began to support the family by selling clothing and textiles to tourists at the beach shacks. Life is far from easy for beach-sellers. Licences are expensive and sellers – almost always women – often face extra demands for money from various official and unofficial 'authorities' or their wares may be confiscated. That would leave them with no means of earning a living.

Ratuja's elder son got work as a waiter and their joint income keeps the younger ones in education. Her elder daughter is in technical school learning accountancy. The youngsters are in grade school. Ratuja cannot read or write but she is oh so bright and hard-working. She has picked up English, some German, and even a little Russian - well enough to help her in her work. She is determined to help her children into a more secure life, especially her daughters. Life is difficult beyond our understanding for many, many millions of poorer people in India, but especially so for women and girls. Early marriage is common and no haven from abuse of all kinds. Rather, it's often the reverse. Goa has been described as 'soft' India, mainly because it is one of the wealthiest, though the smallest, of Indian States. Twenty-five per cent of the population is Christian. That helps give some impetus for gender equality and respect for women. But there are still more than a hundred country miles to go and it is the courage and enterprise of women like Ratuja who are making a difference.

Ratuja hopes, eventually, to have a licensed, beach shack shop so she can increase her stock, her turnover and her income. This year she filled some gaps in my holiday ensemble and though she hasn't given me a taste for consumer shopping as we know it, I'll gladly walk a kilometre or two along the beach to where she is planning to open her shop to see her again. It will be a simple opportunity to support the local grass roots economy and it can make a difference to the future of women like Ratuja and their children. A Marathi name, 'Ratuja' means 'daughter of truth'. Our Ratuja is much more – she is also a daughter of inspiration.

Chris Kilpatrick

**

And on another beach...
With Refugees to the Seaside

The summer's day dawned clear and bright – if not a trifle chilly. Today, five refugee families, who had recently begun to settle in Northallerton, were to travel to Scarborough to meet fellow countrymen who had also been welcomed elsewhere in North Yorkshire after fleeing from the Syrian conflict. The sunny morning heralded a first, whole day outing, during which local volunteers would be hosting the 10 parents and their 18 children, ranging

Hither and Thither...

in age from six months to 10 years. The initial sense of anticipation was more about the coach experience, I felt, than the imminent refugee get-together. Once aboard the coach I ran through the safety instructions, before explaining that the journey would cover around 60 miles and take us over the glorious moors and then down to the sea at Scarborough. Sadly, as we progressed, one child after another began to feel sick, so the coach driver pulled into a layby to enable them to recover and take a sip of water. A mile or two later two adults began to feel unwell and this interruption was repeated a further four or five times. Finally, we reached Scarborough and found our way to the Stephen Rowntree Theatre, whereupon the widespread nausea mysteriously disappeared. Everyone was looking forward to the events of the day, to meeting fellow Syrians and sharing stories of their new lives in Britain. The Syrian women had dressed especially for the occasion in ankle length coats with embroidery around the bodice and wrists, along with colourful hijabs. The men, however, were attired simply in jeans and casual jackets!

In the foyer was displayed an array of imaginative and colourful art & craft work contributed by the various Syrian groups from all over the county. Then, once in the theatre, we heard not only speeches of welcome from the Refugee Council but also accounts by Syrian men who had been in the UK for a few years of how well they and their families had been greeted and helped to settle. The children were assembled separately to learn a drumming routine for a later performance to us all.

For lunch, the Syrian wives had all contributed delicious specialist dishes – which set us up perfectly for a period of happy entertainment. The drumming sequence was a big hit, both with the participants and their proud parents. And memorably, in conclusion, all the men and their young sons took to the stage (women in Syria do not dance in mixed company) to demonstrate some traditional dance routines to the accompaniment of Arabic music. The pride on the faces of the fathers as they showed their sons the steps was a wonderful sight.

As we left the theatre the sun was shining warmly, so I suggested to our children that we should go down to the beach for an ice cream. That seemed to meet with universal approval and within minutes we all found ourselves on the sands. My first task was to select a couple of the older children to accompany me to the kiosk, where we placed an order for 40 ice cream cones. The three of us carried these carefully back to the families, who by now were sitting down making sandcastles. The arrival of the ices having put a temporary stop to this serious activity, I turned my back and began to talk to the Syrian wives about the earlier events at the theatre. Clearly, they had loved being able to discuss their experiences in Britain and had plans to renew contact with their newfound friends via WhatsApp. Casually, I looked towards the sea and could not believe my eyes. Despite still being fully dressed, the Syrian men were in the water, holding their young children on their shoulders or in their arms, whilst all the remaining children were following them out into the bay. Laughter abounded, without any thought for the minor detail that no one had towels with them or a change of clothes for the homeward journey. This general merriment continued for 20 minutes or so under

the amused gazes of the mothers on the beach – they too were delighted that their families were able to enjoy the warmth of the sun and the sea! But they remained fully clothed in their heavy wool abayas.

Still full of excitement, the children were chatting twenty to the dozen on the return coach ride. No one mentioned feeling cold and certainly no-one felt sick! Perhaps England was going to be good, after all!

Sue Bush

**

Be careful how you pack...
Hidden Danger

Imagine my security official at the airport. You've probably encountered a few of his over-zealous counterparts on your own air travel adventures. The final frontier at the threshold.

We know it has to be done in these days of terrorist danger, but just see the serried ranks of innocent victims waiting patiently in line for the compulsory mini indignity (at least) to be foisted upon them. Passengers are forewarned to prepare for their potentially deadly bottled water to be confiscated, along with any pharmacy item holding more than the odd tablespoonful. Then they must hoist their possibly dubious hand baggage into a tray; transfer jacket, hat, belt, shoes, bumbag etc. into another; spectacles, watch, keys, coins, jewellery, comb, mobile into a third, while their sinister I-pad is suspected independently of preparing to do its worst. Through the X-Ray machine it all goes.

But of course you yourself and any clothing you still retain are certainly not beyond further suspicion. Off you go though more high tech paraphernalia. Probably arms raised, on to body frisking, along with the handheld magic wand scan for good measure. And woe betide you if you fail to satisfy!

Today I fell at this final hurdle. I bleeped wildly around the nether regions, but my simple explanation was not accepted at face value. Unable to be probed, stroked or wanded further in the full glare of other onlooking future targets, I was kindly invited to accompany the officer to a secure private room off stage. There a more experienced interrogator joined us. As they had 'confiscated' my glasses, I couldn't easily read their wall chart, outlining the lengthy security rigmarole of assorted warnings and reassurances: so it was laboriously intoned to me to satisfy the red tape criteria. Ditto, signed in on their pad of suspects' names.

Then the serious business began. On command, my trousers dropped to the floor to expose, as I had promised them, a pair of pale blue Fat-Face shorts with a range of poppers and zips to a multitude of pockets. It had seemed to me a good idea to wear them, rather than add unnecessary weight to my cabin bag. The wand now proceeded to embark on another wonderful session, playing assorted tunes up and down them. Lots more panicky patting of the pockets too. Glances were exchanged between my minders. Were they next going to insist on the 'full-monty', I wondered? The ultimate airport conundrum; to

Hither and Thither...

take off or not to take off, that is the question. Did I look to them like a man with interesting orifices guarding undeclared surprises within?

Disappointingly for you, dear reader, apparently not. Though my hand luggage, containing tiny pairs of silk knickers and spotty pink bikini bottoms destined for my daughter, might have raised more than the odd eyebrow and given them a little more encouragement for a new line of attack if the investigation had proceeded in that direction!

Anyway, fortunately for me, my naive complacency was vindicated without further ado. I was apparently a free man again – while my over zealous officer stayed behind to enjoy a few words of advice from his senior. With re-hoisted trousers in place once more over my guilty secret, off I went, now unsupervised. Only to get into fresh trouble back at the 'coal face' for trying to retrieve my belongings from an unexpectedly sensitive section of their countertops. And the little tray containing my specs etc seemed to have temporarily disappeared. Clearly, now that I was deemed innocent, no one was interested in my future destiny.

Time to put it all behind me, I thought, but ironically I was immediately given the chance to offer anonymous feedback on my experience. As I exited the scary zone, I spied four smiley faces displayed along a voting stand, in colours ranging from red through oranges to green. I was invited to express my approval or otherwise of my experience by choosing and pressing the most appropriate button. So I did...you can guess...

Paul Bowes

**

Walking towards holiness...
Pilgrimage into Silence!

There is a particular challenge, not simply in stepping over a threshold into something new, but also in spending time – dipping in and out – and then going back to normal life, as happens on pilgrimage or whenever people go to a place of worship. What does the liminal time do to make 'normal life' different?

Both ideas involve much to ponder within the context of clothes. Pilgrims have always worn 'uniforms' to mark their state/status. This taps a rich seam. I once heard a pilgrim remark, 'We know the pilgrimage has started when you put your hat on' (a hat I wore year after year and only on pilgrimage, although I had not realised it was so).

Officiants in places of worship wear robes – not just to mark their official status but also to signify it as a space between heaven and earth. I always used to get irritated by the bejewelled glitz of the Orthodox hierarchy but now understand it too has its place.

Beyond the 'threads', pilgrimage is a challenge and an adventure. It stretches across all faiths and none as people make the effort to visit places or undertake journeys significant to them. The bustle and noise of an airport, the noise of tramping feet, the hooting of buses and lorries, the chattering of folk sharing and encouraging, the pounding of exhausted hearts and lungs. All these are the stuff of pilgrimage. The places may have been made sacred by the past – by people, events, myths – and perhaps the core of all that is important. But also places made sacred today by the hopes and values of those who continue to travel such routes. The many books, academic dissertations, films or maps of pilgrim routes old and new seem to belong in a realm far from that of a small group of people meeting regularly in a quiet room or chapel – sitting quietly waiting on God in the silence. And yet... the two worlds do share a threshold experience.

For many years I have walked on pilgrimage in the company of others from Western European countries. We walk with the minimal of belongings, sleeping in village or church halls en route. Living simply and worshipping ecumenically, we have time to discuss matters of importance, to share stories, to learn about each other and ourselves, to observe life along the route – people, places, views, the natural world. But even as we walk together, there are many times when silence is paramount. Prayer is rooted in the very walking. We do not need speech to be aware that next to us our neighbour is struggling.

In this focused time we live in the present. The needs of the moment lead to a real understanding of many spiritual clichés:

i) We share each other's burdens, we feed each other
ii) We know that 'slough of despond'
iii) We fight with the giants of fear - the fear of responsibility (be it map reading or cooking supper or holding up the others)
iv) We know *'we have left undone those things which we ought to have done; and we have done those things which we ought not to have done and there is no health in us'*
v) We take on new challenges and surprise even ourselves
vi) We learn to let go of ideas and objects that we thought were essential

Most importantly in the pilgrim experience – with the tramp of boots or rhythms of train and bus comes a silence deep within. A silence that is every bit as valuable as the silence of sitting alone. Thus does travelling on age-old routes to exotic holy places link with the holy space of the humble living room.

Our journey to that silence within, however short or long, strenuous or easy, is to a meeting with the other, and others. To face challenges and distractions. To be ourselves, vulnerable and open, sharing and receiving – alive to love incarnate.

Sheana Barby

**

Camino Hills

Gods, they knew, lived in the high hills:
They brought gifts – food, sons, rams at a pinch –
Built cairns to honour and to guide.

Romans knew the point of skull hills, too,
Hung their keepers' larders with torn flesh:
'We are gods now: these,
The secular monuments of our power.'

Then churches be-crossed the hills,
Monuments to death, visited
By the penitent, eyed warily
By those in the valley who knew
Gods were still harsh, powerful, capricious.

Now hills speak again of secular power –
Crosses replaced by wind farms, pylons, aerials,
Taking earth's power into human hands.

Hills of a new sign – *ruach*, blowing wind,
Broadcast messages, person to person words:
What for the travelling pilgrim?
We lift up our eyes to the Pentecost hills.

John Lansley

Through the Vestry Door
(editor)

A Reflection

Encountering on the Journey

...your journey can be a place of encounter for you, sacred and unique to you and your Becoming, a place where the invisible and visible, in yourself and in all creation, can become reconnected. For the Celts there was never any shadow of doubt that these two worlds, the visible and the invisible, the material and the spiritual were one...interwoven, as surely as the air we breathe and the food we eat come together to give life to our bodies. Margaret Silf.

Travel involves many decisions, planning for that transition before the journey is embarked upon. When? Where? How? What shall we take? What will the weather be like? How can we fit it all in? What can we leave out? Some journeys are intrepid and dangerous. One can find oneself in a landscape without a map. Lostness can be terrifying. It is humbling to consider just one example of many from the animal world. Penguin mothers leave their chick eggs in the tender care of fathers huddled together to survive in horrendous, blasting, icy weather conditions, whilst they travel for months to scavenge food from the hostile ocean, risking being eaten alive themselves in their attempts to harvest for their chicks. If they do return, they arrive depleted and exhausted to feed their young and their hungry mates They don't choose to go on these journeys as we usually do. They are irresistibly drawn to go. They have to go. But sometimes we have to obey that intrepid, unexpected call to the unknown too. Do you recognise that imperative in your life?

After half a life-time in the South, in answer to such a call we moved to the mysterious North, an area 200 miles distant that we had rarely visited before. We left our beloved family home, our bookshop and publishing business and our retreat centre. Our five children were by then travelling on their own chosen journeys. All four of our very elderly parents were still independent and self-sufficient, so maybe the time was right for an 'adventure'? We dared to leave all that was safe, familiar, tried and tested. My friend offered me a challenging image. That of an ocean-going liner, strongly constructed, built for exploration, ready for sailing the high seas, and she asked the question, 'Is it right that it should languish, magnificent, impressive and majestic for decades in the dock?' I always remember that question when I am hovering on the threshold. I think of my mother saying, 'You never regret a bold decision.' Yet ironically this gifted, creative, intelligent, feisty woman had always found that difficult. But she was right, I have discovered. Well, thus far 'at any rate', as we used to say in my native Birmingham.

Nowadays, I frequently travel on trains as I keep in touch with my scattered family. Generally, that is more relaxing than battling with the ever increasing road traffic,

Hither and Thither...

but a fellow train-traveller's recent experience taught me never to be complacent.

'Our train manager will be along shortly, so please have your tickets and travel passes ready for inspection,' came the announcement.

It suddenly became obvious that there was a fracas across the aisle from me. A peer of mine, another elderly grandma on her way to see her family (we had had this conversation) was showing her ticket – right destination, correct day of travel but used in error, it transpired, on an incorrect company's train. 'I'm sorry, you can't use this one, madam. It is not appropriate for travel on this train. You will either have to get off at the next station or pay the full fare from York to King's Cross.'

She began to cry, and the full, busy coach gradually settled from quiet to silence. On it went for almost 15 minutes, which felt like a lifetime. Terrifying... At first she had tried reasoning...'I don't have that much money with me and no card. I booked these tickets weeks ago.' Panic...and then...a young professional woman stood, approached the guard/train manager, said, 'I will pay the £120,' handed over her card, and returned quietly to her seat, sat down and continued working on her laptop.

The coach remained in silence, as if in suspended animation, until one by one, over the next few miles, other passengers went along the aisle to this young woman with five, ten and twenty pound notes. It had taken this act of reckless, abundant, uncynical generosity to release and enable others in theirs. Phew, what an experience! And what a learning curve for us all.

Stuff often happens to me on trains. In spiritual terms we do speak frequently of the journey being more significant that the destination!

Homilies

Travelling up the Stalk

John 14 :5
Thomas said to him, 'Lord, we don't know where you are going, so how can we know the way?'

I was beginning to meander around a local Food and Craft Fayre. It was a bustling occasion, with glistening Yorkshire sausages, shiny glazed crispy meat pies, mouth-watering baking, exotic gins, rural cheeses, lovingly crafted shopping bags, peg bags, handbags, tote bags, cards and vintage jewellery, enticingly arranged around a courtyard and hall. The sun was shining and men in 'pinnies' were cooking on a barbecue some home-made and very-superior-indeed burgers.

Just before entering the hall I paused to look at an attractive little cart affair, loaded with yummy jams and marmalades with little gingham caps topping the lids. Hmm! Marmalade with Amaretto...yes please. A youngish woman took my money and then looked at me again, 'You are the vicar who took my dad's funeral, aren't you?' That threshold occasion has suddenly returned to enrich this unexpected encounter. We embraced warmly and then she pushed up her sleeve, exposing a beautiful dragonfly tattoo. She pointed to all the dragonflies around her cart and on her brochures.

'We have dragonflies on everything possible in our family now,' she said. 'It was because of the little book you gave us when my dad died. Little Laura (granddaughter) could not cope at all with losing her grandad. They were very close, and then you gave us 'Water Bugs and Dragonflies'. That just transformed everything and made all the difference. It helped her so much and we were all so thankful, which is why we have this dragonfly symbol of transformation all around us now.'

G.H.P.

In that story a family of water-bugs lives at the bottom of a muddy pond. Around they go, getting on with day to day life, but every so often they see one of them looking tired and somehow quite old, and eventually it goes off up a handy stalk…up…up until it can no longer be seen. The ones left behind at the bottom of the pond all wonder what is at the top of the stalk and why their much-loved bug does not come back and explain where it has gone. They have a meeting and decide that the next one to go off up the stalk will come back and tell them. So let us follow this one…

Up it goes, tired and slowly, and finally lands at the top of the stalk on to the large flat leaf of a beautiful water lily. Hmm. Seemingly no longer in the water, but somewhere quite different. Exhausted after all that effort, it rests and has a big sleep. And one day when the sun is warm, it wakes, and stretches itself out. Its crusty shell slowly and gently bursts open and as it leaves, it finds it is completely transformed. No longer is it a brown bug, but it is amazingly beautiful; it has wings and it can fly. It remembers that it is now to go back down the stalk and tell all its friends and family what has happened to it, but no matter how hard it tries, its new amazingly beautiful body does not allow it go back into the water.

Oh dear. It can't keep its promise, so what now? It lies in the sun a moment, and then begins to stretch. As it unfolds the fragile but strong new wings, it finds it can take to the air, flying around in a stunningly different world, more free than it has ever been.

And so the transformation of the water bug into the dragonfly echoes our own crossing of that threshold from life to life. It is a mystery, we do not understand it, but God's woven fabric of creation around us shows us that anything is possible!

It is a powerful and yet true story. Now when I see the granddaughter to whom I have given this fable, she usually asks me if I am ready to go off up the stalk yet. I am not quite sure what this means!

**

The Landscape Changes Overnight

Mark 4:35-41
'Teacher, don't you care if we drown?'

What a turbulent story. Hard to grasp its full impact intellectually. How often in my spiritual journey am I wrestling, tossed about, anxious and very definitely out of control, as if the waves are breaking over me, so that I almost sink. Concentrating on the resources of learning, study aids, knowledge and understanding, yet missing encountering Jesus

Hither and Thither...

himself. I am experiencing this account in all its anxiety, fear, panic, irrationality.

I recall another book, a simple, humble offering by a gifted poet and cartoonist Michael Leunig, conveying our search for God, the soul or the Divine spark in everyday life. We sail along on calm seas for years, trusting that God walks alongside us. We come to church, read the Bible, say our prayers and hope things go along much as they always have. But of course, there comes a time when the storm blows up.

Here comes the cartoon.

A little stick fellow in a tiny rowing boat, without oar, sail or rudder. A tiny crescent moon, and a few scattered stars, so we know it is night time. It is dark. And here is how the landscape changes overnight.

God bless this tiny little boat

And me who travels in it

It stays afloat for years and years

And sinks within a minute.

And so the soul in which we sail,

Unknown by years of thinking,

Is deeply felt and understood

The minute that it's sinking.

'The waves broke over the boat so that it was nearly swamped.'

There was Jesus, the one on whom his friends depended, asleep on a cushion, seemingly oblivious to the danger. What about their faith, then? And what about ours when these times come; when our fears and anxiety threaten to submerge us?

With an open heart in prayer, ask Jesus to speak to you through this passage. Dare to wake him up! Quietly reflect on the storms in your own life, which threaten to overpower and even destroy you. Those times when you are buffeted by circumstances whirling around you.

There may be less than healthy addictions, temptations of longstanding pattern; ways of reaction and response which you wish you could alter. It might be a crisis such as sudden redundancy, retirement, broken and damaged family relationships, debilitating illness, even the diagnosis of terminal illness. More acute than any other anguish which presents itself in my ministry is that of 'bereavement'. Sometimes involving the physical death of a loved one, but also where there can be no ritual acknowledgement of the full consequences of a devastating loss. For example, children who don't come any more, divorce, the slipping into dementia of a loved one, a treasured friendship unaccountably rejected. All these situations can leave us bewildered, in an alien landscape without a compass. Tossed about, almost swamped as the turbulent waters break over us. We feel helpless. And as Christians, we sometimes wonder why we cannot take more strength and hope from our faith. Jesus can feel absent or at best asleep on a cushion somewhere in the recesses of our heart. 'Who is this whom even the wind and waves obey?' Because, actually, it is very scary to lose control and then have to surrender our hand on the tiller, and trust that he will still the storm.

Yet we come to God as we are. God comes to us as we are. Not as we think we ought to be. With our hearts full of turmoil, paralysis, or like stone. That is how we are asked to step into the boat with him. With honesty, in all the mixture of who we are, at every stage of our journey. Our fears and anxieties do not go away suddenly. They go slowly, and some we may be being asked to still live with. But we do have to remember to wake him up now and again, because of course he cares if we drown!

The buffeting of the boat is actually an integral part of the mystic journey. The gracious gift is not only that God consents to live in our hearts, but rather that we dwell in the heart of God...always, whatever the weather! Wherever we are on the threshold of our journey.

**

The Cage of Freedom

Exodus 20. Galatians 5:1, 13-25. Luke 9:46-48
Do not use your freedom to indulge the sinful nature; rather serve one another in love.

The story of the Ten Commandments begins with setting the scene for a very special journey, as the Israelite people move from slavery into the Promised Land. The people of God went through the waters into freedom. Now they are free. They can go anywhere they want to go, and do anything they want to do. Where will they go? What is the best way?

Well, that ability to choose brings responsibility. The best way of living is not the easiest. Sometimes things go wrong. Even though the commandments seem restricting, in that they are fairly didactic, in fact to live them is life enhancing and brings true freedom to live in the best possible way. Paul's letter to the early church in Galatia says, 'It is for freedom that Christ has set us free'. We achieve this, not by being under strict law, but by living in the Spirit. When we truly do that, we feel love, joy, peace, kindness, goodness, faithfulness, gentleness and self control. Against such things there is no law. And they are essential for building up the free and healthy life of any community, if it is to be built up rather than broken down.

Here is a metaphor which might help consider this idea of freedom. I was on a two year course for spiritual growth. One of my fellow students was a young minister who spent a whole week locked in a cage called 'the Cage of Freedom' with one of his friends

Hither and Thither...

outside his church. They were in there praying and hoping to 'live' the message for the city people that Christians believe God offers freedom for wherever we are trapped, cornered, angry, having made poor life choices, and being forced into poor behaviour patterns which are not life freeing. They depended even for food for that week on what was offered to them.

A highly intelligent person of middle age spoke to me recently of how all his life he had been totally God focused and passionate, so much so that because God's creation is bountiful and free, and he had believed that we were not to restrict ourselves with rules and boundaries and social conventions. He said, 'But just lately I am wondering whether actually all my apparent freedom (for example, I am not monogamous) is making me more constrained and imprisoned than anyone I know.'

The Israelites went off to freedom in the promised land, leaving their slavery in Egypt. But before long they were all arguing and whinging, because they did not know how to handle it. In order to be free, they needed God's guidance on the best ways to live; the boundaries, the guidelines. It is a bizarre paradox. The passage from Luke is set on the journey to Jerusalem and begins with a private row about who is the greatest. Problems will always occur on our journey too, and that is the reason why we need to lay markers down.

Our hope and trust in love must be that all the flowers and all the fruits of tomorrow are in the seeds of today. There are risks. The Christian life of freedom is costly and that is also a paradox. But are we going to remain unlived, for fear of change? Or are we going to be released to a new freedom? Like the Israelites, where will we go? What is the best way to cross this threshold?

> *Come to the edge.*
>
> *We can't, we are afraid.*
>
> *Come to the edge.*
>
> *We can't, we'll fall.*
>
> *Come to the edge.*
>
> *They went there*
>
> *And he pushed them,*
>
> *And*
>
> *They flew.*

G. Apollinaire (1880-1918)

A Final Musing

Dressing for Dolphins

Hmm! I think I might.
I had been on an expedition to Cromarty (yes, of shipping forecast fame) on the bus; an adventure day off from my retreat house. I wanted to revisit the cheese-shop. So there I was now, with my new cheese parcels, replete after a lunch of langoustines in garlic butter, when I spied from the window a sign next door, 'Dolphin and Wild Life Trips'. 2 hours. 2.00pm. 1 space left.

'Well,' I thought, 'I would be back in time for my bus.' Good job I had worn my dungarees and mac. 'Dolphins and other wild-life, here I come!' The vintage clothes and book shops would have to wait until next time.

I approached the office whence the expedition began. As I entered, I thought that there must be another trip on the way out, maybe to the Arctic Circle or some distant part in the North Atlantic. Because out came apparently androgynous figures (you could only see a nose), walking, legs akimbo, in identical suits. Thick padded waterproof trousers and matching long jackets with hoods pulled up. Indications under the hood hinted at thick elasticated ear protectors, goggles, and the final encompassing item of clothing was a life jacket. I was just in time to hear the instructions on how to operate the life enhancing inflatable nature of that garment. Phew. Thank goodness I was only going out on a tripper boat, on a dolphin trip.

However, on crossing the threshold, there on the counter was MY identical sailing outfit too, awaiting my robing! They did help me to put it on as I tried to keep a brave face on this unexpected situation and turn of events. I followed the others down to a locked gate on the harbour steps and I could not see a boat for the life of me. Then, Oh my goodness. It was a Rib Ride. For those who do not know, these are black and red blow up, raft like water vehicles which look like the rib cage of a whale or some vast water creature. I have seen them in Devon. They move like speedboats, thundering over the waves; you can hear them banging up and down from up on the cliffs. Why do I never learn to check things out? Then it became a matter of pride (always comes before a fall) to get my leg over the edge and on to one of the tiny seats which have to be straddled for the next two hours. NO STANDING! Panic! Is my ageing body up to this?

Well, of course we saw no dolphins along the coast-line, in the middle of the

Hither and Thither...

North Sea or anywhere else. But we did encounter some seagulls and a shag or two in passing. We did however have a close-up of the oil rigs, those mysterious erections, and a bit of an excursion around them at a great rate of knots.

'Terrifying, yet exhilarating' has been my reflection. Followed by a word of warning to myself for whenever I next risk crossing a hitherto unknown threshold...'if the appropriate clothing looks beyond my comfort zone, so might the experience be too!'

Time for Change...

LETTING GO

Throw your dreams into space like a kite, and you do not know what it will bring back, a new life, a new friend, a new love, a new country. – *Anais Nin*

Not I, nor anyone else can travel that road for you. You must travel it for yourself. It is not far. It is within reach. Perhaps you have been on it since you were born, and did not know. – *Walt Whitman*

I always find beauty in things that are old and imperfect, they are much more interesting. – *Marc Jacobs*

My mother was right. When you've got nothing left, all you can do is get into silk underwear and read Proust. – *Jane Birkin*

But perhaps neither gain nor loss. For us, there is only the trying. – *T.S. Eliot*

Life Is not so simple as a loom. What you weave, you cannot unravel with a tug. – *Madeline Miller*

...you can't save time. You can only spend it wisely or foolishly. – *Benjamin Hoff*

Through the Wardrobe Door
(Contributors)

Parting is such sweet sorrow...
Rich Rags

How uplifting is the joy which can be found in seizing small remnants of beautiful cloth and turning them into something fresh! That makes me realize how much I over-value the consumeristic things in my life, including shop-bought new clothes. These never have the same heart and soul. But actually they can have more than one life too.
   My Mum loved her clothes and was very particular about what she wore. She took care of them and it really mattered to her how she looked. When she died ten years ago, my sisters and I sorted her clothes and belongings. Many of the outfits were familiar to us from family occasions and weddings. We decided to donate them to a hospice charity. I offered to transport the clothes to a shop which wasn't near where any of us lived, as none of us wanted to see Mum's beloved clothes in a shop window or on the racks. This meant that I had to fill my small car right up to the ceiling with bags of Mum's clothes. What I soon realized was that my car smelt of Mum! I also sensed that I was driving around with Mum's life all around me - as represented by all of her treasured outfits. I didn't rush to take them to a charity shop. I found that I wanted a short transitional time to experience the intimacy of being so close to her scent in those beloved clothes. Without trying to sound melodramatic, it almost felt like being back in her womb. This final threshold echoing that earliest one. After a few days I finally took them, with rather a heavy heart. And though strangers, the women volunteers in the shop that day showed such respect and kindness to me. They accepted the clothes with such compassion, almost as though they were my Mum's ashes.

Sue Woolmore

**

Clothes taking on a new life...
Coats Re-born

'A Monmouth Street laced coat' was a byword a century ago, and we still find Monmouth Street the same. Pilot greatcoats with wooden buttons have usurped the place of the ponderous laced coat with full shirts; embroidered waistcoats with large flaps have yielded to double breasted checks with roll collars; and three-cornered hats of quaint appearance have given place to the low crowns and broad brims of the coachman school; but it is the times that have changed, not Monmouth Street. Through every alteration and every change, Monmouth Street has still remained the burial-place of the fashions.
   We love to walk among these extensive groves of the illustrious dead, and to

Time for Change...

indulge in the speculations to which they give rise; now fitting a deceased coat, then a dead pair of trousers, and anon the mortal remains of a gaudy waistcoat, conjuring up and endeavoring, from the shape and fashion of the garment itself, to bring its former owner before our mind's eye. We have gone on speculating in this way until whole rows of coats have started from their pegs, and buttoned up, of their own accord, round the waists of imaginary wearers; lines of trousers have jumped down to meet them; waistcoats have almost burst with anxiety to put themselves on; and half an acre of shoes have suddenly found feet to fit them, and gone stumping down the street...when our eyes happened on these shop windows, there was a man's whole life written as legibly on those clothes as if we had his autobiography engrossed on parchment before us.

Charles Dickens (Sketches by Boz)

Normally, I don't think much about previous owners of the garments I buy there, but I am addicted to charity shops because of the elements of surprise and discovery. The few times I have been into new retail clothes shops recently, I never felt inspired at all. Although I must say I could get very inspired by the Vivienne Westwood shop in Leeds. But I would look ridiculous, and as for the prices!

Actually, there is one garment from a charity shop for which I have a special affection and for its previous owner, and that's my Alexon lined raincoat which is black on one side and fake leopard skin furry on the other. This beautiful coat came replete with the slightly metallic smell of old ladies' face powder, which I have never been able to remove. So, I can't help wondering about the personality of the person from whom I have inherited it.

My favourite thing about this coat concerns the opportunities it presents. Such as when I met my good friend in York and turned my black coat inside out while she was in the ladies to be all in fake leopard skin by the time she emerged, as an evocative tribute to my glorious Aunty Doreen. Licensee of The Odd Fellow's Arms in Pocklington, she was under five feet tall and pretty much as broad (or so it seemed). Never seen without full makeup and her earrings, she had a big heart, was incredibly generous and as tough as old boots. What a wonderful combination. At her funeral the vicar explained that he had only been in post for six weeks and yet he knew he would miss her very much. He said he would especially miss the hats on Sundays!

Gill Montia

**

Gently and graciously re-fashioned for another generation...
Kilts

I have some precious memories of my beloved Grandpa. During the First World War he had served in a Scottish regiment and was wounded at the Battle of the Somme. His regimental kilt returned home with him and had been stored in the attic until thirty years later, when he decided to make three small kilts out of it, one for each granddaughter. I remember the kilts had white bodices attached and they were very itchy! My sisters and

Letting Go

I were so proud of them – an act of love from Grandpa, especially reminiscent of those days of 'make-do-and-mend'. Every time I see a kilt now, I think of him. He never completely recovered from his war injuries, but that didn't stop him from making the kilts, or from making beautiful furniture and me a wonderful tree house!

Grandpa was a gentle, musical man who was a friend to everyone. He often listened to music and he loved singing. He even made us learn all the Carpenters' songs with him. I remember when he would tell us stories from the trenches and we would sing 'It's a Long Way to Tipperary' and 'Pack up your Troubles in your Old Kit Bag' at the tops of our voices.

Above all though, I will always treasure his special crafting of our kilts – as an item of 'threads' that crossed the threshold between the generations.

Thank you, Grandpa.

Sue Graham

**

Daring to let go of the 'busy' day...
The Practice of 'Sacred Idleness'

Two of my URC's most exciting recent developments eventually came together. For the past few years, a small group of very dedicated and hard-working volunteers have created a most beautiful, fruitful and peaceful garden from an overgrown plot of land next to the church. In its short life this garden has already given much pleasure and purpose to many and now a first Quiet Day (springing from a new relationship with the Quiet Garden Trust) will combine with the even newer practice here of contemplative prayer. Once a week, a small group of people (some church members, some not) meet for a short time of such prayer in the church 'cottage' under the umbrella of the Julian Meetings.

I have been privileged to take a very tiny part in both these initiatives and I was excited at the thought of this special day. A group of about 20 people gathered – some from our own church, some from the town locality, and others from as far afield as Newcastle! We had facilitators for practical matters so that we could be fully inclusive and no-one would feel in need.

After a short introduction and opening worship on the theme of the five (maybe six?) senses, we were invited to spend the day where and how we wished. We could use the rooms in the church building itself, the cottage (a less formal and cosier setting where gentle music played) or our Secret Garden. The garden has a range of places to sit and be quiet – benches, a patio area, little arbours and seats in nooks of the garden – which all give a different perspective. We were also provided with a 'mindfulness' trail to direct reflections in particular places of the garden. Strategically placed baskets or pots contained natural objects from the garden to use as a focus for contemplation. To inspire, prompt and support our reflections, contemplation and prayer – to explore and discover – we were offered a selection of quotes, thoughts and bible verses organised around the five senses.

Time for Change...

We eventually assembled for lunch (a choice here too – silent or talking!) and finally came together at the end of the day for a short time of reflection and celebration.

It was a day of such abundance – different environments, different inspirations, delicious food and drink, someone to talk to if we needed that, but most importantly for us all, I think, the time and space to practise 'sacred idleness', to just be, with our thoughts, our prayers and our own minds and with permission to 'do' nothing. One of the participants described it as 'a gift'; she hadn't realised how tired she was and the day had allowed her to slow down and pause.

From a personal point of view:

In the morning, I immediately chose my favourite little sheltered arbour in the garden and was invited to contemplate 'protection from the buffeting of the storm', aided by a basketful of natural objects – a poppy seed head, a stone, a small branch, a fir cone – to examine and use as a means of reflection. It was to be a quiet day, but my head was noisy so many things I wanted to think about without the everyday distractions. While contemplating the perfect symmetry of the poppy seed head and the precise mathematical positioning of each part of the fir cone, I contrasted the perfect patterns of the natural world with our chaotic human minds and lives.

Later I spent time in many other areas of the garden – particularly enjoying the sunshine after a rain shower – as well as in the cottage and in the church – I didn't want to miss out on anything!

The silent lunch was a particular experience for me. I am quite a chatty person (never having an unexpressed thought, someone once said!) and I often feel the need to fill a silence, admiring those who do not. During lunch it was a blessing to concentrate on the food – aware of others but without feeling the impulse to talk. Bliss!

When we all came together at the close to share our experiences if we wished, I described myself as feeling 'full'. At certain times in my life I have had a sense of 'hunger', wanting something, not food, but not knowing what it was I lacked. This was the complete opposite – the time, space and opportunity (especially in the garden) provided the nurturing and balm that my soul required. In church the following Sunday there was mention of 'the bread of Heaven', and I realised that was what had filled me completely that day.

Alexa Barber

**

Incoming tides...
Crossing the Causeway

Crossings, just the word, makes me smile and sends my mind to a calm place. I particularly revere our special a place of blue skies, white clouds and bright, deep blue sea. I don't need to close my eyes to see myself stopping at the edge of the Causeway, just to gain a view of Holy Island. A view I picture at any random time when I am least expecting it. There must really be a reason why I am jerked into that memory, a memory which is as real as this page. A memory that I can almost touch, just as one can touch this paper.

The journey across the Causeway always surprises me in that it is actually almost three miles long. When I begin and can already see the island, it looks as though it

must be much shorter. I look and see the wet sand and the gulls who feel safe to land on the still and shallow pools, left by the retreating waters. To preen and talk into the wind. I watch the walkers who stride across the wet, soft ground with sturdy boots or bare feet, following the pilgrim posts. Some bend into their task and lean on their walking sticks or long shafts. Some huddle together and wonder how long it will take. I wonder how they will feel when they reach the safety of the island. Perhaps as I do, although I doubt if anyone could feel quite as I do.

    The water tower comes into view and, as the causeway road curves, I see the high dunes with their salt-loving grasses. Grasses which hide birds and wildlife that people travel miles to see. Large lay-byes, cut from the road and to the side, are usually filling up with cars. Seaweed and flotsam often trapped there until the next tide. Not much farther along, I see the castle perched high on the rock, which Lutyens recreated from an early Tudor interior. It usually sparkles in the sun, and still I am on the road which carries me across. I feel liberated, happy and as though I live there; which I sometimes do for two or three weeks as the tide wraps and unwraps itself around the island. The familiarity is wonderful in that first, bursting moment of arrival past the carpark into the village. A village now crammed with eager people, and when they have gone back across to the mainland, I go out and breathe it all in again. I visit the familiar places as I have done for oh such a long time, but I cannot easily make the tortuous walk up the many steps to the castle now.

    I look forward to gazing out upon the island, over its fields, the long grasses and the many birds who flock and croon and fly up and dart around suddenly. I know a number of people there; enough to feel I belong for that short time. Enough to visit the places I always visit. The ruined Monastery and its excavations, the first one to be desecrated by the Vikings when they decided to stop trading with the island and instead to plunder.

Time for Change...

And the old church. Anglican now but Catholic in places. The churchyard which holds, according to my father when he would take me to visit, his great aunt Margaret. So I visit the tall gravestone and say hello to this lady. She looks across to the small harbour with lobster pots and creels stacked high. I can picture my father, turning and smiling to me and saying hello to her as well. These places all have to be visited, with a wonderful familiarity. I visit family and friends whilst I stay on the island sometimes, going back and forth across the causeway, with the same smile and pleasure.

One visit held a memorable, special surprise. An otherworldly sight hove into view. A fully-masted sailing ship, with white sails shining like diamonds. It dropped anchor as I stopped to watch and furled its sails in classic style. Just outside the small harbour, in deeper water. Part of the Tall Ships race had decided to overnight off-shore; the crew took advantage of the local hostelry and enjoyed dinner and drinks. I learned this later, as in the morning the ship had gone as quickly as it had arrived. Like the island, it seemed magical.

I look forward to returning each year and just the thinking makes me smile and I visit the familiar places in my mind. The Crossing is always the start of it. I am smiling now. Perhaps like those happy gulls who bob in the shallows and talk to the wind, I also have the memory bobbing happily in my mind. And I talk to the wind of my crossing, that threshold from one world to another.

Cris Reay Connor

**

Urgently searching for an explanation...
In the Consulting Room

I am watching the receptionist as she looks at her computer. She exudes an air of frustrated misery whilst scrolling across the screen, her mouth set firmly as she studiously avoids eye contact with me. Eventually, she says, 'Take a seat,' and turns away to continue prioritising the computer.

There is only one other patient in the waiting room, so there are plenty of seats available. I choose not to sit, although my legs are hurting and I have a sharp pain in my back. 'You might be waiting for some time,' the receptionist says as she notices I have remained standing in the waiting room. 'It's okay thanks,' I reply. I want to remain standing so that when I see the doctor, he will still observe the fasciculations, or muscles twitching, in my legs. It is the only outward sign of my problems, yet during six years undergoing investigations for a myriad of strange symptoms for which I have never received a diagnosis, I have been in constant pain, all over my body, and have suffered from extreme, bone-deep fatigue which is disproportionate to normal physical activity.

In due course I am called into the consultant neurologist's room, where he is seated, with three other people perched on their chairs like meerkats at the side of the room. The consultant asks me to take a seat on the other side of his desk and explains that the three observers are junior doctors and medical students. 'So, why are you here?' he asks. 'And what do you expect to get from this appointment today?' 'I would like to have an explanation for what is wrong with me so that I can have some treatment which will help to relieve my pain. I want to be able to get on with my life, to be physically active and be

Letting Go

able to work.' 'Well, I can tell you now that you're not likely to get that,' the consultant says.

My heart sinks. His manner seems to me to be very cold and unsympathetic. I feel that I am a nuisance to him and that he already thinks I am wasting his time. He begins to elicit the complex medical history from me, and he looks increasingly frustrated. I can sense that he is losing patience. I am trying to be as clear as I can about all of the symptoms, but they are multiple and nebulous, and it is very hard to be concrete and specific.

He asks me to stand up whilst he examines me. At one point I am stood facing the wall with the consultant and the junior doctors behind me, and I have been asked to lift up my skirt whilst they all look at the backs of my legs. I am praying silently that they will be able to see the muscle twitching, and I feel very exposed. Will they be thinking how horrible my white Irish skin is? Might they be thinking how ugly my cellulite is? I am holding my breath at this point and willing the whole thing to be over.

Then he asks me to lay on the examination couch. Without any warning, he proceeds to lift my top to expose my abdomen. He starts flicking the skin and turns aside to his junior doctors, saying, 'I don't suppose we will see anything here after a twin pregnancy, will we?' I feel ashamed about my tummy fat. I close my eyes and lie silently whilst the consultant does various tests on my hands, arms and legs. Eventually the examination is over and I am invited to return to the chair. 'Well, I can't see anything wrong with you,' the consultant says. 'I will arrange for you to have some further tests, an EMG and nerve conduction studies, plus blood tests. I expect that they will all be normal.' 'So, what can be causing all of my symptoms? I am not making things up,' I say, and I feel the need to tell him that I am a strong person. That I am not neurotic or a malingerer. I just want to feel well and to live life fully. 'I suspect that the problems are due to migraine,' he concludes.

Just before leaving, I tell him that I am currently reading a book about somatisation, 'It's All in the Mind', which was written by a psychiatrist, Suzanne Sullivan, and is an exploration of how a physical illness can be manifested due to a psychogenic cause. 'Maybe the problem is all in my head?' I say, almost jokingly. The consultant does not reply.

I sit down on a bench in a small park near the hospital to ponder and rest my legs a bit before continuing my journey home. As I later travel on the train, slumped on my seat with dejection, I suddenly sit up straight and I pick myself up by the bootstraps with the bold decision that I am going to finally abandon pursuing a medical diagnosis. I am tired of feeling persistently unwell. I have seen so many doctors and spent so much wasted time being referred to various specialists over the years and it really has not achieved anything positive. Despite being a highly trained, specialist nurse myself, I make a commitment to change my approach from attempting to find a traditional resolution. It is truly a threshold moment in my quest to find an explanation.

I have always been open to and interested in alternative methods of healing, and I have received treatments such as Reiki, massage and acupuncture previously. Although these activities felt pleasant in the short term, they have never actually resolved my physical pain. I have also experienced counselling many times, the first being when I was training to be a counsellor myself. Yet I do not understand what it is within me that blocks me from manifesting good health. What is it that I am still needing to learn? There

Time for Change…

must still be a missing piece of the jigsaw in this learning process which I need to discover in order to find an answer.

There is a six month wait to see an NHS counsellor, so I meanwhile decide to make an appointment with a homeopath. 'So, what has brought you here today?' Alison asks. I like her immediately and I feel that she is listening properly as I begin to tell my story. She does not interrupt my flow as I describe my physical symptoms and expalin how this has impacted on my life over the past few years. At one point I start telling her about a previous long relationship with an Indian man, and as soon as I mention his name, she stops me mid-sentence and asks me to stop talking and get onto the couch. She tells me that the moment I mentioned his name, my whole energy changed.

'This is where you are holding your pain,' she exclaims to me. And as she says it, I know that this is true, because I can feel an actual physical sensation of pain and pressure rising within, in my heart. I want to cry and I am swallowing hard. She places her hand on my forehead. 'Tell me more,' she says.

Another threshold is approaching…

Jackie Marsden

**

An inspirational colour choice…
Yellow

Following a re-decoration of the hall, we were trying to decide where to site a mirror. Off I went to consult 'Interior design with Feng Shui', a book which had lain unopened for years. On the back cover I read that yellow is the colour symbolising longevity. I felt something click inside as I remembered that during my cancer treatment I had started to buy yellow clothes – a colour I had never much worn before. Not content with blouses and dresses, I went on to paint all the walls of my bedroom in a lovely shade of honey. Similarly inspired, my latest acquisition is a golden wool throw for the bed.

Hilary Clark

**

The gift of the healing properties of song from life to life…
The Threshold Singers

Now grown to over 200 independent but affiliated chapters worldwide since its conception by Kate Munger in California twenty years ago, the Threshold Choir offers peace and wellbeing to people in the community who are moving from life to life. By focusing on singing for those on that unique threshold.

One such example concerns Margot, who first met Threshold singing on holiday in Findhorn, little realising how important this soothing gentle music would become in the lives of herself and Dave. Hear their unfolding story…'A decade ago we moved at last to our retirement dream home. Two weeks later my husband was diagnosed with a grade 4 spine tumour. Four months on, he became very ill and needed 24/7 care for a further six months until his death. Over that time all my other work and activities ceased. All except

Letting Go

Threshold singing. I continued to meet with this amazing, kind, generous-hearted group of women, who I am now privileged to call my friends, to sing, deepen, soften, blend voices and hearts and bring comfort to others, to ourselves and to my husband. For many weeks we practised our singing where he lay in a hospital bed downstairs in our cottage. As he grew weaker and more poorly, we gathered twice to offer him 'proper sings'. He loved it all; it brought him comfort and peace – and sometimes cake!! At his funeral, all the women sang for him, standing beside his coffin. They sang his favourite song: 'So Many Angels'. Angels indeed.'

The chapters meet regularly to learn and rehearse a selection of songs, specifically written and chosen to soothe and support those who are critically or terminally ill. The appeal of the songs is widespread and not religiously oriented. Without any formal audition process, they perform mainly in places that offer 'end of life' care, such as hospices, to groups of residents. But they also offer a more intimate 'bedside' or 'home' service where up to four members of the choir sing to one individual and the family/friends/loved ones. Songs are selected, taking into account an individual's personal musical tastes, spiritual inclinations and level of receptiveness. Sound has many healing qualities which touch both givers and receivers, enhancing feelings of serenity, deep peace and, within that moment, surrender.

Editor from conversations with members of the local chapter

The Vigilant Bride

Emblazoned by the setting sun,
Lichen cloaked sentinels
Guard shrouded graves,
Groomed by grazing sheep.
No-one left to cherish names
Once deeply etched
'In loving remembrance',
Now worn to obscurity.
Loved in life, forgotten in death,
Skeletal corpses,
'Treasures in heaven',
Cocooned in Gaia's womb.
Elegies no longer whisper
To old swollen mounds,
Now drawn into Earth's bowels
Like foetid flesh.
Years do not age the souls
Of fathers, daughters, mothers, sons,
Mingling in the evening mist,
Where one tormented groom,
Ripped from his bride by cruel war,
Mortal dreams and futures snatched,
Awaits her arrival.
Her weary body picks
A path between the shrines.
Rheumy eyes still burn with tears,
Remembering when
Her gallant soldier, stretchered home,
Mind broken, body bloody and torn,
His final battle over,
To rest within his tomb.
His name is not forgotten,
His grave shows no neglect,
His spectre hangs,
watching,
waiting,
Whilst she prays that soon,
They'll meet again,
Souls reunited.

Sue Thorn

Through the Vestry Door
(editor)

'Life Will Never be the Same Again...'

For the unborn child, the mother's womb is the total story of what it means to be secure, but the time comes when this security is shattered, and the baby plunges into the birth canal to be expelled, as it must seem, into a hostile new environment. – Margaret Silf

I know the unbelievable pain and agony which a mother passes through in the liminal experience of giving birth, so how much more scary must it be for that tiny creature, feeling squashed and squeezed and carried helplessly along in all the chaos and urgency? The birth canal is the crossing place from one certain world where all its needs are met to the next where everything is more uncertain. For most babies this new environment is not inherently hostile and birth usually becomes the doorway to a much fuller way of life, but it cannot know that at the time.

As human beings we meet up with numerous crossing places in the natural order of things, which require a letting go in order to move on. We have to let go of the breast of our mother, leave home to go to playschool, to 'big' school; maybe to university, to our first job. We may have to face our children leaving home and sit disconsolately in an empty nest. We may find ourselves facing challenges for which we do not feel prepared. Or encounter resistance, a block on the chosen path, so that we have to let go of our dreams maybe. I even let go of my vintage clothes recently! And so on until ultimately to death when we leave this life behind.

And there are many others. Letting go of a home, the workplace into retirement, facing the bereavement of a loved one, a life-changing illness. We let go of land as we cross the sea or fly through the air. We drop a letter into a post box, sometimes in hasty error; likewise nowadays an email, and it may all need unscrambling later!

My incredible elder daughter had to 'let go' at nineteen of ever being able to lead the glorious, gifted life she had planned, after suffering from Leukaemia and being irreversibly damaged by the too harsh treatment administered to save her life. And my other incredible daughter has had to let go of the company of her sister, with very limited access to her. In fact, we all had to let go of her to a great extent as she eventually had to emigrate to a very hot country just to stay alive, and we rarely see her. We never completely let go of having to 'let her go', of course. She knows what it is to have been in excruciating pain of every description, but I think it is true to say that she touches the lives of everyone who encounters her, with joy.

Margaret Silf speaks of crossing anxiety thresholds. She uses the very powerful image of a causeway to open up a possible way through what seems to be uncrossable waters. Sometimes our times of change and crisis feel more like being squeezed through a small space and driven along a narrow path into the unknown, with the sea swirling either

Time for Change...

side of us, and the tide sweeping in behind us, cutting off any possibility of retreat.

What might be our causeways at these times? The solid ground underneath us which enables a safe crossing? Who or what have been these safe causeways in your life? The places where you can let go in safety, the places where chaos becomes calm and hope? In mine they have generally been people and in the circumstance of my strangulated hernia crisis, the hospital and medical services, and I am truly thankful.

I have walked in my ministry alongside many who are on a causeway, in the hospital, parish and hospice. Funeral care for people's families became one of my greatest privileges. I especially felt it an honour to be trusted by those who did not 'want anything too religious' for their loved one, but 'not a Humanist one either'. Without exception they were looking for hope.

One thing I have learnt in my spiritual life is the wisdom not to be busy busy all the time. I can stop, take time out and be quiet and be still. I do not need to be needed! The world can manage without me managing all the time!

On a recent retreat, because I had time to stand and wait, I saw one of the neatest and most satisfying letting-go processes I have ever encountered! I am on the top of a hill overlooking a small woodland; below sprawled an eccentric shaped field beyond which, lapping at its boundaries was the Moray Firth, still and sparkling blue in the sunshine. Across that water, along its banks and beaches, lay the spreading town of Inverness. I had watched the farmer and tractor in the field over the week. He just seemed to go back and forth, back and forth, cutting the same dullish grass, over and over. Round and round he went. On the third day I met him at his gate, his crossing place from his farm to the lane. 'Is it going to be hay? For your animals for the winter?' I asked him. His face transformed and lit up. 'Yes, and I am baling this afternoon at last while we have the sun. It's been a terrible year for it.' This I must go and watch, I think. In the afternoon, I went down to the gate and sat on it to wait and see! Two tractors now, circling round each other. One with my farmer inside the cab, still seemingly going round cutting and chopping, and I see he is also transforming his field into perfectly straight ridges and furrows, such that the other tractor can come along and scoop up. Where on earth was it all going? He only had a smallish looking trailer container at the back. Every so often it stopped, reversed a little and moved on. It came to where I sat, turned round, backed up and lifted a lid, then slowly let go of its cargo. Rolling out and down the slope came an enormous, perfectly contoured bale of hay, compacted and bound with twine into a great golden cylinder. Mystery and majesty. How have I lived in the country for years and never seen this process? It made me chuckle with joy. At the end of the afternoon I returned to The Coach House, passing the hill viewpoint to see a transformed golden field, mown with faintly discernible, devastatingly straight, closely cropped tracks and all these wonderful huge cylinders scattered around the field, immaculately harvested to provide nourishment for the winter. The birds were there also, flying around in excitement, so they must have found a nourishing harvest too!

Finally, I recall that gentle man in the pub who had come to visit me. He eventually died at a time in the parishes as one of about a dozen over six weeks, one hard winter. The village was reeling in shock as it seemed to have lost so many of one generation. I went from home to home, sitting with their grief and planning the funerals in

Letting Go

their church. They were all the keepers of the stories, the born and bred, and it was vital quietly to acknowledge that another threshold had been reached in the life of that village.

Homilies

Can I Ever Forgive Myself?

John 11: 1-44
Take off the grave clothes and let him go.

'Unbind him. Let him go free,' commands Jesus, speaking of the grave cloths which had bound Lazarus. Jesus heals Lazarus to set him free. Jesus heals Legion in this story to go free. 'Go and tell people what God has done for you.' How does our faith help free us of that which binds us and prevents us from being fully alive? Experience of life has taught me that difficulty in issues of forgiveness can be what binds and constrains so many of us. It may be very painful even to be offered the opportunity to confront this most difficult of challenges.

'As we forgive those...' are words of the most familiar Christian prayer of all. Are we able to forgive those who have hurt us? Do we feel guilty if we can't? Do we find ourselves left feeling a 'victim', or angry, bitter, full of self-justification, contemptuous? We may even bear long-lasting consequences in our bodies via stress-related symptoms. Perhaps someone is not able to forgive us for some hurt which we have consciously or unconsciously caused. That's sometimes even harder to deal with, because it means having to face in ourselves that which is difficult to acknowledge. We may long to be forgiven where we know we've hurt, yet now find that forgiveness is withheld.

When we express our hurt, 'helpful' people may advise, 'You have to let it go.' Such advice can cause a heaping on of further self-blame. How can you possibly let go 'as if it had never been' of something that has damaged you so much? Something which has seared you to the bone? The core of your being? And yet, that is how God in His infinite mercy forgives us.

Henri Nouwen writes, 'Those who love us wound us too. That's the tragedy of our lives. It's what makes forgiveness from the heart so difficult. Because it is precisely our hearts that are wounded'. So how can we use this image of the wounded heart to help us to move from the place of the victim, the place of bitterness and rage, the place of self-justification, to a place where we can reclaim our own power in Christ, and not let these events continue to dis-able the rest of our lives.

To understand that forgiveness is a process which can take years, rather than be a one-off act, offers hope, because the process of liberation can then also commence. Nouwen continues, 'Not only can we then begin to set the person free from the negative bonds which exist between us, but we set ourselves free from the burden of being the offended one'. We can begin to untie the knot (which interestingly is also the same word in Greek for forgiveness). We can cease to pull these people with us, dragging them as a heavy load. Do you recognise that? Ball and chain?

Time for Change...

It can be a huge temptation to continue justifying our own stance both to ourselves and to others, thereby clinging in a way to those who have hurt us. Also, of course, when we reach a place of forgiveness, we may discover that we cannot force those we now want to forgive into accepting our forgiveness. They may not be able or willing to do so, nor accept that they have ever wounded us. They may even no longer be alive. The truth is that the only people we can really change are ourselves. And that forgiving others is first and foremost about healing our own hearts. Forgiving is not forgetting. It is learning another way to remember. Not a once and for all, but an ongoing process.

Healing in forgiveness, then, is not a 'letting go', but a scar grafted on to the heart. The paradox of a healing that entails the hurt becoming incorporated into our own being as part of a learned and acquired wisdom. Some of that is to do with acknowledging the reality of the pain, but also in having the courage to face oneself honestly. And I think it usually means some process of humility too.

Scars form and change over many years. When touched they remain tender for a long time. One of my sons was quite severely scalded as a baby on his arm. He says that he never knew until he was about nine that he was the only person who had these marks or scars on his arm. I asked how he felt about them now. He said that he liked them. And that they were part of him and one of the things which made him unique! We are precious to God. Like my son's scars, ours contribute to the preciousness and uniqueness of who we are and are pointers to what we can become if we accept them..

I close now with these words of encouragement and hope, written by 14th century Julian of Norwich. She writes then, for those we have hurt...for the times we hurt ourselves...or those who have hurt us:

'Though we sin continually he loves us endlessly. If there be anywhere on earth a lover of God who is always kept safe from falling, I know nothing of it, for it was not shown me. But this was shown; that in falling and rising again we are always held close in one love'.

**

Born Again?

John 3:1-17
Flesh gives birth to flesh, but the spirit gives birth to spirit.

Born again? How can that be? And what has it to do with power? This passage from John's gospel heralds the forthcoming death of Jesus, following his conversation with Nicodemus about being born again. Jesus juxtaposes the fundamental certainties of humanity, birth and death, to teach about that mystery of new birth for all people through his death. He teaches us, through all the mess of our humanity, about that paradox where power and humility and submission meet and are reconciled on the cross.

Jesus has raised this image of being born, so I invite you to reflect with me on that concept. A new baby is not born instantly, nor arrives in the beak of a stork, all clean and ready-made. Birth is a process which begins in its creation, months before it comes to pass. It is a process which can be long, painful, potentially hazardous, at times lonely, and

Letting Go

very messy. It is a process which manifests as awesome power but requiring submission, relinquishing of control and the laying down of all dignity, trustingly and absolutely, into the hands of the midwife. If that is what it is like for the mother, so must it be for the baby. That is what it is to be born as a created human being, and why I know that to be born again in Christ is a process which may last all my life and even beyond to complete, and it will probably also be messy.

Jesus' teaching of the threshold of rebirth is followed immediately by foretelling his death on a cross. 'The Son of Man must be lifted up, so that everyone who believes in him will have eternal life'. How can this be? The man Jesus in humility and submission endured his living flesh being hammered into dead wood, releasing a power which made the earth tremble. This death on the cross was long, painful, terrifyingly lonely, and very messy. It too was a process where power and new birth required a submission, a relinquishing of control and a laying down of dignity in absolute trust into the hands of his heavenly father. The cross. That place where power and humility meet and are reconciled. Where death becomes birth into a new way of being.

So where does power fit into Christian living? Power can be a very difficult concept. Our knowledge and experience of the consequence of power in the world can so easily cause us to fail to look beyond its negative manifestation in abuse, destruction, the diminishing of others in relationship, of violence in state and religions.

And it is equally as easy to misunderstand humility. We can so easily put ourselves down inappropriately. I'm hopeless at doing...' 'I'm not clever enough to...' 'I don't think I've been a good enough mother, father...' 'I'm not a powerful person. I can't make any difference to anything.' 'It must have been my fault.' So, what could this outward expression of apparent humility be covering?

Nelson Mandela suggests it can be fear: *'Our deepest fear is not actually that we are inadequate. Our deepest fear is that we are powerful beyond measure. It is our light and not our darkness, which frightens us. There's nothing enlightened about shrinking. As we let our light shine, we unconsciously give other people permission to do the same. As we are liberated from our fears, our presence automatically liberates others.'* Similarly, Jesus says here, *'Whoever lives by the truth comes into the light, so that it may be seen plainly that what he has done has been done through God'.*

And that of course is the key to the whole paradox. Power is actually part of God's world, shot through with the light of his glory. 'God did not send his son into the world to condemn the world, but to save the world through him'. He consecrated that creation by his presence within it, by his birth into humanity and his death on a cross from which he stoops to lift us up. Humility in Christ is not about putting ourselves down, being a doormat, or a 'martyr' to every cause, but a daring to hand over our own fearful and fragile power, into those nailed hands, which turn our faces into smiling and our hearts into loving. In the joy of recognizing the 'me' as part of the greater story, we then give others permission also to dance a new dance.

Birth is a letting-go and a moving on. Death is a letting go and a moving on. Both the 'no' and the 'yes' are equally part of empowered living, in humility.

Thanks be to God who is still prepared to bless us, and use the mess in the purpose of his love.

Time for Change...

A Miner Miracle

2 Timothy 1:1-7
These are the things you are to teach ...

A few years ago, the world's newspaper headlines for a week were, 'Praying for a Miner Miracle'. The world has watched and waited...and prayed for miners trapped deep underground as the cavity was filling up with water. Maybe the most significant moment in all the horror was to discover that a chapel, a sacred space, had been created within the horrific entombment. Every last one was eventually freed. Some fell to their knees as they emerged into the light to give thanks to God. As often at times of crisis and tragedy, great heroism was certainly manifest in this case with the gentle, caring rescue work, whilst the mountain cracked around them; people pray who would not necessarily do so. It appears to be an automatic response for the human spirit to reach out to the Divine. To pray alongside others in solidarity is powerful and palpable.

Because prayer is not only about words, it is about experience. It is about relationship. If you have difficulties in your life, or deep joy to share, you will usually share them with the people to whom you are closest, with someone you trust; with someone with whom you don't have to put on an act. That all evolves out of a nurtured relationship. How do we nurture our relationship with God? How are we growing in that relationship? Do we need a special place where we feel we can do this more easily? Some speak of nature for them being the place where they feel closest to God, or their garden, some in church in worship, others in an empty church! At home? What about in the Corona crisis lockdown?

In Timothy's 2nd letter, we see the influence of his grandmother Lois and his mother Eunice. But it is rare, I imagine, that family prayers and Bible readings regularly happen in Christian households today. Remember the big family Bibles inscribed with family trees over generations. 'Old fashioned', we might say. I suspect other faiths, eg Muslims would regard Christians as odd in this respect, since in their religion, as in many others, the home is still the obvious place where faith is nurtured and practised.

The miners made a sacred space where they were. An unlikely venue! Could that inspire us to do the same in our homes. A place where we can go and just be there before and alongside God. The Bishop of Whitby challenges us here to do just that.

'Our scriptures are works of art, not just books of rules. Read them with wonder and care. Read them often. Read them to each other. Read them at home. Dialogue with them and let their words release the knowledge of God to you'.

A Final Musing

Angels at Westminster

...I alight at King's Cross and find my way through the maze of the underground to Victoria where I am journeying to see my two grandson choristers sing in a concert at Westminster

Letting Go

Cathedral.
    I will have a two hour wait. 'See you in Pret a Manger, Mum,' said Jeremy. I call into a very posh fragrance shop to ask for directions to this cafe. An assistant looks at me sympathetically and, pointing, says in a slow American accent, 'We have several of those in this country, there is the one closest to us, over there.' Yikes, am I not speaking the right language, or do I just look very elderly, and like the country mouse which I am?'
    Not a relaxing experience. I bought some packaged food and drink and struggled with a tray, my yellow satchel and suitcase up some spiral stairs signposted 'Jobs' and found an empty table, to be surrounded by people working frantically on laptops. Hours later I was whisked away to a noodle bar, perched on a high stool to hastily consume noodles with chopsticks, with only fifteen minutes until the start of the concert, picking up a' dry white' on the way with Elaine, while Jeremy hurried off to buy some tickets!
    Collapsing in exhaustion amidst a congregation of about 2,000, I settled myself in expectation and relief at having finally arrived. We were asked not to applaud at the concert's conclusion as that was not an appropriate response to the death of Jesus, but when that moment came, we would be invited to join with the choir in a response known as *strepitus*, which would involve the stamping of feet and banging of books. 'Hmm, unusual,' I thought.
    This evening was to become one of the most sacred and memorable moments of the whole of my life.
    The Stabat Mater by Palestrina reflects the anguish of Mary, the mother of Jesus, as she watched her dying son hammered into the rough wooden cross of a criminal. It soon became apparent that the whole evening's music, including Allegri's Miserere (grandson Oliver singing the alto solo), had been choreographed into an occasion where we were not merely observers, but in it and of it. The singing was sublime in that acoustic. Throughout, the choir in small groups would appear at different points in the cathedral. We were surrounded and embraced by this heavenly music. A small group of boys would be singing above our heads; at one point a very tiny boy left the main body of the choir at the front as if he was just wandering off, and that little treble slowly made his long winding way up the steps to join some more mature voices high in the East. All the time the lighting of this awesome cathedral was changing subtly, when suddenly, towards the climax and crescendo, mainly in the dark, the two large pillars at the front appeared to be shaking and dissolving into a trembling mist...and this continued terrifyingly, such that one also trembled. Yes, it was actually incense but, integrated with the heavenly voices that pierced the soul, it was as if...we were there. Then the silence of the ending of the beginning...
    ...and next a roaring and a banging began, seeming to shake the cathedral into an earthquake which had shaken and changed the world for ever.
    Stunned, we departed round to the school to say 'Goodnight' to those little boys who were glowing with the experience we had all shared. The pure music had come from their souls, touched ours and changed everyone in some mysterious way. How do they do it?
    Yes...truly it felt that angels, whose main work is to praise, adore and worship God, had crossed the temporal threshold that night, so that we all went out...changed.

Time for Change...

The Maypole Dance...

POSTSCRIPT

'May, on a tree, has its own symbolism – the white flowers and bright green leaves signalling Spring as the start of life's journey.'

'The maypole is a symbol of the tree of life.'

'Added symbolism derives from the ascent up the spiritual path in a spiral – the sort of journey Dante took up the mountain.'

'Some of the older original maypole ceremonies used large trees shaped like a cross, at the top of which were 'goodies' – treasure.'

'The slippery pole with traditional presents at the top symbolised the unattainability of the treasure of the spiritual realm.'

'The dancing venerates the holiness of trees in early faith – symbolises unity, wholeness and community – protectively surrounding.'

Through the Vestry Door
(editor)

Community and church in the maypole dance.
Re-configuring...

My daughter Emma writes...*Particularly interesting is that the 'modern day' Maypole and tradition of dancing with ribbons was all down to John Ruskin in Victorian times! He saw rural customs and traditions which held communities together as a way of counteracting the increasing debauchery, squalor and moral decline in the cities. He encouraged a new Christian and family focus, and the dancers tended to be children from local churches...*

By contrast, more than a century later, an analysis in 'That was the Church That Was' opined thus...*The collapsing of the Church of England is embedded in England's changing social structure in its deepest joys and sorrows. When class structure fell, it brought the bishops down with it and the stitches and threads started to come undone as well. The Church of England has become the only organisation where the customers are always wrong. They can only return when people once again see that the church exists for them.*

At the end of my House for Duty lay ministry there became the great unravelling, like a piece of knitting slipped from the needle and pulled this way and that. Can there be any redemption of such unravelling? Can the garment be recreated?

...And then, ten years later, came the story of the disappearing roof. One dark autumnal night the whole of the lead from the Brafferton church roof was stolen and water poured in, mercifully avoiding the organ, but soaking everything else. The village was devastated, but it was like an Old Testament story...an apocalyptic tale...a wake-up call to test whether the somnolence of either people or diocese could be shaken up. It was.

The village people said, 'This is our church. It is important for our community.' The diocese said, 'If so, it is you who will need to find the money to replace it.' Within eighteen months this small village raised £120,000, but then they looked around and asked, 'We have invested our money in this building where hardly anything happens, including regular services (worship), any longer. This is indeed the church for our community, so what is its purpose? How is this church existing for us, now?' Wondrously, God breathed new life into this chaos.

The Spirit did indeed move upon the waters of Brafferton, that threshold parish on the boundary, almost falling off the edge of the diocese. Its future is now in the hands of a group of passionate, committed, energetic, mainly lay people, and 'stuff' happens' there and the ministry is growing in a fundamentally different way. I had felt seventeen years ago that my post was a pioneering role, responding to the Church of England's call to 'think out of the box'. Now I see it was just a beginning, maybe or small part of it, the model of ministry it offered being built upon now by an even more radical lay team, jumping right out of the box! The threshold has been crossed, in an imaginative, creative and non-institutional way.

The Maypole Dance...

All denominations are seriously short of paid clergy/ministers; so much is in flux. Renewed energy, money and activity are being expended on training lay Christians for leadership, but it was ever thus. A much more radical solution is required. The reality of vicars/ ministers being in charge of 5/6/7 churches is surely unsatisfactory. Once one person in a place routinely served a single church. Does that person still need to be 'ordained'? Needing to be properly trained, supported and fully accountable, of course, but a part-time, local lay person would surely be more effective in relationship with the people than a remote ordained figure. (I have heard such 'absentee' posts called 'Sacraments on wheels', ie priests travelling around burning fuel in these times of awareness of climate change.) But how ever could this possibly work while the mysticism of the ordained remains theologically paramount? Maybe the words of the new Archbishop of York, Stephen Cottrell, speak helpfully into this debate, as in the Church Times he calls on the Church of England to be *'simpler, humbler, bolder and more diverse'*. Hmm. Humbler?

Olwyn Marriage writes ironically, *'The priesthood of all believers is the best kept secret in the Church of England'*. I was reminded of these words as I subsequently worshipped and ministered in various ways for ten years in a United Reformed Church, where it is the congregation who make any final decision re process and ministry at a local level. I knew this was going to be a different prospect when my 'welcome interview' took place at an elegant table in Betty's Tea Rooms with one of the elders! I saw this trust of the laity played out there over the years, even in major issues such as 'Would we be prepared to marry same-sex couples in our own church?'.

My varied experiences in Yorkshire have shown me both discouraging and encouraging glimpses of the future possibilities. Discouraging mainly that much of the hierarchy couldn't accept my ambivalent formal role as exercised via a 'lowly' Reader status – not even as an official bridge between themselves and the people. But encouraging in that to the people in the communities this made little sense...formal status was much less important than personal qualities. 'Go and love the people.' That matters the most.

Aspirations must be lifted off the page and brought to life.

Unfortunately...So many of these radical ideas simply languish for decades, but maybe this could be the time for a new dance.

The maypole traditionally heralds the re-birth of Spring. My risky post maybe signposted one way to revive the parish model. Like the maypole, it crafted a 'multi-coloured' thread, weaving a rich pattern of traditional English community life, with the village church at its heart. How now could the dance form and reconfigure?

With the help of many people, including the contributors to this anthology, it has been a privilege to ponder the challenging lessons to be learned.